Dear Reader:

The book you ~~are now holding~~ is a ~~part of~~ St. Martin's True Crime Library, the imprint *The New York Times* calls "the leader in true crime!" Each month, we offer you a fascinating account of the latest, most sensational crime that has captured the national attention. St. Martin's is the publisher of Tina Dirmann's VANISHED AT SEA, the story of a former child actor who posed as a yacht buyer in order to lure an older couple out to sea, then robbed them and threw them overboard to their deaths. John Glatt's riveting and horrifying SECRETS IN THE CELLAR shines a light on the man who shocked the world when it was revealed that he had kept his daughter locked in his hidden basement for 24 years. In the Edgar-nominated WRITTEN IN BLOOD, Diane Fanning looks at Michael Petersen, a Marine-turned-novelist found guilty of beating his wife to death and pushing her down the stairs of their home—only to reveal another similar death from his past. In the book you now hold, PLAYING WITH FIRE, John Glatt examines a startling case of death and arson.

St. Martin's True Crime Library gives you the stories behind the headlines. Our authors take you right to the scene of the crime and into the minds of the most notorious murderers to show you what really makes them tick. St. Martin's True Crime Library paperbacks are better than the most terrifying thriller, because it's all true! The next time you want a crackling good read, make sure it's got the St. Martin's True Crime Library logo on the spine—you'll be up all night!

Charles E. Spicer

Charles E. Spicer, Jr.
Executive Editor, St. Martin's True Crime Library

TITLES BY
JOHN GLATT
FROM THE TRUE CRIME LIBRARY
OF ST. MARTIN'S PAPERBACKS

Playing with Fire

Secrets in the Cellar

To Have and to Kill

Forgive Me, Father

The Doctor's Wife

One Deadly Night

Depraved

Cries in the Desert

For I Have Sinned

Evil Twins

Cradle of Death

Blind Passion

Deadly American Beauty

Never Leave Me

Twisted

PLAYING WITH FIRE

THE TRUE STORY OF A NURSE, HER HUSBAND,
AND A MARRIAGE TURNED FATAL

John Glatt

St. Martin's Paperbacks

PLAYING WITH FIRE

Copyright © 2010 by John Glatt.

Cover photo by Westend61 GmbH / Alamy.

All rights reserved.

For information address St. Martin's Press, 175 Fifth Avenue, New York, NY 10010.

EAN: 978-0-312-36517-2

Printed in the United States of America

St. Martin's Paperbacks edition / March 2010

St. Martin's Paperbacks are published by St. Martin's Press, 175 Fifth Avenue, New York, NY 10010.

10 9 8 7 6 5 4 3 2 1

ACKNOWLEDGMENTS

On a freezing Saturday afternoon in late January 2009, I arrived at the Lakin Correctional Center, where convicted murderess Shelly Michael is incarcerated for the gruesome murder of her husband Jimmy and then burning her house down. Located on the West Virginia border with Ohio, Lakin is home to some of the most dangerous female prisoners in the state.

Heavily made up and wearing a short-sleeved cream-colored prison uniform, with her inmate number, 45996, embroidered on the breast pocket, Shelly was brought into the visitors' room. There I was waiting at a table with her parents Michael and Kathy Goots and her friend Mary Childers.

After I shook her tiny hand, I asked what had happened to bring the one-time respected pediatric nurse here.

"It's been hell on earth," she replied sadly. "I survive by keeping busy and praying a lot. This has strengthened my faith . . . I read the Bible every night."

She still declares her undying love for Jimmy, claiming that she's an innocent victim and the real killer is still out there.

"All of a sudden my husband was ripped away from me," she said, using her hands to emphasize her point. "It was so horrible. I was a mess. I just wanted to be buried with Jimmy.

Then I was arrested and put in jail. It was such a shock. Life couldn't get worse."

When asked how she survives with the prospect of spending the rest of her life behind bars, the 35-year-old former cheerleader stares blankly into space.

"What keeps me going," she replied, "is that I know that if I had been the one that had been killed, Jimmy would be there fighting for me, tooth and nail."

Although Shelly spent two hours with me, later making her parents, sister Jennifer and lifelong best friend Renee DelViscio available for interviews for this book, she later waged a campaign from Lakin to stop publication. Even though she has exhausted all appeal processes, Shelly believes she will eventually get a new trial. She has hired a private investigator, who she now claims has uncovered information that proves her innocence beyond a shadow of a doubt. But when asked for details, she refuses to divulge it.

In the months following my prison visit, Shelly Michael sent a flood of letters to me and the Executive Editor at St. Martin's, Charles Spicer, demanding we halt publication.

"The book will only serve to interfere with the investigation," she wrote me in early September 2009. "Hinder our ability to find the truth, and further undermine my innocence."

During many months of exhaustive research for this book I was helped by many people. Firstly I thank Shelly Michael for telling me her story. I am also indebted to her parents Michael and Kathy Goots and her sister Jennifer Barker and her partner Jamie.

I owe special gratitude to Jimmy Michael's parents Dennis and Ruth, his brother Steve and cousin Daniel Twigg, for sharing their fond memories.

This was a complicated story, and I would especially like to thank Morgantown City Fire Marshal Captain Ken Tennant and fire chief David Fetty for their great patience in explaining the finer points of arson investigation. Thanks also to Monongalia Prosecutors Marcia Ashdown and Perri

DeChristopher, Morgantown detectives Paul Mezzanotte, Chris Dalton, Sgt. Harold Sperringer and Sgt. James Merrill of the West Virginia State Police.

Thanks also to: Shawn Alt, Ginny Armistead, Renee and Eric DelViscio, Courtney Dunn, Tom Dyer, Stephanie Estel, Jeremy and Tara Miller, Reggie Ours and Keri Whitacre.

I would also like to thank my editor at St. Martin's Paperbacks, Charles Spicer, his assistant Yaniv Soha, my agent Peter Miller and Adrienne Rosado of PMA Literary and Film Management and M. William Phelps for his help and being a real gentleman.

And as usual I am indebted to Gail, Jerome and Emily Freund, Debbie, Douglas and Taylor Baldwin, Gertrude Gurcher, Danny and Allie Tractenberg, Cari Pokrassa, Virginia Randall and Annette Witheridge.

Under American law a convicted defendant is entitled to appeal his or her conviction, in an effort to overturn the jury's finding of guilt. Shelly Michael's appeal has been denied by the West Virginia Supreme Court, but she has still the option of challenging her conviction by petitioning a Federal court to grant a writ of habeas corpus. As of going to press, no such petition has been filed.

CONTENTS

PROLOGUE   1

CHAPTER 1   The Cheerleader   5
CHAPTER 2   Only Bad Girls Do It   12
CHAPTER 3   West Virginia University   16
CHAPTER 4   Settling Down   25
CHAPTER 5   The Hunter   29
CHAPTER 6   Stephanie   36
CHAPTER 7   Chasing Jimmy   40
CHAPTER 8   6PACK   48
CHAPTER 9   545 Killarney Drive   55
CHAPTER 10   Scandal   62
CHAPTER 11   Shelly Michael, Nurse   67
               Practitioner
CHAPTER 12   Ultimatum   74
CHAPTER 13   Labor Day   81
CHAPTER 14   Chicago   87
CHAPTER 15   Thanksgiving   93
CHAPTER 16   A Living Death   102
CHAPTER 17   Tuesday, November 29   106
CHAPTER 18   Flashover   113
CHAPTER 19   Detective Paul Mezzanotte   122
CHAPTER 20   "I Wish I Would Have Loved   129
               Him More"
CHAPTER 21   "She's Not Grieving Right"   137

CHAPTER 22	Homicide	144
CHAPTER 23	"Maybe She Drugged Him"	153
CHAPTER 24	The Grieving Widow	161
CHAPTER 25	The Funeral	167
CHAPTER 26	"More Like Lovers Than Friends"	173
CHAPTER 27	"A String of Lies"	178
CHAPTER 28	Seventeen Minutes	191
CHAPTER 29	"Maybe That Iron Fell Over"	207
CHAPTER 30	God's Way of Punishing Her	214
CHAPTER 31	A Deep Excavation	223
CHAPTER 32	"Linear and Logical"	231
CHAPTER 33	The Arrest	235
CHAPTER 34	"I'm Not Guilty"	241
CHAPTER 35	The Media Trap	244
CHAPTER 36	"Not in Morgantown"	251
CHAPTER 37	Razed to the Ground	260
CHAPTER 38	Indignant	267
CHAPTER 39	The Trial Begins	274
CHAPTER 40	"A Death Without Mercy"	278
CHAPTER 41	Cold	288
CHAPTER 42	"I Made a Huge Mistake"	293
CHAPTER 43	The Defense	310
CHAPTER 44	"'I Value Honesty'"	317
CHAPTER 45	"The Cruel and Unusual Manner of This Murder"	334
CHAPTER 46	The Verdict Is Unanimous	344
CHAPTER 47	"There Is a Very Dark Side to Your Character"	349
CHAPTER 48	Justice4Michelle	360
EPILOGUE		365

"I wanted that picture perfect traditional American family."
—*Shelly Michael, 2006*

"To be buried while alive is, beyond question, the most terrific of those extremes which has ever fallen to the lot of mere mortality."
—*Edgar Allan Poe—"The Premature Burial"*

PROLOGUE

It had been a long night on the neonatal ward of Ruby Memorial Hospital, and respiratory therapist Shawn Alt was looking forward to a good sleep. But as he was finishing up a twelve-hour shift, things suddenly got busy, so he stayed on an extra forty-five minutes.

"When I clocked out, it was late," he remembered. "It was close to eight o'clock."

There was a heavy rain and fog as he came out of the hospital's front entrance, still wearing scrubs. But it was unseasonably warm for November, with temperatures later reaching a near record 60 degrees.

As 37-year-old Alt—who also was a volunteer fireman—had that Tuesday off, he planned to sleep in the Star City Fire Department's bunker room, to be on call in an emergency. But first he drove home to shower and change into his day clothes.

Alt lived at 574 Killarney Drive, in the prestigious Suncrest section of Morgantown, West Virginia, just about a mile away from the hospital. By 8:10 a.m. he was reversing his Dodge Ram truck into his driveway.

"It was still drizzling when I got out of my vehicle and smelled something burning," he recalled. "It had the odor of a house on fire."

From his experience as a firefighter, Alt could easily distinguish the smell of a simple chimney fire from building materials like insulation and furniture. He recognized this as a house fire.

His first concern was that his own house was burning. So he slowly walked around its perimeter, inspecting it from all sides. Then, satisfied it was not on fire, he stood in his driveway, looking around for any smoke in the neighborhood. He saw nothing burning, but as a precaution he called a firefighter friend, to see if any fires had been reported in Suncrest, leaving a message when the call went to voice mail.

Then he went into his house to shower and change. But when he came out at about 8:20 a.m., he could still smell burning. After taking another look around and still not seeing anything, he got into his truck and pulled out of his driveway, turning left onto Killarney Drive.

At the top of the hill, he came to a stop sign at the intersection with Eastern Avenue. As he slowed down, he saw his neighbor Shelly Michael's distinctive silver Ford Expedition, backing out of her driveway. She turned left in his direction and stopped, directly facing him across the four-way stop.

Alt was well-acquainted with the smartly dressed, attractive young mother-of-two, the second wife of successful entrepreneur Jimmy Michael. Shawn and Jimmy had studied respiratory therapy together, staying in touch after his friend had started his own home medical business. They now lived four doors away from each other, and often chatted.

But Shelly was different. Alt knew her from Ruby Memorial, where she was a pediatric nurse practitioner. But he was always very wary around her, as she could be very moody.

"There were times when you didn't know whether you should approach her," he said. "That day, when I saw her facing me at the stop sign, I just threw my hand up and waved. She didn't give me acknowledgment. She then sped off through the stop sign."

On his arrival at the Star City fire house, Shawn Alt discovered that no fires had been reported in the area. So he went into the bunker room, lay down and immediately fell asleep.

Just after midday, he was awoken by a colleague, saying he had a phone call. The mother of a Morgantown firefighter friend was calling, to report a huge fire on Killarney Drive, a couple of doors down from his house. She had just driven past, seeing numerous fire trucks, and people crying in the street. Although the fire was now out, she asked if he could drive over and find out if any firefighters had been hurt.

Alt left immediately, and on the drive back received an emotional call from his friend Reggie Ours, informing him that Jimmy Michael's house had burned down and their mutual friend had not made it out alive.

"He told me Jimmy died in a house fire," said Alt. "And I said, 'That's where I'm headed.'"

Soon afterwards, he arrived to find his house blocked off by firemen and police, as the nearest fire hydrant was in his yard. Then he walked over to talk to a fire investigator, who was dismantling a hose line.

"That's odd," Alt told him. "You know I smelled something burning this morning, and then I saw his wife leaving the house."

Then, with nothing further he could do, Alt got back into his truck to return to the fire station. A few minutes later, he received a call from a detective on his cell phone, ordering him back to the fire scene immediately.

A few minutes later, Shawn Alt was directed through a security barrier to a police cruiser, where Detective Paul Mezzanotte was waiting for him. The burly homicide detective had arrived at 545 Killarney Drive several hours earlier, after a badly burned body had been found in the second-floor master bedroom. Although it hadn't been officially identified, it was believed to be Jimmy Michael.

Even though it was early in the investigation, the detective already had grave suspicions about the fire. First, the horribly charred body had been found in bed in a sleeping position, with no signs of him trying to escape. And second, the only damage to the two-storey house was the totally burned-out bedroom, with the rest of it virtually untouched.

Then Detective Mezzanotte had been told about Shawn Alt's claim to have seen the presumed widow leaving the house, and he wanted to know more.

When the volunteer firefighter recounted seeing Shelly Michael backing out of her driveway at 8:20 a.m., Detective Mezzanotte asked how he could be certain it was her. Alt said he had known both the Michaels for many years, and had often seen Shelly's silver Ford Expedition, with its distinctive 6PACK vanity license plates.

"I found Shelly's car and saw the license plate," recalled the detective. "Everything that he had said checked out."

Two hours later, Detective Mezzanotte interviewed Shelly Michael at a neighbor's house, where she was being comforted by friends. He was immediately struck by the supposed fire victim's wife's strangely calm demeanor.

When asked about her husband Jimmy and what could have possibly caused the fire, she was evasive, complaining of being unwell.

"I've handled a lot of death investigations," recalled the detective, "and her reaction to me wasn't of normal grieving. I don't ever remember seeing her cry. She seemed very cold and very calculated."

CHAPTER 1

The Cheerleader

Shelly Michael was born Michelle Lynette Goots at the United Hospital Center, Clarksburg, West Virginia, on January 29, 1972—the first child of Michael and Kathi Goots. Her great-grandfather had come from a small town in Italy, emigrating to America at the beginning of the 20th century, settling in West Virginia.

Nestled in the rolling hills of north central West Virginia, Clarksburg lies where the West Fork River meets Elk Creek. Known as "Jewel in the Hills," it was founded in 1785 and named for General George Rogers Clark, an American Revolutionary War hero known as "the Conqueror of the Old Northwest," for forcing the British to cede the territory to America as part of the 1783 Treaty of Paris.

Clarksburg's most famous son was Thomas Jonathan "Stonewall" Jackson, who was born there in 1824, leaving at the age of 18 to go to West Point. During the Civil War, it was an important Union Army supply depot, and the remains of Union earthworks are still on display in Lowndes Hill Park, attracting thousands of Civil War buffs each year.

In the 19th and 20th centuries, Clarksburg owed its prosperity to coal mines and natural gas fields. It was a flourishing industrial and shipping center, producing high quality glass and metal products. But in the second half of the 20th century, the town fell into a deep decline, with the population dropping from 32,000 in 1950 to just 18,000 today.

Michael Goots' father John Batista, known to everyone as J.B., was born in Clarksburg, working most of his life as manager of the Broughton Dairies. His wife Geraldine bore him nine children, and Michael was born on November 18, 1950.

A good-looking, ambitious boy, he was always fascinated by his Italian heritage, dreaming of one day seeing the old country for himself.

At 16 he met Katherine Grant, who was two grades below him at Notre Dame High School, and they started dating.

"It was love at first sight," recalled Michael.

"I'm not so sure I would categorize it that way," said Kathi. "But we go a long way back."

The two teenagers courted in local church coffee houses, going dancing on the weekends. After graduating from Notre Dame, Michael went to refrigeration school, before getting a job with a local company called Wuchner Equipment.

In early 1971, 18-year-old Kathi found herself pregnant. So on June 11, the young couple were married at the Immaculate Conception Catholic church, moving into a trailer on Chub Run Road, in Mount Clare, just outside Clarksburg.

The following January, Kathi gave birth to a beautiful baby girl. They named her Michelle, after her father.

"She was a good baby," recalled Kathi. "I was lucky."

Soon after Michelle's birth, Kathi's father William Grant died from alcoholism. Then Kathi, who was also now working for Wuchner Equipment, hired a babysitter to look after the new arrival.

In summer 1974, Michael Goots moved his family out of the trailer to 204 Grant Street in Clarksburg, next door to his parents. He then began an extensive remodeling of the whole house.

At 2 years old, Michelle, who had been dubbed "Shelly Bean" by an aunt, had eye surgery for strabismus, a condition where one eye cannot focus with the other.

Soon afterwards, Kathi became pregnant again. On

November 11, 1975, she gave birth to another daughter, who they named Jennifer.

With a growing family, Michael and Kathi worked long hours to make ends meet, employing nannies and babysitters to look after their daughters.

When the owner of Wuchner Equipment died, Michael Goots took over the company, renaming it Thermex Refrigeration. He appointed Kathi as office manager, officially incorporating the new company on the Bicentennial.

"July fourth, 1976, is the day we started," remembered Kathi. "Well, that's what we put on our business papers and everything."

Over the next few years their new company prospered. As Michael worked long hours and was on call around the clock, he rarely saw his two little girls. Shelly would later remember one of the many nannies her parents employed, as being "very strict," often hitting her with a paddle if she misbehaved.

As her grandparents, two aunts and an uncle all lived on Grant Street, Shelly's father's house became the "neighborhood hangout." Some of the little girl's earliest memories are of playing hide-and-seek and kick-the-can with her cousins.

At the age of 5, Shelly started kindergarten, soon impressing her teachers with her keen natural intelligence.

"She was just real high-spirited," said her mother. "Bouncy and tomboyish, and she liked just about everything."

At kindergarten, the tiny dark-haired girl became best friends with Renee Orme, whose parents were close friends of the Goots family.

"We were baptized on the same day in the Immaculate Conception," said Renee. "Our first interaction was in kindergarten, that's how far back we do go."

One afternoon, Shelly was walking home from kindergarten with an aunt, when they saw a woman get hit by a car and thrown into the air and injured. Shelly suspected it was her mother, still lying on the ground awaiting medical help. And as her aunt led her away from the scene, she kept asking if it was her mother, but the aunt refused to answer.

Later Shelly discovered it had indeed been her mom, who spent several days in the hospital with a broken hip.

On April 23, 1979, Michael and Kathi had their third child, a baby boy they named Matthew, who would complete the family.

That summer, Shelly and Renee started at St. Mary's Elementary School, in Clarksburg. It was part of the Catholic School System, with nuns providing a strict religious education. All the girls had to wear severe navy blue uniforms, and Shelly was embarrassed by her mother making her wear a plaid jumper with matching tie on school picture days.

Years later, Kathi admits to having been a disciplinarian, imposing an 8:00 p.m. curfew and always expecting her children to be well-behaved. She laid down strict rules to be followed at home and would punish the children if they didn't obey.

"I was very very strict," she explained. "I guess I was a little too strict maybe."

Michael, who was seldom at home, left the children's discipline to his wife.

"But we had no real problems with Shelly," said Kathi. "She might lip a little . . . but that's about all."

Shelly would later describe her parents as "not very affectionate people," complaining that she rarely received "hugs and kisses." She also felt that her father did not give her enough "quality time," as he was so busy building his business.

Shelly hated her mother's curfew, as her friends were allowed to stay out playing far later. Often, after doing her homework, Shelly would sit alone in her bedroom, playing her favorite Blondie and Michael Jackson singles over and over again on her record player. When MTV was launched in late 1981, she became addicted to watching music videos.

She and her best friend Renee loved participating in the annual St. Mary's Christmas pageant and other talent shows. They once dressed up as the Go-Go's, performing their big hit that year, "We Got the Beat," as well as giving several roller-skating performances.

It was the first time Shelly had performed in front of an audience, and she loved it.

At the age of 9, Shelly claims to have been sexually molested by someone close to her family, who forced her to masturbate him.

"[I]t made me feel terrible inside," she later wrote. "I never told any one about it because I was too ashamed."

That same year, she started cheerleading for Pop Warner, the junior football and cheerleading organization dating back to 1929. Her mother enthusiastically pushed her into cheerleading for the Clarksburg Bears junior football team. Over the next few years, she would become her daughter's biggest fan, attending every game Shelly cheered in.

"She really loved cheerleading," remembered Kathi Goots. "It just struck her . . . and just stayed with it."

Cheerleading soon became *the* most important thing in Shelly Goots' life. She loved the applause of the crowd, when she back-flipped across the football field. And it fulfilled a deep need she would always have, to be admired and respected.

Years later, she would complain that her father was usually too busy to see her in action, writing about her excitement on the rare occasions when he did.

In 1984, a Clarksburg newspaper wrote a story about Shelly and another student making it to the final of the Junior High Division of the Individual Cheerleading competition. There was a photograph of the grinning 12-year-old, holding a giant pom-pom.

The now yellowing clipping remains one of her most treasured possessions.

In May 1985, Shelly started junior high at Notre Dame High School, where her father had gone. Renee Orme went along with her, and they both immediately tried out for the cheerleading squad.

At the time it was a requirement that cheerleaders do back-handsprings, so the tenacious 13-year-old spent weeks practicing hour-after-hour to perfect her technique. But she kept falling on her neck, and just could not get it right.

"She stuck at it," recalled her mother. "In junior high she wouldn't or couldn't do a back-handspring. And I was working on it [with her]. Her cheering advisor said, 'Michelle, if you can't do your back-handspring, you're going to have to sit over there, and we're going to stop the practice until you do it.'"

Eventually Shelly mastered it, quickly learning a lot more throws and tumbling tricks.

"Cheerleading was my life," she later recalled. "I loved everything about it."

Shelly was proud to be a Notre Dame cheerleader, going along as they won several state championships. She loved being known in town as the best, delighting in wearing the squad's "trademark" pigtails, fondly known as "Mickey Mouse ears," in their hair.

"That was something she was always passionate about," recalled Renee, also on the cheerleading squad. "It was just something that was an important part of her."

By the time Shelly joined Notre Dame High School, she was a driving force behind the cheerleading team. She modeled herself on the squad's experienced coach, Carol Morrison, who was from Kentucky.

"One of my 'idols,'" Shelly later wrote. "I wanted to be just like her; a successful career woman, an excellent cheering coach, and a great mother and wife."

But Shelly Goots didn't just make a name for herself, cheerleading on the football field. She was also a straight-A student, and at the top of her class in science and math.

"She excelled academically," recalled Renee. "Always great grades. It seemed to come easy to her."

Shelly also found time to run track, swim and play basketball. She was an active member of the student council, on the yearbook committee, manager of the school store, a member of the Key Club and the Spanish club, and vice-president of the National Honor Society.

"She did it all," remembered her sister Jennifer, who was two years behind her in school. "And she was very popular."

According to Renee Orme, Shelly never had a single enemy in high school.

"She had no airs about her," she said. "She was just this little tiny girl with a lot of energy."

As his business prospered, Michael Goots took off alternate weekends from work to devote to his family. He would take his three children camping in the mountains, or to the race-track, where he competed in truck and stock car races. And they also vacationed at Virginia Beach, Niagara Falls and amusement parks all over the East Coast.

"Shelly's family was loving, supportive and tight-knit," said Renee Orme, who joined them on several vacations.

On Christmas Eve, three generations of Gootses would gather at grandfather John Batista's house, for the traditional family celebration.

"We'd have a big family get-together," said Jennifer. "Shelly played a big role in it."

But Jennifer had problems growing up in the shadow of her over-achieving older sister.

"We didn't get along all that well," she admitted. "I guess there was too much sibling rivalry. Shelly's super smart, super athletic, super everything."

Later Shelly would explain that her need to excel masked feelings of deep insecurity and low self-esteem. Although she was an exceptionally pretty girl with the perfect body of an athlete, Shelly considered herself plain and unattractive. In her early teens she developed bad acne, making her insecure around boys.

"Most of my friends were very pretty," she later recalled. "I was just referred to as the 'nice' one."

CHAPTER 2

Only Bad Girls Do It

Kathi Goots was particularly strict with her daughter Shelly when it came to boys. Shelly was forbidden from calling them on the telephone, always told it was the boy's place to call her. And even then, she could only talk on the phone for half-an-hour.

"My mother always taught me that sex was bad," Shelly later wrote. "And only bad girls did it."

Her mother also forbade her being in a car alone with a boy until she was 16. Shelly later complained that all these rules scared boys away, and believed that that was exactly what her mother had wanted.

In summer 1986, Shelly Goots started dating a boy named George Lamb, considering him her first "real" boyfriend. They dated for a year, breaking up after she accused him of cheating.

Then she had a brief relationship with another boy named Brad Skinner, but ditched him, as she did not have "strong feelings" for him.

That summer, Michael Goots bought some land at Circle Drive in Mount Clare, just south of Clarksburg, to build a new house for his family. When Kathi first saw it, she thought he was "crazy," as the land was nothing more than an overgrown hillside. But Goots insisted on buying it, and once he began excavations, his vision of their new house slowly began to take shape.

Every weekend Michael, Kathi and their three children moved into a trailer on the property, spending all day moving dirt, cutting down trees and digging a pond. It would be two years of hard, backbreaking work, until it was ready to move into.

That Labor Day weekend, Shelly, now 14, went with friends to the Clarksburg Italian Heritage Festival. They were at the Sheraton Hotel, when she started drinking vodka and orange juice. Eventually she got drunk, and was taken home to sleep off the effects on a couch.

The next morning, her mother smelled alcohol on her breath. Although Shelly insisted she had not been drinking, her punishment was to spend all day seeding her father's property in the 90-degree heat.

A few weeks later, Shelly was stopped for shoplifting at a clothes store in a local mall, but never prosecuted. She would later describe the incident as a bad joke.

"I'm still ashamed of it," she later told detectives. "Friends were shoplifting from Ames, and I ended up carrying the bag out. [I] knew that it was shoplifting, but I went along."

Everything changed for Shelly on her 16th birthday, when her parents bought her a black Ford Escort GT. Soon she was driving her friends to McDonald's, or around the Notre Dame parking lot.

After school, Shelly would tell her mother she was going to study in the library, but instead she and Renee drove to their boyfriends' high school to hang out together.

That summer, Shelly and Renee were sunbathing at the Quiet Dell Pool in Clarksburg, when they met Sean Messe and Patrick Lance. Pretty soon all four became inseparable, spending weekends at local clubs like Hammerheads and the Long Beach Inn, drinking wine coolers or beer.

"We would double-date together," remembered Renee. "She had a couple of what you would categorize as serious boyfriends through high school."

Shelly and Sean were together three years, and he gave her a "promise" ring, pledging to marry her eventually. She loved cheering for Sean's football team, showing off in front of his friends and family, by executing perfect back flips up and down the gym floor.

In March 1989, Michael Goots' dream home was finally completed, and his family moved in. His elder daughter was now a high school senior, working as a part-time waitress to make extra money. She helped him run electric cables through the house, as well as painting and fastening drywall.

That first Christmas in the new house, Michael Goots hosted the annual family celebrations, as he would do from then on.

Shelly Goots turned 18 on January 29, 1990, and seemed to have everything going for her. She had just been voted the student "most likely to succeed" by her classmates.

In May, Shelly graduated as salutatorian with honors, with a grade point average of 3.90, and her parents were delighted.

"It was very good," said her mother. "Of course, you've got to realize that there were about twenty-six people that were actually in the class, as it was a very small Catholic school. But she was still salutatorian."

At her senior prom, Shelly's date had a bet with friends that he could have sex with her that night. Later she discovered the wager, writing that she was "so proud and thankful" that she had stuck to her principles and only allowed him to kiss her.

After she graduated, Shelly found a summer job as a cashier, as she and Renee began applying to several universities. The two friends were accepted by four of them, and opted to attend Xavier University in Cincinnati, Ohio.

But just before their first semester, they decided Ohio was too far away from their parents, instead choosing West Virginia University (WVU) in Morgantown, just 34 miles northeast of Clarksburg.

Several days before she was due to leave for Morgantown, Shelly's beloved grandfather John B. Goots died after a stroke and complications from diabetes and heart disease. Shelly, who had always been close to him, was devastated.

"That was especially bad," remembered her mother. "The day she was leaving to go to school was the day we had the funeral."

CHAPTER 3

West Virginia University

It would take Shelly Goots a long time to feel comfortable in Morgantown—a town twice as big as Clarksburg, with its sprawling WVU campus.

Morgantown was first settled in 1772 by Colonel Zackquill Morgan, the son of Colonel Morgan Morgan, reputed to have been the first white settler in the region later to become West Virginia. In 1785 the Virginia Assembly chartered the territory along the banks of the beautiful Monongalia River, holding a lot sale, and Colonel Morgan, who had valiantly fought against the British in the American Revolutionary War, was awarded the charter to establish fifty acres in the eponymous Morgan's Town.

In February 1838, the town was incorporated and renamed Morgantown. A quarter-of-a-century later, it became part of the newly created State of West Virginia.

West Virginia University was founded in 1867 as an all-male institution, with just six faculty members and six students. At that time WVU tuition was only $8 per term, as well as $3.50 a week board and lodging.

Over the next twenty years, WVU grew rapidly, and in September 1889 the first ten women were accepted on campus. By the 1920s, WVU had become one of the preeminent colleges in the South.

The Mountaineer athletic legacy dates back to fall 1891, when a group of WVU students took on a team from Washington & Jefferson College, Pittsburgh, in the newly invented game of football. The match was played in a cow pasture outside Morgantown.

Over the years, the Mountaineers have included many other sports like baseball, basketball, soccer and wrestling. The "Old Gold and Blue"—WVU official school colors—and the distinctive Mountaineer logo, are common sights in Morgantown.

College life revolved around the Mountaineer football team, and freshmen had to run around Mountaineer Field in a group before every game—compulsory to attend.

In recent times the Mountaineers football team has had one of the best records in the Northeast Conference. In 1986, Mountaineer Field was expanded to 63,175 seats. Two years later, the Mountaineers had their first ever undefeated season, culminating in a win over the University of Notre Dame in the Fiesta Bowl.

When Shelly Goots arrived in Morgantown, she set her sights on becoming a WVU cheerleader. But it would take almost a year before she got the call.

In their freshman year, Shelly and Renee roomed together at the Arnold Hall Dormitory on Price Street. Shelly was majoring in Pre-Pharmacy and Renee in Business. It was an exciting time for the two childhood friends, and they enthusiastically threw themselves into WVU college life.

"It was the first time we had been away from home," remembered Renee. "We would go out and have a good time as any eighteen-year-olds would. It was a fun place to be."

Shelly remembers that first year as "amazing," boasting that although she "partied a lot," she still managed a 4.0 grade point average.

But her mother remembers Shelly's freshman year slightly differently.

"She was just lost," said Kathi Goots. "She went from a class of twenty students to two hundred—from a very structured high school to a large university. The first year at college was very rough for her."

After a few months of struggling with her courses, Shelly switched majors to Nursing.

"She was going to go into Pharmacy," said her mother. "But she had some difficulty with the chemistry."

Gradually Shelly settled into college academics, applying herself to her studies.

"She was home in our dormitory every night," said Renee, who had also switched her major to Journalism. "She was just there to study. We lived in a strict environment. She didn't seem to wander or go around with boys."

Although Shelly supported herself with student loans and grants, her father paid the rent. Her sister Jennifer, who would follow her to WVU a couple of years later, often came to visit. But most holidays and birthdays, Shelly came home to Clarksburg, spending time with her long-time boyfriend Sean Messe.

According to Shelly, the relationship soured when she announced that she wanted to try out for the WVU cheerleading squad. When Sean told her that only sluts became college cheerleaders, as all the players were perverts, she ended their three-year relationship.

Shelly and Renee lived down the hallway from a couple of other girls from Clarksburg, and they all went out three nights a week to one of the many downtown bars and nightclubs.

"We had a great time," Shelly recalled, "but it was all clean fun . . . We just drank our beer or mixed drinks, danced our butts off, and went home to crash in our rooms."

Renee said that during that time, Shelly never once brought a boy back into their dorm room, explaining that it would have been difficult, as students had to check in and out at the front desk.

"We lived in a strict environment," she recalled. "You couldn't do much."

For 1991 Spring Break, Renee drove Shelly and two friends to Daytona, Florida, in her father's new Ford Probe.

Shelly would later describe it as "quite a trip," after they were kicked out of a bar before receiving a speeding ticket.

Another night, carrying a case of beer up to their hotel room, they were stopped by an undercover policeman. Before giving them a citation, the policeman made Shelly and her friends call their parents, informing them about the underage alcohol ticket.

Shelly expected to be in "deep trouble" when she got home. But the incident was never mentioned, her father giving her a new Dodge Daytona Shelby Z sports car instead.

In May, Shelly and Renee moved out of the dorm for their sophomore year, finding an apartment on Stewart Street with two other girls. That summer, though Renee left town, Shelly stayed in Morgantown, getting a job as a cashier at Gabriel Brothers clothing store. And as her friends had left for the long summer vacation, she started making new ones.

She became inseparable from a fellow Gabriel's employee named Pat Black. They would socialize together every weekend, but according to Shelly their "special" relationship was strictly platonic, and they never even discussed dating.

In February 1992, 20-year-old Shelly Goots started dating a handsome student named Bruce Adkins, who was also in the Air Force Reserve.

"We met at a place we worked together," she recalled, "and we dated for a while."

By spring, she found herself pregnant.

"I was so afraid to tell my father," she later wrote "because he was an old fashion, Italian catholic man, and girls like me just don't get pregnant without being married."

When Shelly told her father, he was "adamant" they get married and legitimize the baby. But after meeting Bruce, her parents changed their minds.

"There was talk of [marriage]," recalled her mother. "But he wasn't ready to be a father, or a husband either."

Renee Orme was shocked by the pregnancy, for although

they shared an apartment, she had no idea Shelly even had a boyfriend.

"That took me by surprise," remembered Renee. "That relationship and the obvious pregnancy that resulted. I wasn't even really aware of the gentleman until I found out she was pregnant. She was going in her direction and I was going in [mine]."

In May, Renee moved into her sorority house, while Shelly briefly lived with Bruce Adkins and his brother in an apartment on Ross Street.

Years later Shelly would recall being "very excited" to be pregnant, saying that Adkins had been very supportive and she would have married him, if he had only asked.

Shelly continued her studies as long as possible, and then her mother moved to Morgantown to help her through her final trimester.

"She just kept on trucking," said her sister Jennifer. "She's a very versatile person."

On December 17, 1992, Shelly Goots gave birth in Clarksburg to a baby boy she named Alec. The day he was born, she was photographed cuddling her "little Goob." For the next few months her mother helped her cope with her new baby.

A couple of months later, Shelly and Bruce broke up, as he still refused to marry her. Then in May, soon after her 21st birthday, Shelly returned to Morgantown with baby Alec, moving into the Timberline Apartments. She cut her course load to become a part-time student.

"She went back to school for the next semester," recalled her mother, "and I went to Morgantown and spent as much time as I could with Alec. It was difficult, but you just bond together and do it the best way you can."

As a young unmarried student mother, Shelly received benefits from Aid to Families With Dependent Children, as well as food stamps.

Soon after Alec's birth, Shelly resumed her rigorous exercise routine. When he was 7 months old, she tried out for the WVU cheerleaders, encouraged by her friend Pat Black.

"I had always wanted to be a WVU cheerleader," she explained. "I decided to go for it."

And Black was with her when she received the call informing her that she had been accepted into the cheerleading squad.

Kathi Goots fully supported her daughter's dream to resume cheerleading, sharing in her future triumphs.

"Yes, she started cheering," her mother remembered. "I went to all the games with Alec. He was just a little thing."

As Shelly was on the second-tier squad, below varsity, she only cheered home games, so she would not have to travel with the team. To help her, Bruce Adkins looked after Alec during the twice-weekly practices. Then Kathi would take the baby to home games, to see his mom in action.

The first time Shelly performed in front of the thousands of fans at Mountaineer Field, she found it "almost indescribable."

"Shelly did back-handsprings," recalled her proud mother, "down the whole length of the field in front of sixty-five thousand [cheering fans]."

The highpoint of her first season was cheering for the Mountaineers when they beat Miami during a heavy snowstorm to cap an undefeated season. And Shelly loved looking up into the stands, to see her mother and baby Alec waving to her.

Over the next two years, little Alec Goots became something of a mascot to the other cheerleaders, who nicknamed him "Bubba."

That fall, Shelly Goots was accepted into the WVU Nursing program, soon proving to be excellent in the field. She had decided to study child development, with a view towards becoming a pediatric nurse one day.

"When she started college," said her sister Jennifer, "she knew that's what she wanted to do."

Kathi Goots recalls her daughter always having an affinity for babies and young children.

"She always loved to be around babies," she said. "Anybody who had a baby in the family—she was right there."

In June 1994, 43-year-old Michael Goots had a serious heart attack. He recovered after having stents placed, but would need medical care from then on.

A few weeks later, Pat Black took Shelly and a few of his friends to the Buffalo Wild Wings restaurant, on Morgantown's High Street. Later they were joined by Rob Angus, a WVU student friend of Black's, who soon struck up a rapport with Shelly.

Shelly made the first move, asking him to hold her hairbrush for her. And later, when she went over to the juke box to play some records, he followed, inviting her out on a date.

"He did not seem like my type," she remembered. "I was not completely thrilled or excited . . . but I did not want to hurt his feelings, so I said yes."

As a young mother with a small child, Shelly had not dated anyone for a long time, feeling that her romantic choices were limited. On their first date, the ruggedly handsome mustached student, who was eight months younger, "treated [her] like a queen," and she thought him "a great 'smoozer.'"

They soon became serious, after Angus met Alec, immediately forming a strong bond with the little boy. Shelly was delighted, deciding he would make a great father for Alec.

"She seemed to really like Rob," said Renee Orme, who had been appointed Alec's godmother. "She said he had a great personality. They had fun and he treated her well. I honestly think she was looking for companionship and somebody to be the father-figure for her son."

Soon after they started dating, Bruce Adkins returned to Morgantown after a few months away, to propose marriage. He said he had had a change of mind, begging Shelly to marry him, and provide a family for Alec.

But Shelly refused, saying she had moved on and was seeing someone else. Adkins was very upset, but walked away gracefully, finally settling down in Ohio with another woman.

That summer, Rob Angus drove to Clarksburg, to formally ask Michael Goots for his daughter's hand in marriage.

"He came down to talk to Dad about it," remembered Jennifer, "before he actually made it official."

Rob immediately hit it off with Shelly's father, and the rest of her family liked him too.

"He's a good storyteller," said Jennifer. "So he's the life of the room, and he's got a story for everything."

In September, soon after Shelly and Rob got engaged, she became pregnant. Shelly had an abortion in Pittsburgh, later claiming that Rob told her it was not a good time to have another child.

After her "difficult" abortion, Shelly claims their relationship deteriorated into bitter arguments and constant fighting. She wrote of having never really known her fiancé, wondering if he had just changed towards her or had always been a "total fake."

That Thanksgiving, Shelly's grandmother Geraldine Goots died, and she returned to Clarksburg for the funeral. It was an emotional time for the family, as Shelly and her mother started planning for her upcoming wedding.

Her sister Jennifer urged her to call off the nuptials after Shelly confided her reservations with all the problems they were having. But as the invitations had gone out, she decided to go ahead, as her son Alec really loved Rob.

That football season, Shelly Goots went to a tournament in Philadelphia with the WVU cheerleading squad. It was the first and only time she would travel out-of-town with the Mountaineers.

During an after-game party, she began drinking beer, commenting how she thought one of the trainers was cute. The next thing she recalls is waking up in a hotel room, with the trainer on top of her having sex.

"I was so intoxicated," she later explained, "that I do not remember how I got there, [or] how the encounter started."

The next morning she returned to her own room, feeling "humiliated and filthy." Shelly maintains that she never told anyone what had happened, being uncertain if she had been raped or "had went along with it" [sic] under the influence of alcohol.

"I can not remember for certain," she wrote. "That was the end of my cheerleading career at WVU. I never tried out again after that."

CHAPTER 4

Settling Down

On July 22, 1995, Shelly married Rob Angus at the Immaculate Conception Catholic church in Clarksburg. Her two-and-a-half-year-old son Alec, dressed in a tuxedo, was ring-bearer.

"Robby was standing up there at the altar waiting for Shelly to come in," remembered Kathi Goots. "And Alec came in and just ran up the aisle, yelling, 'Daddy, Daddy, Daddy!' So Robby held him during the entire ceremony."

The 23-year-old bride looked stunning, wearing a low-cut pure white silk wedding dress with a long veil, and holding a corsage. The dashing groom wore a tuxedo and a rose in the buttonhole.

She would later recall telling herself as she slowly walked down the aisle that she would grow to love him.

Renee Orme, who had graduated WVU the previous year and moved to Philadelphia, was a bridesmaid.

"It was a decent-sized wedding," she remembered. "Shelly seemed happy and . . . in retrospect . . . she wished it didn't happen. Although at the time . . . you wouldn't have thought anything else leaving the wedding, other than 'These are two people who are happy to be getting married.' "

After a brief honeymoon, Rob Angus moved into the Timberline Apartments with Shelly and Alec. A few months later, BOPARC the Morgantown Board of Park and Recreation Commissioners, where Angus worked as a part-time caretaker, provided them with a small house in a town park to live in.

Soon after the wedding, Bruce Adkins suggested that Rob officially adopt Alec as his own son.

"Alec and Rob jumped at the chance," Shelly would later testify, "because they really bonded. So we just all agreed."

But that was perhaps the only positive thing in their marriage. Shelly claims the marriage soon imploded in "anger and violence." She "began to hate" her new husband, describing herself as "a loveless witch."

She later wrote of daily screaming matches in front of little Alec, culminating in physical violence from both sides.

Jennifer Goots, who was now a student at WVU, would make daily visits to look after Alec, and witnessed the acrimonious marriage first-hand.

"He knew how to push her buttons," remembered Jennifer. "They were better not together, that's for sure."

Around Christmas, Shelly became pregnant again, after missing a birth control pill. She wanted the baby, asking Rob to undergo marriage counseling, but he refused.

In early 1996, Shelly and Rob Angus visited Renee in Philadelphia for the first of several visits.

"They loved going to New York," said Renee. "So we would drive into New York to see a show or do something."

Although they now lived far apart, the best friends kept in close touch with each other.

"Sometimes we would talk weekly," Renee remembered. "It would just depend [on] what was going on in her life."

But Renee had no idea of the turbulent state of her best friend's marriage, as Shelly always kept up the pretense of having a "perfect family."

In May, Shelly Angus began her sixth year at WVU, with one more year remaining until graduation.

"I think she slowed down a little," said Jennifer, who married her boyfriend Joe Barker in June 1996. "She had Alec and was going part-time for a little while."

In September, thirty-nine weeks pregnant, Shelly was charged with shoplifting a pumpkin Halloween costume for Alec at Ames Department Store in Star City. She later claimed that it had been a mistake, and she'd put the costume in her bag and forgotten about it.

"I was accused of shoplifting," she would later tell police. "It was purely unintentional. I did not mean to leave the store with an unpurchased thing, but, you know, it was just my word."

A few days later, she was found guilty by a female judge, who commented on her being so heavily pregnant in the dock.

On October 3, Shelly gave birth to a baby girl they named Kylie. Shelly was proud of having carefully scheduled classes so she did not have to take any time off school to give birth.

"I had her on a Thursday," she recalled, "and was back to school one week later [sic] on Monday."

Shelly and Rob loved their new daughter, and little Alec immediately bonded with her too. Every Monday morning, Kathi Goots would dutifully drive in from Clarksburg to look after her new granddaughter.

For 1997 Spring Break, Shelly left her family to go to Myrtle Beach, South Carolina, with some of her WVU college friends.

A month later—after seven years as a student—she finally graduated WVU with a Bachelor's Degree in Nursing, and a minor in Child Development.

"I have always been sort of an 'over-achiever'," she explained, "and I was very proud and excited to finally be an RN."

A few months earlier, Shelly had been offered a nursing job at the Pediatric Intensive Care Unit (PICU) at WVU's Ruby Memorial Hospital. In June she became a registered nurse, licensed by the West Virginia State Board of Examiners at a salary of $28 an hour.

She loved working with the young children in the PICU unit, finding her new job "thrilling and challenging."

Soon after she started her new profession, Renee visited Morgantown with her new boyfriend Eric Del Viscio.

"They were living in the park," he remembered. "[Shelly] was running around with the two kids, because Kylie had just been born. She was obviously busy with that and taking care of the house."

Eric was eager to make a good impression on Shelly, as he knew she and Renee were very close.

"I tried not to be too forward," he recalled. "So I was laid back. I took my time. But she was very nice."

During the brief visit, he was impressed by Shelly's organizational skills, and how well she balanced her new nursing job with being a mother.

"She's a hyper-kinetic person," he said. "There's just not a lot of grass under her feet."

Before long, Nurse Shelly Angus was making a big impression on her PICU colleagues.

"She was all about flirting with the boys that we worked with," remembered PICU respiratory therapist Stephanie Michael. "Cheerleader moves in the unit. She just came over and did this high kick to her ear, and just kinda giggled and kept walking."

Another respiratory therapist, Reggie Ours, was amazed when he first met Shelly.

"She still thought she was a college cheerleader," he remembered. "She loved the attention."

About a year after she started working at Ruby, Nurse Shelly Angus met Stephanie Michael's husband Jimmy, who was working the same weekend shifts. When things were slow in the PICU, they would sit around with the other staff, watching NASCAR races together on television, or chatting.

There was an instant attraction between Jimmy Michael and Shelly Angus.

CHAPTER 5

The Hunter

Jimmy Michael was born in Cumberland, Maryland, on February 20, 1972, exactly three weeks after Shelly Angus. The second son of Baptist pastor Denny Michael and his wife Ruth, Jimmy grew up steeped in a religious family tradition going back generations.

His grandfather Ralph Andrew Michael was a pastor, as was his Uncle Larry. Jimmy too would devote his life to being a good Christian and trying to serve God.

Lying 75 miles due east of Morgantown on I-68, Cumberland is etched into the deep shadow of the Appalachian Mountains. It was named for King George II's son Prince William, the Duke of Cumberland. As Colonel George Washington's first military headquarters, it played a major role in the French and Indian War.

Cumberland was a flourishing industrial city in the early 19th century, supplying coal, iron ore and timber from the nearby mountain ranges. But after the Second World War many factories closed, sending Cumberland into a deep decline, its population falling by almost half.

Denny Michael was raised on a hobby farm just outside town by his father Ralph, who worked for a light and heating manufacturer, and mother Lorna Lee. He went to Fort

Hill High School on Greenway Avenue in Cumberland, where he met a pretty student named Ruth Stinson.

"We were high school sweethearts," remembered Ruth. "I was fifteen and he was seventeen when we met."

They were married on May 19, 1966, and nearly three years later, they had their first son Steve, followed by Jimmy in 1972.

Denny worked for NCR Corporation for twelve years, before buying Mel's Business Systems and going into business for himself.

"I was an entrepreneur," he said. "I always brought in real estate, but I never fooled with the stock market."

During his eighteen years running Mel's Business Systems, Denny bought and sold land and property, always turning a tidy profit. Then he found his vocation, spending thirteen years as pastor of the Mineral Heights Baptist Church.

"I was a pastor, and I ran a business too," he said. "I was always dabbling in stuff."

His two sons Steve and Jimmy were as different as night and day. Steve was tall, athletic but not academically inclined, while Jimmy was short, overweight and a gifted student.

"He was the typical younger brother," Steve remembered. "As boys, we always fought . . . and we tried to get each other in trouble. I was always the athlete and he was the smarter one, I suppose."

Their father saw himself in his younger son, and they always had a special relationship.

"He was my footprint," explained Denny. "He said to me one day, 'Dad, you're a hard act to follow.' "

After attending Northeast Elementary School, Jimmy went to Washington Junior High. He sat next to a little girl named Kerri Whitacre, and they instantly became friends.

Kerri says their parents had grown up together, and first remembers meeting Jimmy as infants at family gatherings. But it wasn't until junior high that they began an enduring friendship, lasting the rest of his life.

"We had a brother–sister relationship," she explained. "We

were very close. He watched out for me and I watched out for him."

The young boy loved to listen to music, spending hours with his cousin Kelly, listening to their favorite records. Jimmy especially liked Elvis Presley's "Hound Dog," playing it over and over again.

As a child Jimmy—or Jimbo, as he was nicknamed by the family—had a quirky sense of humor that endeared him to everyone. He always knew how to make people smile.

"Once he had toys scattered all over the bedroom," recalled Denny. "His mother said, 'Jimmy, before you get in that bed, clean all those toys up or you're going to get a whipping.'"

She then left to do some chores, returning in a few minutes to find the light switched off and the bedroom in darkness.

As she started walking in, Jimmy said, 'Don't turn the light on! Don't turn the light on!' So she turned the light on and the toys are still scattered all over. She said, 'Jimmy, I told you to pick those toys up.' And he said, 'I told you not to turn on the light.'"

When Jimmy was in the 8th grade, his father taught him how to hunt deer. A couple of years earlier Steve had disappointed him by showing little interest in hunting, but Jimmy loved it.

From then on, every Thanksgiving—the first day of the hunting season—Denny would take his youngest son out with him. And over the years hunting provided a bonding experience between father and son.

"Jimmy loved hunting," said Denny. "And he was pretty good. We hunted with rifles and a little bit of bow. I won't kill anything unless I'm going to eat it. When I was growing up, that was a way of life."

Denny also took Jimmy fishing in a lake in upstate New York, and each summer the whole family vacationed at the beach or went to amusement parks.

Like their parents, Steve and Jimmy both went to Fort Hill High School, although they were two years apart. Once again, Jimmy and Kerri Whitacre sat next to each other in class.

"He was the guy everybody wanted to be around," recalled Kerri. "He was likable. He was funny. He was upbeat."

All through high school, football-loving Jimmy was overweight and highly self-conscious about it. He was nicknamed "Chunk," and although he good-naturedly laughed it off, his weight would always be a problem.

"Jimmy was really overweight when he went to high school," said his mother. "But it never stopped him from having a lot of friends."

His cousin Daniel Twigg grew up with Jimmy, witnessing his constant battle with obesity.

"He always had weight issues he struggled with," said Twigg, "but was very, very confident."

The Michael family lived in a large house with a swimming pool, and Jimmy often invited all his football teammates over for swimming.

On one occasion, his high school football coach ordered Jimmy to go on a diet or be banned from the sport, saying that his excess weight made him too accident-prone.

"So he lost the weight," said his mother. "We'd come home and find him [swimming] with twenty kids."

Growing up, Jimmy Michael was "reckless," always getting into bad scrapes and hurting himself. Once his father watched him ride a trail bike in the church parking lot, and get hit by a car.

"He flew off and landed clear upon the hood of this car," said Denny. "Then he saw me coming across the yard, and jumped up, saying, 'Nothing wrong with me, Dad, I'm fine.' Because he thought I was going to whip him."

So when Jimmy asked his father to buy him a motorcycle for his sixteenth birthday, his father refused.

"No way," Denny told his son, "because you'll kill yourself on that highway."

* * *

Jimmy always got good grades, deciding at a young age that he wanted to go to medical school and help sick children.

"He was always ambitious," said his mother. "I still have a letter that he wrote in the first grade . . . that he wanted to be a pediatrician."

He would also discuss his dreams for the future with Kerri, always his closest confidante.

"He was very optimistic," she recalled. "He knew he was going to go into the medical field. And Jimmy was a person that, if he had a goal, he was going to reach it. He was very disciplined."

In high school, Jimmy fell deeply in love with another student named Pamela Ross (not her real name). They were together for two years, but her mother didn't approve of the relationship, eventually causing their break-up.

"He was truly in love with her," recalled Ruth. "Her mother didn't want her to have a steady in high school, so she made it pretty rough. And it nearly broke his heart."

Ruth says her son took the break-up badly, sinking into a deep depression.

"He kind of scared me," she remembered. "I thought maybe he was suicidal."

While they were breaking up, Jimmy was writing a class paper on death and dying. One day Ruth read his notes, and was relieved that he could never imagine killing himself.

Finally, Denny had to give his son a man-to-man talk, to help him get over it.

"He came home one day, carrying on," remembered his father. "So I just took him in the bedroom and I said, 'Look, when you get your college education, you'll have plenty of women. There's a lot of young girls out there, looking for someone with a good head on their shoulders. That's the kind of girl you want.' He straightened up after that and he was fine."

When Jimmy and Kerri graduated together in the class of 1990, he was her escort at a graduation party at a friend's house.

"We shared graduation night together," she said. "We had

fun, sitting around sharing high school stories. We talked about where we and our friends were going, and what we were going to do with our lives."

As a graduation gift, Kerri gave Jimmy a scrapbook she had made to commemorate their schooldays together.

Soon after he graduated, Jimmy wanted to go to James Madison University in Harrisonburg, Virginia. But Denny insisted he go to Allegany College in Cumberland, Maryland, so he could keep a close eye on his son.

"Jimmy wasn't mature enough to handle a big school," explained Ruth, "because he'd probably go partying. He needed that extra year."

So that fall, Jimmy went to Allegany College to study respiratory therapy, with a view toward going to medical school one day. He then moved into an apartment close to the family home, with another student named Reggie Ours.

"We became very good friends," said Ours. "He was a good guy."

With just four students in their respiratory therapy class, everyone socialized together. And it was not long before gregarious Jimmy invited everyone over to his parents' house, to go swimming in the pool.

"A lot of us ended up over at his house," remembered Ours. "And his mom would cook for me every once in a while."

Ruth Michael thoroughly approved of Reggie Ours, believing him a good influence on her son.

"They were like 'the Odd Couple,'" she said. "Reggie was the neat one."

Although Jimmy's old school friend Kerri Whitacre was now studying psychology elsewhere, they still kept in close touch.

"We always had a running joke," she said. "Who would get their doctorate degree, and if we'd get it by the age of thirty?"

And Jimmy—still battling weight problems—was constantly teased by his roommate about his obsession with skinny girls and cheerleaders.

"I would come home to the apartment and he'd be watching a cheerleading competition on ESPN," remembered Ours. "He liked the cheerleading girls. He always did. Little skinny cheerleading girls."

And Reggie always teased that Jimmy needed a good fat woman to take care of him.

CHAPTER 6

Stephanie

In May 1992, at the age of 20, Jimmy Michael graduated with an Associate's Degree in Respiratory Therapy. He then applied to West Virginia University, being accepted as a Chemistry major.

Then he and Reggie Ours moved to Morgantown, finding jobs as externs at Ruby Memorial Hospital. As Kerri Whitacre was already at WVU studying psychology, she suggested they share an apartment with her boyfriend Seth.

"It just kind of flowed from there," she said. "They all ended up living together."

On Jimmy's first day of orientation at Ruby Memorial, he struck up a conversation with a pretty dark-haired respiratory student nurse named Stephanie, who was five years older than him. There was a mutual attraction, and they soon started dating.

"I remember the first time that I saw Jimmy," said Stephanie. "He was a big teddy bear."

Over the next few months the two externs became close. Stephanie was naturally shy and reserved, while Jimmy's good-natured extrovert character provided a good balance.

Reggie Ours, who also met his future wife Christine that

fall at Ruby Memorial, observed the early days of their relationship.

"They hit it off pretty good," he remembered. "She and Jimmy had a lot of the same qualities. He liked the real skinny girls—the pretty skinny girls—and that's how Stephanie fit in."

Soon after they met, Jimmy brought Stephanie to Cumberland to meet his parents.

"He brought her to the house," recalled Ruth Michael. "I said, 'How old is she?' Because he said she'd already graduated. Five years is not a big deal."

Ruth believes Jimmy and Stephanie met on the rebound. He was still recovering from a broken heart, while she had also just broken up with somebody.

"She was different," said his mother. "I don't think Jimmy was truly in love."

That winter, Jimmy worked hard at his studies, while getting his first real experience of being a respiratory therapist. His naturally calming manner endeared him to his patients, and he especially loved working with children.

"I would ask him how the job was going," said Whitacre. "And he would say, 'It's good. I really like this. I'm helping infants.'"

In early 1993, Jimmy and Stephanie became engaged, and one of the first people he told was Kerri Whitacre.

"And I said to him," she remembered, "'Is this what your heart tells you to do?' and he said, 'Yes, I want to get married.'"

Soon afterwards, Jimmy and Stephanie moved into an apartment together, while Reggie Ours moved into one with his fiancée.

On June 19, after Stephanie became pregnant, Denny Michael hastily married the couple in a secret wedding at his house, without telling the bride's family.

"I think that's part of what happened with their relationship," said Denny. "Because we married them and we didn't tell her parents."

Reggie Ours said that although Jimmy's closest friends were aware of the wedding, they were not invited.

"It was a private wedding," he said. "His dad was the pastor that married them."

A few weeks later, Jimmy and Stephanie went through the charade of a second church wedding, this time organized by Stephanie's parents.

"It was a disaster," remembered Jimmy's mother. "Stephanie's pregnant and she's trying to get her dress up."

Later, after Stephanie's parents discovered the truth about the first wedding, they always resented Jimmy and his parents.

On February 11, 1994, Stephanie gave birth to a baby boy they named James Andrew II, after his father. But he would always be called Drew.

Jimmy was delighted to be a father, taking his new responsibilities very seriously. But there were a lot of pressures on him, as they lived in a house owned by Stephanie and her father.

"Jimmy's making the payments," said Denny. "And he wanted to buy his own house."

So over the next few years, he worked as many shifts as he could in Ruby Memorial, saving for a mortgage. He also studied hard at WVU, getting a Bachelor's Degree in Chemistry.

After graduating WVU, Jimmy had his sights set on going to medical school. But then he learned there was no money left to put him through school, as Stephanie had secretly run up thousands of dollars of credit card debt.

"He was getting ready to go to med school," remembered Denny, "and she sprung all that on him. So that's why he couldn't go. This was the beginning of the end."

In September 1996, Stephanie, now pregnant with their second child, swore out a police complaint, alleging that Jimmy had "pinched" her arm during an argument. She claimed he then tried to placate her by buying her a bottle of her favorite perfume. The following January, she accused him of throwing a shoe through a window of their house in a fit of temper.

On March 14, 1997, Stephanie and Jimmy had a baby daughter they named Jenna Catherine, who would always be known as Jacie. But their new baby did not improve the marriage, and five months later they separated.

Jimmy moved out and bought himself a new house at 88 Brytes Way, so his children could stay over. But he was devastated by the split, confiding in his old friend Kerri Whitacre, who had now moved to Texas after marrying her boyfriend Seth.

"I think they hit bumps in the road, like everyone does in marriage," said Whitacre. "I know there were some financial issues, and they were pretty big bumps."

During their split, Jimmy and Stephanie saw each other frequently because of the children, as well as working the occasional shift together at Ruby Memorial.

Denny Michael was shocked that the marriage had broken down, counseling Jimmy to go back and try to make it work.

"I didn't want him to get divorced," recalled Denny. "Being a pastor, I said, 'You work these things out.'"

In June 1998, Jimmy and Stephanie had the first of several reconciliations, renewing their marriage vows in a special ceremony.

"We were separated for a little bit right after our daughter was born," said Stephanie. "In the meantime he bought a house, so when he said, 'Come live with me, we're going to renew our marriage vows . . . and make this work,' I moved in."

Stephanie and the children moved into Jimmy's new house, but Stephanie's parents did not approve of the reconciliation, and stopped speaking to her.

Soon after moving back in with Stephanie, Jimmy began working night shifts with Nurse Shelly Angus. And within three months he would walk out on his wife and straight into Shelly's arms.

CHAPTER 7

Chasing Jimmy

Jimmy Michael and Shelly Angus found much in common. They were both in troubled marriages with two children, and that summer they became confidants, discussing their marital problems.

"Jimmy and I would talk off and on at work," Shelly later recalled, "I knew he and Stephanie were having issues, and Rob and I were not getting on very well. And we kinda connected that way. We would just sit around in chairs [at] work when it was slow, and talk, chit-chat."

But many believed Shelly pursued Jimmy, considering him a good catch. They think she cunningly preyed on the ambitious respiratory therapist's vulnerabilities, showering him with compliments and attention.

"She set her sights on him," said Reggie Ours, who worked with them at Ruby Memorial Hospital. "I think from the beginning, what drew her to Jimmy was the fact that she knew he had ambition and was going to be successful."

Shelly Angus was Jimmy's cheerleader fantasy come to life, and he just could not believe she could be interested in him. Over late-night and quiet weekend shifts, she began flirting with him. And she would regale him with her patented back-flips through the PICU, even teaching him how to throw her up in the air and catch her in a chair-sit.

Jimmy's friends on the unit teased him mercilessly about his cheerleading stunts with Shelly, only driving them even closer together.

"She still thought she was a college cheerleader," said Reggie Ours. "She loved it."

At this point, Stephanie had no idea of the growing relationship between Jimmy and Shelly. One night she and Shelly were working a shift together, when the subject of old houses came up.

"Then Shelly chimed in," recalled Stephanie. "She lived in a city-owned house where her husband worked. She hated it and wanted to move."

Stephanie then told her about the nice new house on Brytes Way that Jimmy had recently bought, and Shelly's ears perked up.

A few months later, Stephanie would come to regret telling Shelly about Jimmy's new house.

In the weeks leading up to Christmas 1998, Jimmy and Shelly became lovers. Jimmy, who had recently undergone a vasectomy, was infatuated with her, and they started discussing a future together with their children.

Reggie Ours believes that Shelly was determined to break up Jimmy's marriage, exploiting his weaknesses and luring him with sex. But his friend never discussed Shelly, and he had no idea they were having an affair.

"That was something that he kept very private," said Ours. "I have an idea they messed around while he was still married. Shelly was there pushing and pulling at him. And as he was getting closer to her, he was getting further apart from Stephanie."

Late one night, Stephanie was at home when the phone rang. She picked it up and said "Hello." Then there was slight hesitation before the caller hung up.

"I just remember getting this really funny feeling in the pit of my stomach," she recalled. "I hit the return call code and I wrote the number down."

A couple of days later, Stephanie mentioned the mysterious

hang-up to another nurse, asking if she recognized the number.

"And she opened up the nurses' phone number list," said Stephanie, "and the first number on the page was 'Shelly Angus.'"

Stephanie decided to bide her time and not do anything for the moment.

"I just sat back and let it all unfold."

As the holidays approached, Shelly and Jimmy's marriages were both disintegrating. Their spouses were becoming increasingly suspicious that they were being unfaithful, and there was gossip at the PICU about a possible affair between Nurse Angus and Jimmy Michael.

"There were rumors at work," Stephanie recalled, "about them always being together. When she was working all night long, she would be on the phone, giggling and laughing. And then she was cussing somebody."

Shelly and Jimmy were also visiting each other's houses for late night rendezvouses. One time Shelly stayed the night at Brytes Way while Stephanie was away. When they left the next morning, Rob Angus was standing outside with a camcorder. He then called Stephanie, asking what her husband was doing with his wife.

"Jim was disappearing late at night," said Stephanie, "under the guise of needing stuff at Wal-Mart. And I found out she was doing the same thing."

But things came to a head after she found Christmas presents hidden in a closet.

"They were obviously for a woman," said Stephanie, "so I assumed it was something that I or his mother was getting. And after Christmas morning, when no one had received them, I found presents she had given him."

On December 30, Stephanie finally confronted Jimmy about the affair. A heated argument ensued, and he threatened to kill her, as he attempted to physically throw her out of his house. Later she filed her third complaint with the Monongalia County Prosecuting Attorney's Office.

On New Year's Eve, they again argued about Shelly, as Jimmy adamantly denied having an affair. When Stephanie accused Jimmy outright of cheating on her, he lost his temper, warning her that she was going to "get hurt" if she didn't leave his house.

"He just said that she needed a friend," remembered Stephanie. "That she was having problems with her husband. But at that point I already knew that she had lied about him being over her house."

The following weekend, Jimmy asked Reggie Ours and another friend to help him move Stephanie's belongings out of 88 Brytes Way, into a nearby property he also owned.

"Stephanie had no idea he was moving her stuff out," remembered Ours. "I felt bad. I told him, 'I wish you had told me she didn't know we were going to do this.'"

In January 1999, Shelly walked out on Rob Angus and filed for divorce. Six years later, she would tell police that the marriage had broken down over "lack of trust."

"I couldn't trust him for various reasons," she would claim. "He had a problem with pornography, and I feel like when you want to watch pornography, that is the same as cheating on somebody. I felt very strongly about that."

She would also accuse him of screaming, cursing and yelling at 6-year-old Alec.

"I thought he mistreated him," she said. "Several times I'd leave and say, 'We're done,' and just go back. And then I just left for good."

A couple of weeks later, Shelly told her old friend Renee Orme that she had left Rob.

"She called me one evening to tell me they were breaking up," Renee said. "And then she shared with me some of the reasons."

Shelly accused Rob of being "violent and abusive," never once mentioning the new man in her life. It wasn't until that spring, when Renee visited Morgantown with her new boyfriend Eric Del Viscio, that she first learned of Jimmy Michael.

"That came as a shock," recalled Renee. "She had to go to [Jimmy's] house to pick up something, so I rode with her."

During the drive over, Shelly told her she and Jimmy were just hanging out and helping each other through their various divorces. She never mentioned their romantic involvement.

"That was the first time that I met him," said Renee. "That they were friends . . . supporting each other."

Soon after Shelly walked out of her marriage, Stephanie served Jimmy with divorce papers at the hospital. She had wanted to sue on the grounds of his adultery with Shelly, but her attorney told her she would need photographic proof of them in a compromising situation. So eventually she settled for irreconcilable differences.

As a devout Baptist, Jimmy was having great problems coming to terms with divorce.

"I didn't want him to get divorced," said Ruth Michael. "We encouraged Jimmy to try and save his marriage for the kids' sake. We really did."

Denny Michael believes his son's marriage was already doomed, with or without Shelly.

"Jimmy was wrong for seeing another woman while married," Denny said. "I told him he didn't have biblical reasons for divorce, but he went ahead with it anyway."

That spring, as their divorces went through the family court process, Jimmy and Shelly paved the way for their future life together. The first thing they did was to integrate their families.

When they finally met each other's children, Shelly thought Jimmy's kids Drew and Jacie "really sweet." She felt confident that all four children had "hit it off well."

But although Jacie and Kylie immediately bonded, becoming inseparable best friends, Alec appeared to resent the younger Drew, and would always give him a hard time.

A few weeks later, Jimmy told Kerri Whitacre he had met somebody and was getting divorced. She cautioned him to put his children first, saying she didn't feel that a new relationship was what he needed right now in the midst of a divorce.

"I gave him what for," she remembered. "I told him, 'Jimmy, I want you to think with the head on your shoulders, not the part in your pants.' I was very honest with him."

From her talks with Jimmy, Kerri realized that Shelly would flatter him, complimenting him about his looks and playing on his insecurities.

"Jimmy always battled with his weight," she said. "And he would even say to me, 'She doesn't mind that I'm a little chubbier.'"

He told Kerri he loved Shelly and planned to marry her, once their divorces were final. But Kerri said she and his mother had to meet her, before he did anything rash.

"I said to him," remembered Kerri, "'We have to give her our seal of approval.'"

In late summer, Jimmy brought Stephanie to his parents' new house in Centerville, Pennsylvania. A few months earlier, Ruth Michael had briefly run into Shelly at a funeral for a pediatric patient, but this was their first real meeting.

"We liked her," remembered Denny. "She was outgoing and friendly . . . and seemed like she was good for Jimmy."

Jimmy and Shelly went swimming in the pool, and then Denny took her on a tour of their large red brick house, set in five acres of grounds.

"She thought we were extremely wealthy," remembered Denny. "It looked like the mansion on the hill. I'd bought it as an investment. I do construction work myself, and I had put in a pool and a few things."

As Denny took her on a tour of the house, it was obvious that she was very impressed.

"And Jimmy probably didn't do anything to deter it," said his father. "One of the first things she said to me that day was, 'Why don't you go ahead and give us our inheritance?' It kind of hit me funny. Well, I just brushed it off and said, 'Well, I'm spending Jimmy's inheritance.'"

* * *

On September 7, 1999, Jimmy and Stephanie Michael attended a last divorce hearing at family court. They wouldn't be officially divorced until the following February, when the final paperwork was signed.

A couple of weeks later, Shelly and Rob Angus's divorce was final. The family court awarded them joint custody of Alec and Kylie, with them spending Monday, Tuesday and every other weekend with their father, and the rest of the time with Shelly. Jimmy and Stephanie later agreed to a similar joint custody arrangement when their divorce became final.

Soon afterwards, Shelly moved into 88 Brytes Way, immediately starting a full-scale renovation to her own specifications.

"Sure enough, she got my house," said Stephanie. "And he gutted the entire thing for her—put down all new flooring right when she moved in."

Once Shelly had settled in, Jimmy invited Kerri Whitacre and her boyfriend Seth over for dinner. They arrived to find Jimmy's 5-year-old son Drew laying the table for a spaghetti meal, under Shelly's close supervision. When he finished, she inspected the table, noticing the knives and forks were not perfectly straight, and gave the little boy a telling-off.

"She was very punitive," remembered Kerri. "That was my first impression of Shelly. She became very upset with [Drew], telling him he needed to learn how to set the table right."

Kerri, an educational psychologist, was so surprised by Shelly's anger that she later took Jimmy to one side for a talk.

"I said, "Man, she needs to back off him,'" Kerri remembered. "Drew did what she wanted, and he's young. He's just learning."

As the evening progressed, Kerri felt that Shelly was sending her a definitive message.

"She wanted to get across that, 'You and Jimmy may be good friends,'" said Whitacre. "'However, I'm here now.'"

* * *

That Thanksgiving, Jimmy brought Shelly over to his parents', where she met his older brother Steve for the first time.

"She was a lot different from Stephanie," Steve remembered. "She was more friendly. She was more lovey-dovey and more of a friend at first."

And as they sat down to a lavish turkey dinner, Steve told her, "Shelly, if this doesn't work out, Jimmy's turning gay."

CHAPTER 8

6PACK

On March 24, 2000, Jimmy and Shelly officially became engaged.

"I thought maybe he should wait a little while longer," said Ruth Michael, "before he jumped into it again. But I was OK with her. She seemed to like the kids, and we had fun."

Shelly had now launched a charm offensive on her future in-laws, organizing a stream of social events.

"We were always having picnics," remembered Ruth. "Her family was there, and we all got along great and had a good time."

Stephanie was now dating Rob Angus, but neither knew of the engagement. The first Stephanie found out about it was when she read about it in the local newspaper. She burst into tears.

"He never told me," said Stephanie. "I only knew she had an engagement ring because one of the girls at work told me. Then I read about it in the newspaper, and the kids talked about Daddy getting married. It took a couple of boxes of Kleenex."

To make it even harder, Stephanie still worked shifts with Shelly at Ruby Memorial Hospital's Pediatric Intensive Care Unit.

"I had a mortgage to pay, and babies to feed," she said,

"so I had to go to work and put on a happy face. But I can't honestly say I didn't go into the bathroom and cry."

And whenever they were alone, Stephanie says, Shelly would taunt her about losing Jimmy, threatening to take her children away from her too.

"It was vicious," said Stephanie.

Jimmy and Shelly were married on May 26, 2000, at the Goshen Baptist Church, just outside Morgantown. Shelly looked stunning in an ivory dress, and Jimmy wore a dark blue suit.

Later she would describe it as a "very small and quaint wedding," especially proud of having written their own vows for each other.

Ruth Michael thought them very much in love. She was moved to tears as they stood together at the altar.

"If you'd just seen them when they got married," she said. "The way two people [in love] look at each other."

After the ceremony, there was a small wedding reception at the Lakeview Resort. Kathi and Michael Goots looked after the children on the wedding night, so the bride and groom could be alone together in a hotel room.

Their first few months of marriage were transitional, as they merged their two families into one. Always highly organized and efficient, Shelly took charge, while Jimmy appeared happy to take a back seat.

After the wedding, Shelly banned Jimmy from having any further contact with his ex-wife.

"I wasn't allowed to talk to him anymore," recalled Stephanie. "Anything that I needed to discuss for the children had to go through her. I wasn't even allowed to have his cell phone number. I had to tell Shelly what the issue was. She would call Jim and then call me back with a response."

Although nominally raised a Catholic, having had little contact with religion since she was a child, Shelly now became a devout Baptist under Jimmy's instruction. She began going to church every Sunday with the children, even taking a Bible class entitled "How to Be a Godly Wife."

"He brought Shelly into his faith," said Renee Orme. "She took up religion again, where that had been absent for quite a long time."

Later Shelly recalled making "a lot of adjustments," in the first year of their marriage, noting how they had "significantly more stressors" than the average couple, with the two sets of children. She accused their exes Stephanie and Rob of making her family's life even more difficult.

Shelly's parents believe the couple did a fine job of integrating their children.

"If you saw them together," said Kathi Goots, "you would have thought that they were true siblings."

Shelly took great pride in her new customized "6PACK" vanity license plate, proclaiming her long-cherished dream of having *the* perfect family.

That August, Jimmy started coaching Alec and Drew's Evansdale Tigers Little League football team. And for the next five years he was head coach, while Shelly enthusiastically coached Kylie and Jacie's cheerleading squad.

During the August-to-November football season, Jimmy spent three nights a week, as well as Sundays, coaching football. Rob Angus helped Jimmy coach the community team, as well as mow the grass and drive the Tigers' float in parades.

While on the football field, the two men put aside their differences.

"You get past it because you have to," Angus later explained. "[Our relationship] was as normal as any ex-husband/current husband relationship could be, I guess."

That first season, Jimmy and Shelly befriended another young couple named Bobby and Kelli Teets, whose son Tyler played on the team.

"We were both involved with the Evansdale football program," said Kelli. "That's how we originally became friends."

Bobby also helped Jimmy coach football, and over the next few years the two couples would become increasingly close.

* * *

A few months after their daughter's wedding, Michael and Kathi Goots divorced after twenty-eight years of marriage. Michael remained in the house he had built, while Kathi moved to Nutter Fort, a small town just outside Clarksburg.

"I was devastated, because I always thought we had the perfect family," said Shelly. "I was torn between both of them. It was very hard to handle."

Shelly was "mad" at them, feeling "partly" responsible and wondering if her recent divorce had finally given her mother the "courage" to walk out.

On October 3, Jimmy and Shelly invited their families to celebrate Kylie's fourth birthday at Marilla Park in Morgantown. Everyone happily posed for a group photograph in the gardens outside.

Denny Michael was delighted to see his son so happy with Shelly.

"His relationship with Shelly at the beginning was good," Denny said. "He really loved her and wanted it to work out."

That Christmas, the children celebrated twice—once with Jimmy and Shelly, and then again with their other respective parents. It would be the pattern for all future holidays with the complicated shared-custody arrangements for both sets of children.

In February 2001, Stephanie filed yet another complaint against Jimmy. This time she accused him of trying to run her down during a heated argument, with Shelly and Jacie in the car.

Each side subsequently filed protective orders against the other. At a later court hearing, Jimmy plea-bargained no contest to simple assault, so he wouldn't have a criminal record and automatically lose his hunting license.

"I did ask that the charges be dropped," said Stephanie, "if he would attend anger management classes. I did not want to go to court for this."

During their first year of marriage, Shelly believed her ex-husband Rob was "conspiring" with Stephanie against them.

Shelly thought Jimmy "a little insecure" about the children, leading to arguments. He felt she favored Alec over Drew, and was "bothered" that she'd given his son Alec's old clothes, after Alec had grown out of them.

Although agreeing with him up to a point, Shelly thought it a waste of money to buy new ones, when Alec's "hand-me-downs" fitted Drew so well.

As Shelly and Jimmy had identical custody agreements with their ex-spouses, they would have all four children at the same time. The kids now spent many hours a week shuttling between their various parents' homes.

Stephanie would drop off Drew and Jacie at Jimmy's house on Tuesday evening or after school on Wednesday afternoon. And Rob Angus handed over Alec and Kylie on Wednesday morning before school.

"We would then have them the rest of the week," said Shelly, "and the weekend if it was our weekend."

Then Drew and Jacie would be returned to Stephanie on Sunday evening, while Alec and Kylie went back to their father on Monday evening.

"We used to joke that they were human Ping-Pong balls," said Stephanie, "because they spent fifty percent of the week with me, and fifty percent of the week with their dad."

That summer, after refinancing the Brytes Way house, Jimmy Michael quit his job at Ruby Memorial to work for City Pharmacy, a small Morgantown home-health company. It was owned by a man named Shane Cook and his wife, and Jimmy's job was delivering medical equipment to patients' homes and providing respiratory assistance.

"They promised to make him a partner," remembered his father Denny.

Soon afterwards, Jimmy agreed to put Shelly through two years of graduate school at the WVU School of Nursing, for her Master's Degree.

"Her Master's was something Shelly was very driven to do," explained Renee Orme. "Education was very important to her. It was something she loved, and it amazed me how she did it."

Now their joint income decreased, placing an extra burden on Jimmy, as Shelly would now only be working twenty hours a week at the hospital. So to make extra money, Jimmy started working respiratory therapist shifts at Ruby Memorial and several other hospitals around the Morgantown area.

By late 2001, religion and the church dominated Jimmy and Shelly's lives. Every Sunday and Wednesday evening, they attended Calvary Baptist Church in Morgantown, taking the children with them on the weekends they had custody. They soon became close friends with several members of the Calvary congregation.

Born-again Christian Bill Hunt met the Michaels after joining Calvary Baptist Church.

"We became friends," he remembered, "during Bible studies."

They also became close to another young church-going couple named Jeremy and Tara Miller, who taught the Wednesday evening children's program, which all four Michael kids attended.

"We just hit it off," said Jeremy, who had moved to Morgantown a year earlier. "Right away we became friends, and we started doing Bible studies and stuff together. [We] prayed together, walked together [and] lifted weights together."

At least once a week, the Millers would visit 88 Brytes Way for Bible studies, and the Michaels also visited their apartment for the occasional dinner after church.

"It wasn't unusual for us to be over there a couple of times a week," said Jeremy. "We'd also go there on weekends, to have dinner with Jimmy, Shelly and the kids."

Jeremy soon became best friends with Jimmy, considering him a brother. But he would never feel comfortable around Shelly.

"She was always kind of flirtatious," he recalled. "She wasn't afraid to show her tummy or wear shorter shorts."

And he also did not approve of Shelly demonstrating her cheerleader moves before Bible studies.

"It wasn't uncommon for her to do a back-flip and back-handspring in front of folks," he said, "just to show us that she could. She was always just trying to be the center of attention."

CHAPTER 9

545 Killarney Drive

In early 2002, Shelly began pressuring Jimmy to buy a new house, more centrally located in Morgantown. She complained that 88 Brytes Way on Grafton Road, five miles south of central Morgantown, was too far to commute.

"Our family had outgrown the house," she explained. "We started looking for a place in town closer to the schools."

Shelly had set her sights on the tony Suncrest section of Morgantown, and began looking for an empty lot to build a house on. But as nothing was available, she recruited a realtor to find her new dream house.

She soon fell in love with a spacious four-bedroom house at 545 Killarney Drive, on the market for $188,000. She urged Jimmy to buy it, but he was unsure if they could afford it, as their income had dropped since she'd gone back to school.

He confided his concerns to his friend Reggie Ours.

"Jimmy said, 'That's what she wants,'" remembered Ours. "'And every time I mention that I don't think we can afford it, it turns into a huge fight.'"

Finally, Jimmy conceded, and that May they moved in.

The new house was well-situated, just a mile from Ruby Memorial Hospital, and down the street from Calvary

Baptist Church. Built in 1964, it had a full basement, a large living room and four upstairs bedrooms.

"Everything about it was perfect," said Shelly, "the location, the size [and] the yard."

Drew and Alec shared a bedroom, as did Kylie and Jacie. Jimmy and Michelle had the larger master bedroom, across the corridor from the children.

Soon after moving in, Jimmy repainted the house, laying down refinished hardwood floors, while Shelly put up new vinyl siding.

One day Reggie Ours came to visit Jimmy, and was taken aback when he saw Shelly on a stepladder outside, wearing the skimpiest of outfits.

"She was dressed in little teeny shorts and a little top," recalled Ours. "I said, 'Me and you can make a lot of money. Bring another one of your friends dressed like this and we'll get all kinds of business.'"

The new house sat on the corner of Killarney Drive and Eastern Avenue. Directly across the street lived Deborah and Dan Harris, who had a young son the same age as Drew. Over the new few months they became close to the Michaels.

"I was good friends with Shelly," remembered Deborah, who was twelve years older. "And we would see each other often. We spent a lot of time in the yards together . . . most often in the summer when it was warmer. They would occasionally come over to our home, [as] we have a small pool in the back yard."

In the beginning, Deborah thought Jimmy and Shelly had a "good relationship," and were exceptionally close.

"They did everything as a family," she would later testify. "If one of them had soccer practice, all six of them went. They always seemed like they went everywhere together."

But she did notice how Shelly treated her stepson Drew, far worse than the other children.

"She seemed to pick at Drew a lot, unnecessarily, in my presence," said Harris, whose husband Dan was head of security at Ruby Memorial. "Even when the other children were there, she just seemed to pick on him all the time."

Harris also detected a "definite tension" between Shelly and Jimmy's ex-wife Stephanie.

"She did have several conversations with me about the ex-wife," said Harris. "Not a very good situation. It was always negative."

After moving to Killarney Drive, Shelly Michael began molding the children into her version of the Brady Bunch. She dressed all four in identical matching clothes with never a hair out of place, driving them around Morgantown in her gleaming new car with its signature "6PACK" vanity plates.

And it was a common sight for neighbors to see Shelly out in the yard, teaching Kylie and Jacie back-flips and other cheerleading moves, in what she liked to call "the neighborhood hangout."

"I think Shelly always wanted the perfect family," said her new mother-in-law Ruth Michael. "When they walked out of that front door, it was perfection from head to toe. All the same."

Shelly also liked the best of everything. She loved to go shopping at the mall, only buying expensive designer clothes, and furnishing her new home with top-of-the-line items.

"Shelly's very much about the labels of clothes, and 'What are my children wearing?'" said Kerri Whitacre. "And they had to be wearing such-and-such a brand. Jimmy was not like that. He didn't have to buy from wherever and would be satisfied with Wal-Mart."

When Shelly's childhood friend Renee, by now married to Eric Del Viscio, first visited the new house, she was impressed with how well turned-out Shelly and the children always were.

"She did present a perfect package," said Renee. "Her house was always perfect . . . she did push the children every once in a while, but young children do need a little encouragement. Now what went on behind closed doors, I cannot answer to that."

As they got to know Shelly better, Ruth and Denny realized how she always had to get her way.

"Shelly was a perfectionist . . . a very controlling person," said Denny. "Jimmy said she was really feisty, and she could take up for herself. But what he meant was, Shelly gets what Shelly wants."

Jimmy's parents were now visiting Killarney Drive regularly, for the various picnics, holidays and other events Shelly organized.

"She was good at it," said Denny. "Every time they went somewhere, she had it all planned out. But it had to be her way. And so rather than have a confrontation with her all the time, Jimmy just let her do whatever she wanted."

Tara Miller accompanied Shelly Michael on several shopping expeditions over the years, getting to know her well. She noticed a highly competitive streak, which slightly unnerved her.

"I remember one time she came over to our house," said Tara. "They had put a roof on, and I'd said I didn't realize I was scared of heights until I had kids."

Then without saying a word, Shelly climbed up to the roof to demonstrate she had no such fears.

"And she had to press her little self up there," said Tara, "and walk all over the roof just because I said I was scared of it. But, I mean, that was just her personality—she was very attention-seeking."

Over time, Tara discovered another side to Shelly.

"I had several conversations with her," Tara remembered. "I think she had grown up very self-conscious, and people had picked on her . . . maybe she had acne or something.

"I remember her saying things like, 'You don't know what it's like to be a teenager and be picked on,' and stuff like that. So I think she tried to cover up all her insecurities by showing off."

With all four children using the surname "Michael," many of their teachers and neighbors never realized that Shelly was not Drew and Jacie's natural mother. And she did nothing to dispel any misimpression.

On one occasion, Stephanie tried to sign Drew out of school. But when she gave her son's name, the desk clerk gave her a strange look.

"Well that's Shelly's son, not yours," Stephanie was told, before explaining that Drew was in fact her son.

"People would ask me if I was [Shelly's] sister," said Stephanie. "Was I Jacie's aunt? I took it with a grain of salt. It happened so many times that it was funny after a while."

But things were not always so easygoing between the two mothers.

"There was an episode when Shelly met me at school," remembered Stephanie, "because I had [dared] to call Jim myself. She said a word that starts with 'C', that I won't repeat."

Shelly then screamed at Drew, demanding that he come over to her.

"For once, he didn't listen," said Stephanie. "He was so afraid of her that I'm surprised he didn't. But unbeknownst to her, one of the teachers witnessed that whole thing, and finally someone saw what she was like."

On another occasion, Drew came back to Stephanie with marks on him.

"[Shelly] had struck my children," Stephanie would later testify. "There was a mark on my son. I asked that she not strike my children."

Denny Michael also witnessed Shelly's hostility towards his grandson, and how her son Alec bullied him.

"It used to make me mad because Jimmy wouldn't take up for Drew," said Denny. "He felt Drew needs to stand up for himself."

Even Shelly would later admit that there were problems between the two boys.

"My son Alec would pick on Drew," she said, "and that would upset him."

As a trained educational psychologist, Kerri Whitacre believed Shelly felt threatened by Drew's close relationship with his father, and in turn encouraged Alec's apparent hostility to Drew, complaining that he was not as athletic as her son.

"She always wanted Drew to measure up to what her kids were athletic-wise," said Denny. "Like Jimmy, he gets all good grades, but that wasn't good enough. I could see him pushing his son into sports."

Shelly also demeaned her stepson at the dinner table, constantly criticizing his eating habits.

"That was the biggest thing that used to irritate me," said his grandfather. "She was always on Drew about eating. And he couldn't eat an extra piece of chicken unless he looked at her for approval."

Jeremy Miller, who taught both boys in children's church, often had to calm Alec down, as he was hyperactive and had been diagnosed with Tourette's syndrome.

"Alec was pretty rambunctious," Miller said. "And I think it bothered Shelly that Drew was the quieter kid, and just a better kid behavior-wise."

Rob Angus, who had recently remarried a woman also named Michelle, viewed his son's treatment of Drew as a normal "big brother/little brother" relationship.

"Just normal kids' stuff," he later explained. "I picked on my little brother when I was a kid."

In late October 2002, Stephanie came home to find a message on her answering machine from Shelly, informing her that she was taking Drew and Jacie on an extended family trip to Disney World, over the upcoming holiday period.

"Well it was my Christmas," recalled Stephanie. "And there was a rule in our divorce agreement that you had to give two months' notice for vacations.

Stephanie recalls it being two months to the day that she got the message.

"And she left it when she knew I would be out at football practice with Drew. I didn't have much of a backbone, and Shelly would do whatever she had to do to get what she wanted."

On December 10, Shelly organized a tenth birthday party

for her son Alec at the Valley Worlds of Fun amusement park in Fairmont, West Virginia. The guest of honor was a chubby little boy named Christopher Hiddy, who was in Alec's fourth grade class and suffering from a terminal illness.

"Christopher was a very special patient of Jimmy and [mine] at the hospital," Shelly would later testify. "He pretty much lived in the hospital."

Shelly got permission from Christopher's heart doctor for him to attend the birthday party.

Soon afterwards he died.

In January 2003, Shelly organized her family trip to Disney World in Orlando, inviting Renee and Eric Del Viscio and Bill Hunt and his new girlfriend along. It was the children's first time on an airplane, and they were very excited.

Everybody stayed at the All-Star Sports Resort, and Shelly later compiled a scrapbook of photographs showing the children posing with Mickey Mouse, the Seven Dwarfs and Goofy.

"We went on a family trip to Disney in Florida with them," said Renee. "And it was a wonderful trip, and all six of them interacted wonderfully. It was just a seamless family."

CHAPTER 10

Scandal

In July 2003, Nurse Shelly Michael was suspended without pay for three days for "insubordination," after taking a two-week family vacation she was not entitled to. It was the third and final disciplinary action against her in the six years she had been at Ruby Memorial Hospital.

"We had rented a house in Myrtle Beach for a family vacation," recalled Ruth Michael, "and Shelly told me she was going to be off for two weeks, and I thought, 'That's really nice.' I had no idea she wasn't supposed to take it off."

Her nurse manager at the time, Sally Olynyk, said Shelly had blatantly disregarded an earlier warning not to take the vacation, as she was not entitled to it.

"She was angry," said Nurse Olynyk. "She did not understand why she could not take it—those were her two weeks every year."

Shelly maintained that she was only four hours over her vacation allowance, immediately filing a "rebuttal" with Human Resources.

A few weeks later, Shelly's sister Jennifer, now pregnant with her third child, came out as a lesbian. She announced she was leaving her husband Joe, to move in with her girlfriend Jamie.

"This completely tore my heart apart," Shelly later wrote. "I believed from the bible that God hated homosexuality."

When Shelly tried to "lecture" her sister about her "huge sin," it led to many heated arguments. Jimmy, who also did not approve, banned the children from seeing their Aunt Jennifer and their cousins, saying he did not want them near "that type of lifestyle."

The growing rift between the sisters led to much tension in the family, although their estranged parents accepted Jennifer's decision to get a divorce and live with her girlfriend.

But it would be another nine months until Ruth and Denny Michael learned the true reason why Jennifer and her children no longer attended family events.

"It was like a big dark secret," remembered Ruth. "Actually we knew that Jennifer and her husband had split up, but no one was allowed to say anything."

That summer, the Calvary Baptist Church was disbanded, after Pastor Tim Kraynak resigned to start the Marketplace Community Church. Jimmy Michael, Jeremy Miller and Bill Hunt and their families followed him there.

"We planted a new church," explained Miller, "and we met every Sunday."

Jimmy and his friends were the driving force behind the new church, holding Sunday services in the banquet room of a Morgantown Holiday Inn.

"Jim and I were very involved in the church and ministry there," said Miller. "We were there in the morning setting up for service."

And on Friday mornings they would meet for breakfast in Hardee's, to study Bible passages.

"We found strength through spirituality," explained Miller. "It's a struggle to live a good Christian life with the things in the world. So through the Bible study, we just found strength in that."

Every Sunday, Shelly attended services with Jimmy and the children, teaching Bible to the new congregation's children. But Jeremy Miller always distrusted her motives.

"I think she just went through the motions," he said. "It's part of the 'perfect family' – 'We go to church every Sunday' kind of thing."

That football season, Jimmy Michael coached Alec and Drew in the Evansdale Tigers, while Shelly coached Kylie and Jacie in its cheerleading team. Jimmy was assisted by Bobby Teets, whose wife Kelli helped out Shelly, as her young daughter Regan was a cheerleader.

"We all became very good friends," said Bobby Teets. "Not just my son and their kids played football, but my daughter and their daughters were cheerleaders. In the football season we would spend a lot [of time together]. You're talking four days, five days a week, including games."

Over the next several years the two families would become inseparable.

On the eve of her final exams for her Master's, Shelly drove to Philadelphia to help Renee Del Viscio through the birth of her daughter. It was her third visit to see Renee and Eric, having previously attended her bridal and baby showers.

"She came for the birth of my first daughter Ava," recalled Renee, "to help me take care of her and to teach me what to do."

Although in the middle of writing her Master's thesis, Shelly insisted on making the two-day visit. Then she got up at 5:00 in the morning and drove back to Morgantown, arriving in time to take her family to Sunday church service.

"The energy level was unbelievable," recalled Eric Del Viscio. "She drove here and then stayed up all night with the baby, while she was writing her thesis paper. There was barely any sleep. She did all her work at night to show us how to take care of a kid. I mean, the effort was extraordinary."

As a new mother, Renee found Shelly's assistance invaluable.

"She would help me with my daughter," she said, "and tell my husband [how to] bathe her. Kind of silly things that parents don't know."

A month later in November, Shelly Michael graduated with her Master's Degree in nursing. But it would be another eight months before she was hired as a pediatric nurse practitioner by Ruby Memorial Hospital, after failing a crucial job test and having to retake it.

For their Christmas present, Jimmy Michael redecorated Kylie and Jacie's bedroom in Disney Princesses wallpaper. And on Christmas Eve, Jimmy and Shelly took all four children to Clarksburg, for the annual family celebration at her father's house. Jennifer and her children were noticeably missing.

However, the following spring, Shelly and Jimmy went to a church baptism for Jennifer's new baby daughter. Sitting a few aisles from Shelly at the service, was her sister's girlfriend Jamie.

During the baptism, Shelly seethed with anger, believing her sister was "making a mockery of the church," by "baptizing her daughter in vain."

After the service, a celebration meal was planned at Minard's Spaghetti Inn in Clarksburg. When Shelly asked her father if Jamie would be there, he said she probably would be.

Suddenly Shelly exploded. She ran across the road to Jamie's van, pulled her out and started punching her, screaming, "Leave my family alone!"

Jimmy finally calmed her down and drove her back to Morgantown. A few hours later, Shelly called her mother-in-law Ruth, who was driving back from North Carolina.

"She was hysterical," said Ruth. "I said, 'What's wrong, Shelly?' and she said, 'I just beat my sister's girlfriend up.' And then she hung up."

Ruth then called Jimmy to see why Shelly was so upset. Jimmy expressed surprise that Shelly had called, asking what she had said.

"He told me that they went to the church where the baby was being baptized," said Ruth. "And I guess she interrupted the service."

And that was how Jimmy's parents learned that Jennifer had left her husband for a woman.

"Everything was a big secret," said Ruth. "Jimmy didn't say too much about it, but he didn't want his children exposed to it."

One morning after a Bible study breakfast, Jimmy Michael pulled Jeremy Miller to one side, saying he needed to talk. He told his friend that he had just received a package in the mail, containing one of Shelly's sweaters, along with an anonymous note reading, "Keep your whore wife away from my husband."

"He said, 'I don't know what to do,'" said Miller. "'I don't know who to blame. Why does a lady send me a sweater? Why does my wife deny it all?'

"He didn't know if she was cheating. He didn't elaborate on who it was. He never even mentioned it again."

CHAPTER 11

Shelly Michael, Nurse Practitioner

For Mother's Day 2004, Eric Del Viscio gave Renee a girls' trip to New York, celebrating her being a new mom. She invited Shelly Michael and several other girlfriends along too.

They all met in Philadelphia, taking a limousine to Manhattan and going shopping, before taking in a Broadway show. Then they stayed overnight in a hotel, before returning to Philadelphia.

"Shelly loved going to New York," said Renee. "She was really enthralled with it."

That July, Shelly received her Pediatric Nurse Practitioner Certification, and was offered a full-time job by Ruby Memorial Hospital. As a nurse practitioner, she would now have far more responsibilities than a registered bedside nurse. Although she was under a physician's direction, Nurse Shelly Michael would now be making diagnoses, prescribing and adjusting therapies and evaluating patients. She also had easy access to many of the drugs used in the unit.

"A nurse practitioner tends to function more like a resident physician," explained her boss Dr. Michael Romano, associate professor of WVU pediatrics. "And that is the role of a supervisor."

Dr. Romano had already worked with Nurse Michael when she was an RN, and had had problems.

"I would categorize it as a strained, difficult relationship," he later recounted.

When he had first interviewed her for the vacant nurse practitioner position, Shelly had surprised him: she was emphatic about not working full-time, wanting three ten-hour shifts instead.

"We had a fairly lengthy discussion about her desire to ultimately drop [her hours]," he said. "I had some concerns that it wouldn't work out, but we were willing to give it a try."

He agreed to hire her as the Pediatric Intensive Care Unit's second nurse practitioner, being assigned ten critically ill patients. She was responsible for initial evaluations, conducting physical exams and developing a daily therapy plan. She would be the liaison between the nursing staff and the consulting physicians and specialists, as well as coordinating treatments.

"[Nurse practitioners] are the glue that keeps the unit functioning on a day-to-day basis," explained Dr. Romano.

After working six weeks full-time to get up to speed, Dr. Romano allowed Nurse Michael to drop to three-quarter time in mid-September. But then she wanted to go half-time.

Dr. Romano tried to accommodate her. There was another nurse practitioner he was looking to hire, who also wanted to work 50 percent, and could split shifts with Shelly. But ultimately the other nurse went elsewhere.

On August 7, Jimmy's ex-wife Stephanie married a pediatric nurse named Dan Estel, who also worked at Ruby Memorial Hospital. And after that there was less tension between her and Shelly.

"She would usually be reading me the riot act, until I remarried," said Stephanie. "It was a bit more peaceful because I didn't have to deal with her as much."

That winter, there were growing tensions at the Michael home, as Shelly sunk into a deep depression. She refused to have sex with Jimmy, making him even more suspicious that she was having an affair.

"I had become very hateful, bitter, angry, and inpatient

[sic]," she later wrote. "I was short tempered with both Jimmy and the kids."

Shelly blamed her depression on the moral problems she faced, coming to terms with Jennifer's homosexuality, as well as the stresses of dealing with her and Jimmy's ex-spouses. She began closely identifying with the George Jones classic country and western song, "Life Turned Her That Way."

Her close friend and neighbor Deborah Harris often observed Shelly's mercurial mood swings.

"I would call her moody," Harris later told police. "Up and down. She'd be very happy one time. And another time I might go over and she'd just look at me with a blank stare as I tried to talk to her. I just figured she was in a bad mood, and would leave."

She also noticed a change in Shelly's treatment of Jimmy and the children.

"She would yell a lot, and bark out orders," Harris remembered. "She was harsh with her family, as well as her husband Jim."

And Shelly seemed even more angry at Jimmy's 10-year-old son Drew.

"She seemed to be much harder on him," recalled Harris. "Almost picking at him more. Not just yelling, 'Stop that. Be quiet'—it was more things [like], 'Stop talking that way. Pull your pants up. Don't walk that way.'"

On one occasion, Drew was eating some pudding, when his stepmother became infuriated by something he did with his spoon.

"Drew!" she snapped. "Don't eat your pudding that way."

Her neighbor also noticed how Shelly developed a mania for cleaning her house.

"She'd go on cleaning frenzies," Harris remembered, "and just be really obsessive about certain things about cleaning and where the shoes are, etc."

Shelly constantly complained about Drew to his father, accusing him of misbehaving, even when he had not.

Ruth Michael regularly babysat the children, observing Shelly's treatment of her grandson at close quarters.

"She would tell Jimmy that Drew said or did something," she recalled, "and then when Jimmy asked Drew about it, he would tell the truth. But Jimmy would not believe him."

Then Jimmy began blaming Stephanie for being too lax with his children.

"I said, 'Jimmy, I'm really concerned about Drew,'" said Ruth. "And he said, 'Don't worry, Mom, I'm going to take care of it.'"

In October, Pastor Tim Krynak moved away from Morgantown, dissolving the Marketplace Community Church. Jimmy Michael and Jeremy Miller were very upset, joining the Christian & Missionary Alliance church with their families.

"We had thought of Pastor Tim as a good friend," said Jeremy Miller. "We felt abandoned by him."

After three years working at City Pharmacy, Jimmy Michael was frustrated at still not being made a partner. In November 2004, he decided to leave and start his own home medical supply business.

He asked Renee's husband Eric Del Viscio, a successful Philadelphia banker, for advice about capitalizing on the valuable medical contacts he'd built up over the years. Del Viscio thought it a great idea to start his own business, giving him encouragement and solid financial advice.

"Jimmy had been promised an equity stake in the business," said Del Viscio. "And that wasn't coming to pass. And he said, 'I'm the guy that has all these relationships.' People just liked him, and those doctors would be happy to pass along referrals to him."

Jimmy also consulted his father, who was delighted that his son was showing some entrepreneurial flair.

"I said, 'Jimmy, they're never going to make you a partner,'" said Denny Michael. "'You need to do something on your own.'"

Jimmy's next move was to arrange a business meeting with an old friend named Rich Brant and his partner Susan

Riddle, who ran a real estate and business development company called the Round Table Corporation.

Then, with Del Viscio's help, Jimmy wrote a business plan, and presented it to Brant and Riddle, who agreed to back him financially.

Under their business arrangement, Jimmy secured a personal loan for $60,000, for a controlling 55 percent interest in the company. The Round Table Corporation and several smaller investors put up the rest.

"It was a perfect fit," said Del Viscio, who invested $2,500 himself. "I didn't put in a ton of money, but perversely, it's been the best investment we've made."

That Christmas, Jimmy Michael attended a function at the WVU Alumni Center, striking up a conversation with Cookie Coombs of the Morgantown Visitors' Center.

"He was thinking of going into the medical supply business," she remembered. "He was really gung-ho, and seemed to have all his ducks in a row."

In early January 2005, Mountaineer Home Medical—named for his beloved WVU football team—opened for business. It was located in the same building as the Round Table Corporation on Maple Drive in Morgantown, so his new partners could provide on-the-ground business expertise.

As president and CEO of his new company, Jimmy Michael was ecstatic.

"Kerri, I think this is it," he told his old friend Kerri Whitacre. "I found it."

Jimmy plunged enthusiastically into his new business. He was at his desk at 7:00 a.m. five days a week, and on call 24/7, always keeping his cell phone by the bed. He hired Reggie Ours to work one day a week, making deliveries and setting up medical equipment to his new clients.

"I would help him as much as I could," said Ours. "He told me that he wanted to hire me full-time within a year."

Every Thursday, the new CEO had a weekly status meeting with Rich Brant and Susan Riddle, to go over things and discuss any problems that had arisen. At the beginning,

Jimmy's enthusiasm got the better of him, and he was constantly in and out of his partners' offices with questions.

"We tried to have weekly meetings," explained Riddle. "Otherwise Jim's minutes would go to hours on a daily basis. You had to say, 'Let's hold off until our meeting on Thursday.'"

Soon after Mountaineer Home Medical opened, Jimmy Michael interviewed Brenda Shiflett, hiring her on the spot to run the office. She started on February 21, soon forging a tight working relationship with her new boss.

"I was his go-to girl," she said. "I maintained Jim's office."

As his new office manager, Shiflett was responsible for answering telephones, scheduling patients and following up, as well as insurance pre-authorization and billing.

"He was always working," said Shiflett. "He was just establishing the business, so he didn't turn any patients away."

Besides his work ethic, she also admired her new boss as a deeply religious and a devoted family man.

"Jim and I had a lot of conversations about our relationships with God," she remembered. "That was one of the things that attracted me to working for him. I shared those same values."

But when she discussed her happy twenty-five-year marriage to her high school sweetheart, saying she still considered him her best friend, she sensed this was something lacking in Jim's life.

"I just think he wished he had some of what I had," she said.

Every morning, Jimmy dropped into Jeremy Miller's Ford dealership for a chat.

"I looked forward to seeing him every day," Miller remembered. "He'd have a big thirty-two-ounce cup of coffee and a pen stuck behind his ear. And he always had this smirky smile, like he was thinking something funny."

As Mountaineer Home Medical covered a large area of West Virginia, Jimmy Michael drove to appointments, listening to contemporary gospel radio stations. To make extra money, he continued working shifts at Ruby and Preston

Memorial Hospitals. But his demanding schedule meant that he was seeing less and less of his family.

Now most nights, after his coaching duties, he went to Jeremy Miller's house, as he was helping him renovate the basement. Sometimes he'd stay until 3:00 a.m.

"He was over at the house quite frequently late at night," said Tara Miller. "When Jeremy would get stuck, he would say, 'Call Jimbo.'"

Shelly Michael encouraged her husband to go into business for himself, thinking they could upgrade their lives. But when she realized he was now making less money then before, she was furious.

"I remember Jimmy saying that he'd written himself a paycheck for something like $1,500," recalled Jeremy Miller. "And Shelly was like, 'What is this?'"

Suddenly Shelly began taking an interest in the business, demanding to know why he was not making more money. And she would pressure him, constantly feeding him questions for his new business partners.

"He would ask me questions that were ridiculous," said Susan Riddle. "I wasn't getting it done fast enough."

Finally, she asked if he had a problem with how she was running the company's financial side. He said no, admitting that the questions were all coming from Shelly.

"I don't think she really understood the concept of him going out on his own," said Miller. "That you have to make certain sacrifices in the beginning, to reap the rewards down the road.

"And that's when things started going downhill."

CHAPTER 12

Ultimatum

That February, Jimmy Michael received a call from Eli Henderson, a life insurance salesman from the Northwestern Mutual Financial Network. The referral came from Susan Riddle, who thought he might need some financial advice, now that he had his own business.

Henderson scheduled a meeting at the Mountaineer Home Medical offices.

Jimmy was mainly interested in retirement counseling, but during their meeting he admitted not having life insurance.

"I discussed it with him," remembered Henderson, 28. "That it would be a good idea for him to look at purchasing some life insurance."

The Morgantown-based insurance salesman suggested a $1 million policy, but Jimmy thought $500,000 would be adequate, saying he would think about it. After the meeting, he called his father, who had a lot of experience with insurance policies, for advice.

"He told me he was going to take out a five hundred thousand dollars insurance policy," remembered Denny Michael. "And I told him, 'Why don't you take out a two hundred and fifty thousand dollar policy out, and take the accidental clause, which is double indemnity, and you get five hundred thousand dollars anyway?'

"Most likely it's going to be accidental if something happens to you, because you're only thirty-three years old. And it would be a lot cheaper."

Jimmy agreed it was a good idea, saying he would talk it over with Shelly.

"Then Shelly insisted," said Denny Michael, "that he take a five hundred thousand dollar policy."

The first week of March, after passing a physical examination, Jimmy brought Shelly with him to sign life insurance application forms. He also agreed to take out a $200,000 policy on his wife, as she already had $300,000 coverage through work.

After carefully going through the policy together, which had a $53.51 monthly premium, they signed the separate policies, each being the primary beneficiary if the other died first. And Shelly had her best friend Renee Del Viscio named on Jimmy's policy, as the trustee for the children, in the event of them both dying.

On April 12, Eli Henderson sent them both a letter, confirming their life insurance applications had been accepted.

"Dear Jim and Michelle," it began. "I want to thank you for trusting me with your insurance planning. These policies should help ensure that your primary goals will be met should you die prematurely."

It outlined that they both had a Term 80 policy, with a $500,000 face value for Jimmy's and $200,000 for Shelly.

"I trust our work together has been both helpful and insightful," wrote Henderson, "in addressing your current needs."

A few weeks later, Dr. Michael Romano called Nurse Practitioner Shelly Michael into his office. He told her that as the busy Pediatric Intensive Care Unit would soon be doubling in size, with a new extension to Ruby Hospital underway, she would have to go full-time.

"She did not like that idea," he remembered. "She was very upset. She [said] she wouldn't be able to work full-time."

Dr. Romano complained to Shelly's nurse manager, Sally Olynyk, that her attitude was unacceptable.

"Dr. Romano told me he was going to give her an ultimatum," said Olynyk. "We had ten very ill patients in there, and we were going to go to a unit of nineteen. Dr. Romano desired a forty-hour workweek and was adamant that he have that coverage."

Shelly's behavior did not endear her to the other doctors and nurses at Ruby Memorial Hospital. She had few friends there and was mostly viewed with suspicion.

"She hated her job as a nurse practitioner," said Reggie Ours, who worked shifts with her. "That was obvious. She didn't want to work at all and just wanted the money."

After Dr. Romano's ultimatum to work full-time, Shelly became even more depressed, refusing to have any physical relations with her husband.

"That's when Jimmy would call me up at night," remembered Jeremy Miller. "And he'd want to pray."

Sometimes they would meet late at night by the old railroad, taking long walks together on their favorite trails.

"He was questioning," recalled Miller. "All of a sudden Shelly realized that she needed to work more and not less, because Jimmy's income actually decreased starting the business. She did anything but support him. Instead of focusing on working more hours and helping him release all that stress, she actually wanted to work less."

One night while they were walking, Jimmy confided that Shelly refused to be intimate with him, never allowing him to see her naked.

"Jimmy shared with me that she wasn't having sex with him," said Miller. "She wouldn't even take her shirt off in front of him. It just drove him crazy."

In early May, Jimmy brought a large cardboard box into the office, containing numerous family photographs and pictures, and embarked on a special project to win back Shelly.

"He was making a collage of photographs for her for a Mother's Day gift," said office manager Brenda Shiflett. "A lot of pictures and memorabilia from times before."

And on May 26, their fifth wedding anniversary, Jimmy bought her a one-year-old Ford Expedition SUV, from Jeremy Miller's car dealership.

"My wife and I had actually delivered it over to their house," said Miller. "Jimmy took her out to dinner and then I took it over, backed it into their driveway and left. And when they came back, the car was there."

On Father's Day, Jimmy's parents visited Killarney Drive for the annual family gathering. But for the first time Shelly's parents and sister were absent.

"It was just us," remembered Ruth Michael. "Her family were not there."

And when she asked where her family had gone, Shelly said Jimmy had not wanted them there.

"And I'm going," said Ruth, " 'What's all this about?' "

In June, Mountaineer Home Medical passed the six-month mark, and business was thriving. All of Jimmy Michael's hard work and dedication had paid off, and he was already turning a profit.

"It just took off," recalled Eric Del Viscio. "He was cash-flowing by June [and] you couldn't have scripted this any better. It went phenomenally well."

Jimmy could not believe how successful his new business had become.

"He kept saying, 'Is it really working well?' " said Del Viscio. "And I said, 'Yes.' "

During their weekly telephone conversations, Jimmy would enthusiastically update Kerri Whitacre on his business, often becoming emotional, saying the Lord had blessed him.

"He just couldn't believe how well things were going," she said.

* * *

In July, Deborah Harris's eldest son Ryan, who was serving in Iraq, became ill with a serious potassium deficiency. The Army had sent him to an airbase medical center to recover.

"He told me he just had to stay in the hospital and get well the old-fashioned way," said Harris. "Because they didn't have potassium supplements for him. I was very concerned."

One day she mentioned this to Shelly Michael, saying she was unable to purchase potassium in a GNC store. The nurse practitioner said potassium required a prescription, as it could be dangerous.

The following afternoon, Shelly summoned Deborah Harris across the road to her house.

"She was still in work clothes," remembered Harris. "And she presented me with a small, clear Baggie-type bag. Inside were two big white pills."

Shelly explained that they were a high-strength potassium supplement. When her neighbor asked where they were from, the nurse told her not to worry.

"Send them to Brian," Shelly told her. "Tell him to take one a day, and that'll make him feel better."

That summer, many close to Jimmy and Shelly Michael noticed how their relationship had changed. Ruth Michael stayed over at Killarney Drive two days a week, babysitting all four children. That gave her the opportunity to closely observe her son's marriage.

"I noticed it was different," she remembered. "It was strained and stressed."

Ruth felt tension in the house, making her uncomfortable.

"[Shelly] wasn't as friendly to me," she said. "She was colder to me than she had been before."

She also noticed Shelly no longer treated Jimmy with loving respect, as she had once done.

"Her attitude had changed towards him," Ruth said. "And the way she spoke to him."

One day Ruth was sitting in the kitchen when Shelly tore into Jimmy for helping himself to a second sandwich. His mother looked on in disbelief, as Shelly demanded to know why he was eating so much.

"And I'm thinking, 'Jimmy, please stand up and be a man,'" said Ruth. "'Tell her you'll eat as many sandwiches as you want.' And then she just got stricter and stricter, especially with Drew."

Shelly's neighbor, Deborah Harris, also observed trouble in the Michael home.

"Normally, when I would visit, they would [all] be together," she said. "But [now] he would be sitting in the living room, and Shelly would be in the den. It just seemed like they weren't quite as together."

Late one night, Reggie Ours telephoned Jimmy and he just started to cry. When his old friend tried to calm him down, asking what was wrong, Jimmy apologized, saying he couldn't talk just then, and hung up.

"I went to work with him the next day," recalled Ours, "and he never really said anything about it. But then the following week we talked a little. He said he was having so many problems at home."

That fall, Bobby and Kelli Teets grew closer with the Michaels, after their children all started going to the same schools. Several years earlier, Kelli had even transferred her little daughter Regan to the same kindergarten as Kylie, as the two girls were so close.

For the new school year, the two families began carpooling together, making it easier to take the children to their various schools. They developed a routine where Kelli would drop Regan off at Killarney Drive, then pick up Alec and Drew and drive them with her son Tyler to Suncrest Middle School; Shelly would drive Regan with Kylie and Jacie, to North Elementary School.

"We became really good friends because of football," recalled Bobby Teets, "but our friendship grew because we were around each other so much."

Shelly and Kelli also started going on shopping trips, and once went to Baltimore.

"We were pretty close," said 32-year-old Kelli. "She was the homeroom mom and volunteered at school."

In the run-up to the football season, Drew suddenly announced he no longer wanted to play football and had decided to switch to basketball instead. So Jimmy went along with him as coach, in addition to his football duties. He asked his ex-wife Stephanie's new husband Dan for help.

"He didn't know anything about basketball," said Estel. "And he wanted to coach his son's team, so I agreed, and we were coaching that team together."

As winter approached, Shelly was under increasing pressure to go full-time. With the official opening of the new Ruby Memorial extension only months away, she had to make a decision soon.

Then Shelly suddenly announced that she wanted another child. Jimmy, who had had a vasectomy, refused, saying he did not want to undergo the operation to reverse it.

When he told Kerri Whitacre about Shelly wanting a baby, she was stunned.

"I said, 'And Jimmy wants what?'" recalled Kerri. "Let's talk a minute about what's going on here."

Jimmy told her he thought four children were enough, and did not want any more.

"He'd already told me that she didn't want to work," said Kerri. "And I said, 'Oh, if she has another baby, then she'll really have an excuse not to go to work.'"

Then Kerri asked what Shelly would do all day, if she wasn't working.

"Jimmy said she would probably go shopping," recalled Kerri, "and of course we both chuckled about that, because we both knew how she liked to shop."

CHAPTER 13

Labor Day

On Thursday, September 1, Eric and Renee Del Viscio brought their baby daughter Ava to Morgantown for Labor Day weekend. It would be a homecoming for Renee, who had not attended the Clarksburg Italian Heritage Festival since moving to Philadelphia a decade earlier. During their three-day trip, they stayed at the Michaels' house.

After lunch on Friday afternoon, everyone made the forty-five-minute drive to Clarksburg for the grand opening. Started in 1979 to celebrate the cultural heritage of Italian-Americans in West Virginia, the three-day festival attracts more than 100,000 visitors each Labor Day.

The opening ceremony is a lavish spectacle, culminating in the crowning of Queen Maria, the first queen of Italy.

"It was their first experience of the festival," remembered Renee. "Shelly brought Kylie, and my husband and daughter also came."

After a few hours at the festival, they returned to Morgantown. But several hours later, Shelly and Renee returned to the festival, leaving their husbands at home with the children.

"Shelly and I went back later that evening," said Renee, "to catch up with some high school friends. Her mother was there and her father was there and I believe her sister [too]."

Shelly and Renee met old school friends they hadn't seen for years, catching up on what they were doing.

"We were there until it closed," said Renee. "At which point, Shelly drove us back to Morgantown. We probably arrived back at their house, somewhere around 1:00 a.m. to 1:30 a.m."

On Saturday, Jimmy and Eric played golf, while their wives went back to the festival for a few hours.

"We had a good time," Eric remembered. "He had stopped drinking, but we had a beer at lunch."

In the afternoon they golfed, later drinking several cocktails of Jack Daniel's and ginger ale.

"There was never any indication while we were golfing that there was anything wrong," said Del Viscio. "He said nothing more than the usual gripes a husband would have. [He'd] like to have more sex, which is something I think that all of us complain about."

On the way to Clarksburg, Shelly also discussed her marriage.

"She did share some things with me," recalled Renee. "That maybe their sex life wasn't where it should be. She categorized [her life] as being very stressful and maybe . . . they were not having a relationship like that, as often as he would like. So that was causing a bit of stress in their marriage."

Renee even suggested maybe she and Jimmy should get marriage counseling.

"There was no mention or insinuation that the marriage would dissolve at any point," she said. "It was just that this was a small problem at the time."

Over the course of the weekend, Renee and Eric never saw any tension between their friends.

"Shelly's personality was such that she was the one who dominated any scene," said Eric. "And he was the type that didn't mind that. It didn't bother him. He would naturally step to the background. If he had an issue with anything, I'm sure he dealt with it in private."

According to Eric, Jimmy always stood up for himself.

"He was not a weak character at all," he said. "But he was perfectly fine to let Shelly run ahead and do her thing, and then raise his hand when he thought something was incorrect and say, 'Maybe we should think about this.'"

Renee agreed that there were no signs of anything untoward.

"Everything seemed fine," she said. "He seemed happy. He seemed normal. Their interaction together seemed OK."

The following day, Eric and Renee drove back to Philadelphia. It would be the last time they would ever see Jimmy Michael alive.

A few nights later, Jimmy Michael called Jeremy Miller, saying he needed to talk. Once again they met at the railroad trail, and Jeremy could see how distraught Jimmy was.

"He was questioning Shelly's fidelity," remembered Miller. "She had stayed out all night at the Italian Festival in Clarksburg, and he didn't know where she went or who she was with."

Then Miller asked if he thought Shelly was cheating on him.

"He said he didn't know," said Miller. "I was trying to be a brother to him and I said, 'How do you not know if your wife is [cheating]?' And I told him it was his right to know, because he was her husband. Their sex life wasn't good, and so obviously, when she's not having sex with him, she's probably having it with someone else."

Jimmy also told Reggie Ours that Shelly had not come home after the Italian Festival. He said that when he'd asked her where she had been, Shelly had replied it was none of his business.

"Not an answer you'd expect from your wife," said Ours.

That September, Shelly Michael was suspended from work for three days for "insubordination," after taking another day off without permission. Once again, she denied any wrongdoing, firing off a complaint letter to Human Resources.

As the deadline to the expansion of the Pediatric Intensive Care Unit approached, the pressure was mounting on Shelly to go full-time.

But a few weeks later she was thrown a lifeline.

Bobby and Kelli Teets both worked for the Morgantown branch of Cintas Corporation, the industrial uniform manufacturer. And one of their colleagues, who did embroidery for local sports teams as a sideline, happened to be selling all his equipment.

One night at the Michaels' house, Bobby mentioned that an embroidery machine was available. He said it could be a good business opportunity, as there were four or five local football teams always needing logos and team names to be embroidered on shirts and hats.

Jimmy Michael agreed, immediately offering to back it. So it was decided that Shelly and Bobby—who would have more time to run a business—would start researching the embroidery industry and the equipment necessary.

In early October, Shelly accused Drew of misbehaving. The little boy protested his innocence, saying his stepmother was lying, but Jimmy snapped, taking off his belt and beating Drew with it.

Later that day, after calming down and realizing what he had done, a contrite Jimmy called Jeremy Miller.

"Jimmy had whipped Drew, and he hated it," remembered Miller. "He sobbed like a baby on the phone. He was bawling and hysterical."

The following Saturday Drew was at a soccer game, when his mother Stephanie noticed his arm was covered in what appeared to be grease.

"When I went to wipe it off," she said, "I noticed it was a bruise."

When she asked how he had gotten bruised, Drew refused to discuss it. But then she lifted up his shirt to see if there were any more marks.

"There were bruises up his arms," she said, "and he told me that his father had struck him."

At that moment her cell phone rang, with Jimmy calling to check up on the soccer game.

"I said, 'Drew has bruises on his arm,'" said Stephanie. "'Would you like to explain what happened?'"

Then Jimmy became emotional, admitting losing his temper and hitting Drew, saying how sorry he was.

Stephanie decided not to take any further action. But the following Tuesday a Suncrest Middle School teacher noticed Drew Michael's heavy bruising, and called in Child Protective Services (CPS).

When Drew came home and told his mother that a CPS representative had come to school to photograph his arms, Stephanie called the rape and domestic violence hotline for advice.

"Since he had the bruises, and they had been reported," she said, "I wanted to see if there was anything that I needed to do."

Later that day, Jimmy arrived at Stephanie's house to check up on Drew. Standing at their back-yard gate, he asked his son to come over to him. Then he pulled up his shirt sleeve to see the bruises.

"The color drained out of Jim's face," remembered Stephanie, "and he dropped to his knees and said, 'I'm so sorry, Drew. I didn't know I hit you that hard.'"

Then Dan Estel asked Jimmy to come up on the porch, to discuss what he had done.

"Jim just stood there and all he could do was cry," recalled Stephanie. "He said, 'I'm so sorry. I love my son. I did something that was wrong,' and 'Can you forgive me?'

"It was very hard to look at Jim. He just looked broken in pieces over what he had done. I mean, he was so truly remorseful."

Dan invited Jimmy to sit down at the porch table to talk about it.

"And I excused myself," said Stephanie, "because I didn't

think that he needed his ex-wife to sit in on a man-to-man."

After she had left, Dan asked why all communication regarding the children went between Shelly and Stephanie, circumnavigating him. Jimmy agreed it should change, promising that everything would go through him from now on.

From that moment his relationship with Stephanie improved immeasurably.

"We got along so well after that," she recalled. "I only dealt with Jim from that point on. He was actually joking with me when I would come to pick up the kids."

Dan Estel agreed it was definitely a step in the right direction.

"We didn't have very much interaction with Shelly at all after that," he said.

A few days later, Jimmy Michael met with CPS, agreeing to take counseling from Pastor Kevin Cain of the Kingdom Evangelical Methodist Church. In one of his first sessions, he told Pastor Cain that he and Shelly didn't have "the best of marriages." He said he needed marital help, as he didn't want to give up on the marriage. He also spoke of Shelly being drunk at the Italian Heritage Festival, and not coming home. But he never discussed his suspicions of Shelly's infidelity, saying he wished she would return to the church and recommit to their marriage.

Jimmy was also taking advice from Kerri Whitacre, a qualified family psychologist.

"He felt horrible," she remembered, "and knew he was wrong when he had done that with Drew."

He asked his old friend how he could be a better parent, to ensure that it never happened again.

"We talked about Shelly using Drew against Jimmy," said Whitacre. "I remember saying, 'Jimmy, I understand that Shelly tells you one thing and Drew tells you another. We've got to get something worked out where you guys are all on the same page. Because she can't use your son against you.'"

CHAPTER 14

Chicago

In October 2005, Nurse Practitioner Shelly Michael grudgingly returned to full-time employment at Ruby Memorial Hospital. Her boss Dr. Michael Romano had finally lost patience, telling her to work forty hours a week or resign.

She complained that her life was becoming "even more difficult," balancing her career with her duties at home.

"Dr. Romano had informed me that the position of three-quarters time was no longer available," she explained. "Two-and-a-half days a week was my goal."

She now worked four shifts a week, on weekdays and the occasional weekend. But Shelly felt this placed extra pressure on Jimmy, as she could no longer take the children to school in the morning.

"That made him late for work," she said. "He had to put patients aside. Four days a week was a strain on him. It was making him sacrifice all his work in the new company, so he could be there."

But Jimmy's father refutes that, saying that she was far more selfish.

"She didn't want to work like everybody else," said Denny Michael. "She wanted to do what she wanted to do and she wanted to have it now."

On Friday, October 28, Bobby Teets ran into Jimmy and

Shelly Michael at the high school Mohawk Bowl at Mountaineer Field. He was stunned to see Jimmy so visibly distraught.

"The only time I ever seen Jimmy upset," he later told police, "was that night at the Mohawk Bowl."

Bobby Teets and Shelly Michael were now busy online, researching their plans to start an embroidery business.

Over several meetings to discuss the new project, it was decided that Shelly and Bobby should run the embroidery business from the basement of Killarney Drive.

"Jimmy made it pretty clear that he wasn't going to do a lot of anything on the embroidery," Bobby Teets later explained. "Kelli said she would help every once in a while . . . but it was just going to me and [Shelly]."

After viewing an available second-hand embroidery machine in Morgantown, they decided to buy a new one, and started doing the research.

But there was no money available, as Jimmy had borrowed heavily to start Mountaineer Home Medical. So Shelly came up with the idea of having an embroidery machine manufacturer finance the business.

She was now devoting much of her spare time to learning everything she could about the embroidery business. And while on the computer, she discovered an upcoming seminar in Chicago by the Tajima embroidery machine company, entitled "How To Start An Embroidery Business."

"That popped up online," she said, "and it was a four- or five-hour seminar. We all talked, and that's what we picked to go to. We thought, 'Well that's the best way to learn about it.'"

So Shelly made reservations for herself and Bobby Teets to fly to Chicago to attend the November 17 seminar at the Marriott O'Hare Hotel. She booked them both overnight into a $209 one-bedroom hotel suite.

When Jimmy told Reggie Ours that Shelly was starting an embroidery business, he asked if she was "crafty."

"I said, 'Jimmy, I've never seen her as a crafty person,'"

said Ours. "He said, 'Well she's not. It's kind of odd, but we see it as an opportunity.'"

When Jimmy told his father, he thought it plain stupid.

"I told him," remembered Denny Michael, "'That's the dumbest thing I've ever heard of.'"

And he questioned how Shelly could possibly give up her highly skilled $65-an-hour nursing job to start an embroidery business in their basement.

"I said, 'She's not going to make any money, and they don't pay,'" he remembered. "'And you have trouble getting money from these small teams and church leagues.'"

Denny said he had a friend in the embroidery business, urging Jimmy to call him.

"And he said, 'Well, that's what she really wants to do,'" said Denny. "He was placating her because she wanted to get away from the hospital, and she was going to do it one way or the other."

On November 3, Shelly Michael was involved in a car accident in Clarksburg, and the police were called. Five days later, she fell down the porch steps of her house, injuring her knee. She called Jimmy, who immediately came home and took her to the hospital for X-rays. After being given a painkiller and sent home with a leg brace, Shelly took three weeks' sick leave from the hospital.

But her injury did not prevent her taking Kylie to Pittsburgh for several cheerleading competitions.

While she was away on a weekend trip, Jimmy offered to help Deborah Harris move some firewood in his truck.

"I thought that was odd," remembered Harris, "because generally they went to everything together. If one kid had soccer practice, all of them would go and sit there. But this past summer was definitely different."

When she told Jimmy not to waste his day off, he replied that he had nothing better to do.

"He didn't want to go with her to Pittsburgh," she recalled, "to watch the cheerleading competition."

Since her husband Dan's talk with Jimmy, Stephanie had noticed a drastic change in Shelly's attitude towards her. On Friday, November 11, she and Dan arrived at Killarney Drive with their baby daughter Audrey, to pick up Drew and Jacie for the Veterans Day weekend.

Jimmy came to the door, explaining that they were in the middle of dinner, leaving them to wait in the foyer. A few minutes later he came back, inviting Stephanie and Dan into the kitchen. His ex-wife thought that very "unusual," as it had never happened before.

When she walked into the kitchen, where all four children were having dinner, Shelly was friendlier than Stephanie had ever seen her.

"She asked if she could hold the baby," recalled Stephanie. "Then she held the baby [as] we waited for the kids to finish their dinner."

The following Monday, Bobby Teets started working for Jimmy Michael at Mountaineer Home Medical. After ten years as a deliveryman for RUS Uniforms, recently bought out by Cintas, the 12th grade high school dropout faced a pay cut. So Jimmy had generously offered him a job, saying it would also make it easier for him to work with Shelly on the new embroidery business.

But that first week he only worked three days, as Jimmy had given him Thursday off so he and Shelly could attend the Chicago embroidery seminar.

When Jimmy told Reggie Ours about the upcoming Chicago trip, Ours assumed he was going too, asking if he wanted him to be on call. Then Jimmy informed him that Shelly and his new deliveryman were going alone.

"And I said, 'You're crazy,' " recalled Ours. "And that's when he said, 'I trust her.' I said, 'Well, I trust my wife too, but my wife's not going away with one of my friends to stay overnight in Chicago.' "

At 4:00 a.m. Thursday morning, Bobby Teets arrived at 545 Killarney Drive, to take Shelly to the Pittsburgh airport to get the plane to Chicago. Although it was a business trip, they'd both had the foresight to pack swimming suits in their overnight cases.

They caught a 6:00 a.m. plane for the ninety-minute flight to O'Hare, landing at 8:25 a.m., because of the one-hour time change. On the plane, they started cosying up to one another.

"We were flirting," Teets explained. "It just happened all of a sudden. It was pretty much no more than that on the plane."

Soon after landing at O'Hare, Shelly called Renee Del Viscio on her cell phone.

"She was telling me that she was attending the seminar for an embroidery business," remembered Renee. "That was the first time I had heard of it [or] heard of the Teets family. It definitely hit me out of left field, especially given the sacrifices she had made for her education."

After taking a shuttle van to the wrong hotel, Shelly and Bobby finally arrived at the Marriott Courtyard Chicago O'Hare hotel in Des Plaines, Illinois, taking more than an hour to travel the two-and-a-half-mile journey.

At 10:06 a.m., they checked into the hotel with a Visa card, unwittingly being photographed by a surveillance camera kissing and holding hands at the front desk, like high school sweethearts.

As the seminar didn't start until 4:30 p.m., they had six hours of free time. After leaving their suitcases in their suite, they took a taxi to downtown Chicago to sightsee and go shopping.

"I had never been there, and she hadn't either," said Teets. "So we went to different stores and messed around downtown all day."

And while they took in the sights of the Windy City, they couldn't keep their hands off each other.

"We were kissing," said Teets, "holding hands and flirting."

A few hours later, they returned to the Marriott for the five-hour embroidery seminar. There was a slideshow and a demonstration on a Tajima embroidery machine, as well as a tutorial on how to start an embroidery business.

"It gave you lots of ideas," said Teets, "about an embroidery company."

The seminar finished at about 10:00 p.m., and Shelly and Bobby decided to go swimming in the hotel pool before taking a hot tub.

"They had a pool at the hotel," remembered Teets. "We went down and swam for a little bit and then just went back to the room."

Back in the room they had several cocktails, before having sex on the king-size bed.

"I just got sucked in," Shelly would later explain. "It's ironic, because I value fidelity so highly."

After getting little sleep, they checked out of the Marriott at 4:16 a.m., catching the 6:00 a.m. flight back to Pittsburgh.

"We were both pretty tired," said Teets, "so I think we just dozed off on the plane. I think we might have held hands or something, but that was pretty much it."

On the drive back from Pittsburgh, they discussed what had happened, and whether they felt guilty for betraying their spouses.

But for the moment, they both agreed to keep their affair secret.

"I mean, I had a lot at stake," explained Teets. "I wanted to keep it secret so bad, because I worked for him. I wouldn't have a job if he would have known. And also he was my friend."

CHAPTER 15

Thanksgiving

That weekend, Bobby Teets avoided Shelly Michael. Since his return from Chicago, he was unsure how to proceed, and worried about getting caught. When he took his son Tyler to football practice on Sunday, he tried to act normal around Jimmy, so as not to arouse suspicion.

On Monday morning, he was back at work, but as it was the busy pre-Thanksgiving week, he saw little of his boss.

"We might have lunch a couple of times," Teets remembered. "He was always doing other stuff . . . and I was always doing other stuff."

Shelly Michael also acted as if nothing had happened when she saw Kelli Teets.

"I just didn't say anything," she would later testify. "I don't know if I was hiding it or concealing it well or not."

On Tuesday, November 22, Kerri Whitacre was scheduled to meet Jimmy Michael for lunch in the Boston Beanery, when something came up and she postponed it to the following week.

"It was going to be more than just your thirty-minute conversation on the phone," she said. "And we were going to meet for lunch, anticipating that we would have a couple of hours to catch up."

Kerri was concerned about her oldest friend, wanting to

try to help him sort things out. She knew how upset he must have been to hit Drew, and was hoping he would tell her what was really going on with Shelly.

"I really feel that if we'd had that lunch together," she said, "perhaps more of this would have come out."

In the wake of Shelly's Chicago trip, Jimmy Michael's closest friends noticed a change in him. It was as if he had finally resolved a problem that had been worrying him for a long time. Later they speculated that he may have discovered she had been cheating on him, and was biding his time until after the holidays to get a divorce.

"He said they were having problems," said Reggie Ours. "And things were going to have to change soon. I think he was starting to find out things."

Denny Michael believes his son had finally had enough of Shelly's behavior, and wanted a divorce. But he knew his son would never discuss it with him, after he had been so strongly against his first divorce.

"She wouldn't have sex with him," said Denny. "And he told his friends, 'I don't know what's wrong with me.' And he was alluding to the fact that she was having sex with these other people.

"So Jimmy would not tolerate that for very long. So he was going to pull out. He had to pull out. But of course, we didn't know any of that at the time."

On Thanksgiving Day, Jimmy and Shelly attended a WVU football game at Mountaineer Field. That evening he called his cousin Kevin Coakley, whose printing business was under contract to Mountaineer Home Medical. They discussed how well the business was doing, and Jimmy said he was looking forward to hunting over the Thanksgiving holiday with his father and cousin Danny Twigg.

Jimmy had already warned Bobby Teets that he was going out of town.

"He said, 'You need to be on call on Saturday,'" Teets would later testify, "'because I'm going to be hunting.'"

On Friday, Jimmy went shopping with Drew for new

hunting clothes, because, although Stephanie Estel was scheduled to have the children for the weekend, he was hoping he could still persuade her to allow Drew to go hunting with him in Maryland.

When Jimmy called his ex-wife, she refused. She wanted her son to attend a special family dinner, to introduce her new baby daughter Audrey to the family.

"Everyone that was coming for Thanksgiving was expecting to see all three of my children," she explained. "And I wanted all three of my children there."

Jimmy said he understood and put down the phone. It would be the last conversation Stephanie would ever have with him.

Late Friday night, Jimmy Michael drove to his parents' house in Cumberland to spend the night, so he could make an early start in the morning. After he left, Shelly called Bobby Teets, inviting him over, as the coast was clear.

At 9:00 a.m. Saturday morning, Bobby Teets arrived at 545 Killarney Drive, after stopping off to buy a box of Shelly's favorite Krispy Kreme donuts. The fact that his daughter Regan had spent the night at the Michaels' home, and was still asleep in Kylie's bedroom, did not deter him.

"Since Jimmy wasn't home," he said, "I stopped over . . . early in the morning, just [to be] once again intimate with her."

When he arrived, Shelly led him upstairs to the master bedroom, where they spent the next hour making love in Jimmy's bed, as their daughters slept next door.

"It was fine," recalled Teets. "I mean, she acted OK."

As they lay in bed afterwards, savoring a post-coital moment, Shelly complimented him on his sexual prowess, saying she loved being with him.

"There were times in the heat of the moment," he later recalled, "maybe hugging each other or something like that, [that] she would say, 'I wish I could hold you forever.'"

And Shelly discussed her unsatisfying sex life with Jimmy, saying she no longer wanted to sleep with him.

"She said she wasn't going to," Teets recalled. "And I even said, 'Maybe you should do that—I mean, he is your husband.' But she said, no, she didn't want to do that."

Across the Maryland border, Jimmy Michael was blissfully unaware of what was happening on Killarney Drive. He had set out early from his parents' house and driven the short distance to his cousin Daniel Twigg's farm in Cumberland.

"It was the first day of Maryland Rifle Season," Twigg remembered. "And we always go hunting."

It was a good day's hunting, with each bagging a deer. Twigg thought his cousin seemed upbeat and positive, happily discussing how well his new business was going.

It was late afternoon when Jimmy drove back to Morgantown. He went home to change, before he and Shelly attended a Mountaineers basketball game with Bobby and Kelli Teets.

After the game they all had dinner together.

"I was sitting across the table from Kelli and Jimmy," said Shelly, "and I said to myself, 'What the heck am I doing? This is crazy.'"

On Sunday, Jimmy Michael worked a shift at Preston hospital. After he finished work, he drove back to Killarney Drive to change clothes. While he was there he chatted with his neighbor Steve Negy, offering to pay his children to rake his leaves.

At about 4:30 p.m., he set off back to Daniel Twigg's farm in Cumberland. On his way there, he received a call on his cell phone from Jeremy Miller.

"That was the last conversation we ever had," remembered Miller. "He talked about how much he felt God was blessing his business."

Then Miller discussed Shelly's recent overnight trip to Chicago, saying he would never let his wife Tara go away with another man.

"He really didn't see this guy as a threat," Miller said. "He said the only thing that bothered him about [the embroidery business] was that Bobby would see Shelly more than he would."

"I'm jealous I'm not the one that's with her more," were Jimmy's sad last words to Jeremy Miller.

When he arrived at his cousin's farm, Jimmy Michael was in an unusually reflective mood. Over the next two hours, as they sat in the milking parlor cleaning the deer they had killed, he opened up as never before.

"We had a real long heartfelt talk," Daniel Twigg remembered. "And that was out of the ordinary. His concern was that he couldn't serve the Lord in the way he wanted, because of his marital situation."

Although Jimmy never mentioned that he suspected Shelly of infidelity, or that he soon planned to leave her, Twigg felt that his cousin was carrying a heavy load.

"He wanted to find a way of settling things with the Lord," said Twigg. "And it was bothering him. That was our [last] conversation."

As Jimmy hugged him goodbye, he asked his cousin to pray for him.

It was late evening when Jimmy Michael arrived at his parents' house. After eating dinner, he sat down by the fire in the living room to chat.

"He was in a good mood," remembered his mother. "We talked about a lot of things until about 11:00 p.m. and then he went to bed."

At sunrise the next morning, Jimmy and his father put on their hunting clothes and drove twenty miles to Pocahontas County, Pennsylvania. It was raining with thick fog, but father and son were looking forward to the first day of the Pennsylvania hunting season, and were determined to enjoy it.

"It was Monday and a miserable day," remembered Denny Michael. "One of those days when the hunting was terrible, so we were making all kinds of mistakes."

They set up their portable tree stands in the heavy rain, before climbing thirty-five feet up them to hunt deer.

"I thought Jimmy was happy," said his father. "He was kidding and cutting up."

Before long Jimmy bagged a deer, but after three or four hours with nothing else happening, he became bored and climbed back down.

"He got tired of hunting," remembered Denny. "It was still raining."

Denny gave him the directions back to his truck, so he could drive it back, collect the dead deer and go home.

"He wasn't familiar with the property as well I was," said Denny. "So I'm in my tree stand waiting, and I look down and he's going the wrong way. He was only about one hundred yards away, but there was no way he could hear me shouting."

Two hours later, Jimmy finally found his way back, after getting completely lost in the forest.

"He's all sweaty," said his father. "He got lost. I was just laughing. Usually I'd get mad, because it's just that father–son thing. But it was so funny."

It was already getting dark by the time they arrived back in Cumberland. After hanging up the deer, Jimmy went into the kitchen to say goodbye to his parents, for although the conditions were horrendous, he was driving back to Morgantown, to coach Drew's basketball practice.

"I remember I looked at my clock and it said five-thirty-four," said his mother. "And I told him to be careful, because I'm always cautious of his driving. And I hugged him and told him that I love him. I told him to call me as soon as he got home."

That morning, Shelly Michael was scrambling to find the money for the expensive embroidery machine she had set her sights on. Jimmy had already made it clear that no money would come from Mountaineer Home Medical, and that Bobby Teets would have to get a finance loan with Shelly.

Shelly Michael suddenly arrived at her husband's office without warning, to look into buying a new computer and use the fax machine.

"I e-mailed everybody about the embroidery machine," she later told police. "I guess Bobby kind of thought Jimmy was going to be buying the machine through Mountaineer Home Medical. So I e-mailed them and said, 'I feel really bad if you thought it was going to be this way.'"

She said that if they wanted to pull out, she and Jimmy would go ahead on their own.

A few hours later, Shelly Michael collected Regan Teets and her daughter Kylie from school. Soon after arriving back at Killarney Drive, Bobby Teets arrived to pick up his daughter, who was not feeling well.

"Nothing major happened," recalled Teets. "I was actually on the way back from a delivery. I stopped there and we had talked for a few minutes."

They discussed the embroidery machine financing situation, with Shelly offering to arrange a bank appointment for Teets to request a loan. Then they talked about their affair, and how well they were doing keeping Jimmy and Kelli in the dark.

According to Teets, he told Shelly he had no intention of leaving Kelli and his two kids for her, emphasizing the need to keep their affair a secret.

"I mean," he later testified, "it was just as much my fault as hers as far as the whole sex issue, but I was still intimate with my wife."

A little after 6:00 p.m., Jimmy Michael called Bobby Teets from his cell phone.

"He was on his way back from Maryland," said Teets. "And he was telling me it was real foggy. He said he was real tired."

During the twenty-minute conversation, Jimmy asked about his weekend, and if there was anything that needed to be taken care of at work.

"It was a pretty friendly conversation," recalled Teets.

Earlier that day, Reggie Ours, who had been on call for Mountaineer Home Medical, had left a message on Jimmy's phone asking him to call. He needed to set up an apnea monitor for a new-born baby at Ruby Memorial, and did not know how to do it.

So on his way home, Jimmy called him back, promising to come in to set up the monitor.

"I will be there first thing Tuesday morning," he told Ours, "and I'll bring doughnuts."

By the time Jimmy Michael arrived at the North Elementary School gym in Morgantown, he was exhausted. It had been a long day of hunting, and the drive through the Cumberland Gap through thick fog had really tired him out.

"He said, 'You are going to have to do everything tonight,'" remembered his assistant coach, Dan Estel. "'I have been up since early morning . . . deer hunting.'"

It was just after 9:00 p.m. when the practice finished, and Jimmy discussed Wednesday's arrangements for him to pick up Drew and Jacie after school at their mother's house.

"[It was] very cordial," said Estel, who then drove Drew home with him.

When Jimmy arrived back at 545 Killarney Drive, Shelly was still at cheerleading practice at the West Virginia Gym Training Center. He knew she would be a while, as she had to take Kylie back to Rob Angus's house in Grafton.

So he lay down on his living room couch to watch *Monday Night Football*. At 9:20 p.m. his mother called the house, concerned that she hadn't heard from him.

"I said, 'Why didn't you call me?'" she recalled. "He said, 'Because I had to go to basketball practice.' It was our last conversation."

At about 10:00 p.m., Jimmy called Bobby Teets on his cell phone, as he was buying milk at a Kroger's store. He asked him what appointments he had the next day, but Teets said he did not know.

Then Jimmy brought up the embroidery business.

"I remember him saying," said Teets, "that it seems like we are going to be spending a lot of time together, meaning the embroidery stuff and everything."

* * *

After dropping Kylie off, Shelly drove back to Killarney Drive. On her way she called Kelli Teets to discuss the cheerleading practice. Then she called Bobby Teets, who had just put down the phone with her husband.

Shelly asked him to go home and find his and Kelli's last few tax returns, so she could fill out the application form for the embroidery machine.

"She was actually telling me what I needed, so I could tell my wife," said Teets. "Because my wife knows what that stuff is. I didn't."

Shelly told him that as she was returning to work tomorrow, after three weeks' sick leave, he should bring the forms to her at Ruby Memorial Hospital.

"I didn't know what my day was going to be like," Teets would later testify. "If I was in Morgantown and close to the hospital, I was supposed to call her."

According to Shelly Michael, when she arrived home that night, Jimmy was lying on the couch watching football.

"He was really tired and half-asleep when I got home," she recalled. "I just remember asking him about hunting. I asked him if he got a deer that day. He killed a girl deer that day, and I had to tease him about [it]."

Then she updated him about her progress in buying an embroidery machine.

"He said he was excited for us," she recalled. "I went to the computer to check my e-mails."

At about 11:00 p.m., she went upstairs to Kylie and Jacie's bedroom to watch a DVD of her daughter's last cheerleading competition.

CHAPTER 16

A Living Death

Sometime between eleven o'clock that night and five-thirty the next morning, prosecutors believe, Shelly Michael cold-bloodedly murdered her husband. They think the highly organized nurse had been planning the perfect crime, to be rid of Jimmy. Then she and her children would be able to start a new life, using his $500,000 life insurance.

And the diminutive nurse's murder weapon of choice was rocuronium, a deadly paralyzing drug closely related to pancuronium, used in many states for lethal injections on death row.

In pediatric hospitals the strong narcotic is used to paralyze young children's muscles during surgery, making it easier for a doctor to intubate with oxygen. As a nurse practitioner, Shelly used rocuronium daily on her intensive care patients. At Ruby Memorial Hospital it was designated an unaccounted floor drug like Tylenol, and freely available.

Exactly what happened later that night at 545 Killarney Drive, only Shelly Michael will ever know. But investigators later reconstructed how they believe she carried out her despicable crime, using the evidence and expert scientific analysis.

As her 210-pound husband slept helplessly in their bed in the upstairs master bedroom, Shelly opened her bag, taking out a 5cc syringe with a tiny 23 gauge needle. She flicked off the needle cap, which fell to the floor and rolled under the bed.

The experienced nurse then placed the syringe in a vial of clear rocuronium liquid that she had previously brought home from the hospital. She drew up the medicine, filling the syringe with the full dose of 50 milligrams.

She then got into bed next to Jimmy, who was sleeping on his back like a baby. During her years of nursing she had given hundreds of small children the exact same injection. So she knew how to be gentle, causing the absolute minimum of pain.

In the blinking of an eye, Shelly jabbed the tiny needle into Jimmy's thigh muscle, gently pulling back on the plunger. It took less than a second, and would have felt no more painful than a mosquito bite.

If Jimmy, exhausted by his long day of hunting, had woken up, his wife would have lovingly reassured him. Perhaps she apologized for poking him by accident, telling him that everything was OK and to go back to sleep.

Then Shelly Michael lay next to him, watching the deadly paralytic drug take effect.

Within one minute the drug traveled from his muscle into the bloodstream, making Jimmy feel funny. His arms and legs were becoming weak, and he was having trouble breathing.

Perhaps Shelly continued to comfort him, as he asked what was happening to him. If he had tried to stand up or summon help, she would only have a couple more minutes until he could no longer do so.

By the four-minute mark, the rocuronium had been fully absorbed into his bloodstream. Jimmy was now unable to stand up, and could not support his weight against gravity.

Although he was getting weaker by the second, his mind was crystal clear. He was totally aware of his surroundings and could see and hear everything that was happening to him. But he was powerless to stop it, now being too weak to even raise his little finger.

As his body began to shut down, Jimmy Michael was aware that he was suffocating to death, and probably panicked. Although he was fully conscious, he was perfectly trapped in his own body.

Eight minutes after the injection, the powerful drug flooded through his system. He was now unable to breathe, as carbon dioxide in his body built up and his diaphragm was shutting down, leaving him gasping for air.

As Jimmy lay on his back, he was unable to prevent his tongue from blocking his airways—his body's basic survival instinct kicked in, making him hyperventilate out of fear and anxiety.

In another two or three minutes, Jimmy Michael reached hypoxemia—where his blood oxygen was so low, he began to lose consciousness. The remaining oxygen in his body had rapidly decreased to the point where there was not enough to sustain life.

Two minutes later, Jimmy Michael would have slipped into unconsciousness, and in another five he would have died.

Experts estimate that it took an agonizing thirteen minutes for him to lose consciousness after he was injected him with rocuronium.

Only Shelly Michael knows what she was doing during those thirteen agonizing minutes, as Jimmy battled for life. Perhaps she hovered over him, telling him why she had done it. Maybe she was taunting him about her lover Bobby Teets, and the new life they would have on his insurance money.

At around 5:15 a.m., as Jimmy Michael's body lay on the bed, Shelly prepared for work. She showered and then dressed in a starched white shirt, gray sweater and a black skirt. Then she sat by the mirror, carefully applying her make-up.

When she was finally ready, investigators believe, she took out her electric iron, and plugged it into a socket. Then she placed it face down on the bed sheets alongside her husband's body, turning it up to HIGH.

And at around 6:30 a.m., after one last look at her husband, Shelly walked out of the bedroom and downstairs into the kitchen, leaving Jimmy's cell phone prominently displayed on a countertop.

Then she went into her garage, climbed into her Ford Expedition SUV and drove to Ruby Memorial Hospital to start work.

CHAPTER 17

Tuesday, November 29

At 6:30 a.m. on Tuesday, November 29, Nurse Shelly Michael arrived at Ruby Memorial Hospital. She took the elevator up to the third floor, turning left into the pediatric intensive care ward, to begin a ten-hour shift. It was her first appearance at work since her fall, three weeks earlier.

Over the next several hours, she was as conspicuous as possible, carefully laying down an elaborate alibi. After getting her clipboard, she consulted with the night resident about her ten patients. Then she started her pre-rounds.

Respiratory therapist Reggie Ours arrived for work at the PICU just after Shelly, thinking it strange she was already there.

"She didn't usually get in that early," he recalled. "Usually between seven o'clock and seven-thirty."

A few minutes later, as he was changing an infant's oxygen mask, Nurse Michael, who had been with a patient at the next bed, came over and goosed him.

"She came up and grabbed me in the butt," he said. "That was very odd. It really stood out."

At 7:01 a.m., Shelly ordered an Ativan syringe to calm down a patient while trying to remove a breathing tube. By the time the tranquilizer arrived, the child had calmed down, so she told a nurse to "waste it."

Then at 7:24 a.m. Shelly went into the X-ray room, sat down at the table and called Jimmy's cell phone, leaving a message. Investigators believe that she had earlier left his cell in the kitchen, to be found later.

"Hey, it's just me," she said casually. "I was hoping I could catch you before you left. I need, I wanted to see what was on the lunch menu for the kids, because Kylie ate hot lunch yesterday and didn't really like it. And I was, like, wondering if you could pack 'em something. So, if you haven't left yet, call me back."

A few minutes later, she called her house phone, later telling police she'd gotten a busy signal. Then she called Bobby Teets on his cell phone, asking if he had the tax forms she needed for the embroidery machine. He said he had them, promising to drop them off at the hospital later that day.

By 7:45 a.m., an hour-and-a-half after leaving 545 Killarney Drive, Shelly was becoming concerned that she had still not heard anything about a fire.

"She was very antsy that day," remembered Ours, "and she started getting really nervous."

At 8:00 a.m., she decided to sneak out of the hospital and return to Killarney Drive, just a couple of minutes away. She knew that if the house had not caught fire, and Jimmy's body was found on the bed, it would test positive for rocuronium. So she had to go home and reset the fire.

A couple of minutes later, she walked up to the front desk, informing PICU clerk Nancy Buffalo that she was going to her car to get her pager.

Buffalo thought that strange. During a recent conversation, Shelly had told her she never brought it into the hospital, as nobody ever paged her.

At 8:11 a.m., Nurse Shelly Michael was captured on the hospital's surveillance video, walking past the first-floor cappuccino machine in the east lobby and out of the hospital. Then another camera caught her walking across the parking lot in the heavy rain, to her Ford Expedition.

After starting the engine and turning on the windshield

wipers, she pulled out of the parking lot, turning left on El-
mer Prince Drive. There was little traffic at that time of the
morning, as most of the hospitals change shifts at 7:00 a.m.
Then Shelly made another left onto Willowdale Road, turning left at a set of lights onto Route 705, until she reached
Van Voorhis Road. Then she turned left into Killarney Drive.
It was just over a mile from Ruby memorial to her house,
and she arrived just after 8:15 a.m.

She parked the Ford Expedition in her driveway, glanc-
ing across to the garage, where Jimmy's Mitsubishi was still
parked inside. Then she let herself into the house through
the rear French doors. There was no smell of burning as she
climbed the stairs, walking past the children's rooms and
turning right into her bedroom.

Jimmy's body lay on the bed, just as she'd left it two hours
earlier. The iron was still on the bed and had turned itself off,
so she put it to one side.

Now, prosecutors believe, she probably poured an accelerant over the bedding, before torching it with a lighter. It
would have taken no more than thirty seconds for the bed to
catch fire. And once it was burning, she came out of the
bedroom, closing the door behind her.

After letting herself out the front door, Shelly got back
into her Ford Expedition. She then turned right out of her
driveway to a four-way stop at the intersection with Eastern
Avenue. There, to her horror, was her neighbor Shawn Alt,
stopped directly across from her. When he waved to her, she
pushed hard on the gas pedal, sweeping past him on her way
back to Ruby hospital.

At 8:25 a.m., Shelly Michael's silver Ford Expedition was
photographed by a fourth-floor balcony security surveillance camera at the hospital, pulling into the employee parking lot. She drove up and down searching for a parking
place, finally finding one a few seconds later.

Another surveillance camera captured her at 8:27 a.m.,
walking through the parking lot. This time she had an umbrella up, shielding herself from the heavy rain. A minute

later—exactly seventeen minutes after she'd first left Ruby—Shelly reentered the hospital through the east lobby doors, on her way to the elevator.

Getting out at the third floor without being seen, she went to the front desk, announcing that she would be attending the 9:00 a.m. morning report conference for residents and medical students, something she rarely did.

"She told me she was going to morning report," recalled Nancy Buffalo, who was still at the front desk. "I thought it strange, because [nurses] normally don't tell me when they are going anywhere."

By 9:00 a.m. the staff at Mountaineer Home Medical were beginning to worry why their boss hadn't arrived yet. Jimmy Michael was invariably the first in, usually at his desk between 7:00 and 8:00 a.m. every morning, unless taking his children to school.

When his office manager Brenda Shiflett had arrived at 7:30 a.m. at the Maple Drive parking lot, she was surprised not to see his Mitsubishi in its regular spot.

"Sometimes we fought to get there first," Shiflett would later testify. "We had one computer between the two of us, and the rule was, whoever got there first got to use it."

It was even stranger, as Mountaineer Home Medical had been closed for the four-day Thanksgiving weekend, and as Jimmy had taken Monday off, he had not been there for five days. So he had a busy day ahead to catch up with pressing office matters.

Walking into Jimmy's office, she was also surprised to see a patient package she had placed on his desk the previous evening, still there and unopened. It was essential information that Jimmy would need that morning to set up a newborn baby girl's apnea monitor at Ruby Memorial Hospital's Neonatal Intensive Care Unit. Ironically, he had an early morning appointment across the hallway from where his wife worked.

After Reggie Ours' call the previous day, Shiflett had left Jimmy several messages on his cell phone regarding the package, so she had expected him to collect it on Monday night, if he was going straight to Ruby memorial, instead of coming into the office.

"It had to be done first thing," she later explained. "Because they kept this new-born baby at the hospital overnight, so Jim could set it up."

It was a little after 7:30 a.m. when Bobby Teets arrived, after dropping his son Tyler off at Suncrest Elementary School. He went straight into the stockroom to unpack a shipment of toilets that had arrived the day before.

A few minutes later he received Shelly's call on his cell phone, asking about his and Kelli's W2 forms.

"I was unpacking boxes," he said. "I said, 'I've got the papers in the car. I'll meet you in the hospital as long as I can get around there sometime today.'"

By 8:00 a.m., when there was still no sign of Jimmy Michael, Brenda and her niece Erika Shiflett, who was office secretary, agreed that they urgently needed to track down their boss.

"I started being more concerned about this baby going home," remembered Brenda, "and I knew this needed to be done early."

She called Jimmy's cell phone, but there was no answer. For the next hour she would call repeatedly, baffled as to why he was not answering.

"We always communicated by cell phone," Brenda said. "His phone was always stuck on him. It was a joke. I never saw him without it."

She then went to the stockroom, asking Bobby Teets if he knew where Jimmy was. He said he didn't, but would try his cell phone.

Teets' first task that day was to deliver a toilet seat to a patient's home in Fairmont, twenty miles southwest of Morgantown. He was getting increasingly concerned, needing additional instructions from Jimmy for his schedule the rest of the day.

"So we just kept trying to call Jimmy," said Brenda Shiflett. "I called many, many times."

At 9:05 a.m., when there was still no sign of Jimmy, she told Teets to leave for Fairmont, as the patient needed the toilet urgently.

Bobby Teets drove his 2005 blue-green Pontiac Grand Prix out of Maple Drive towards the WVU Coliseum. He then headed south on Route 119, stopping off at McBee's Exxon Station, using his credit card to buy gas. Then he drove south on I-79 to Fairmont.

At around 9:25 a.m. he arrived at the patient's house. He took the toilet seat out of his car and attached the legs before bringing it inside. While he was setting it up, he chatted with the patient, who was in another room, although Bobby never actually saw him.

On his way back to Morgantown, his wife Kelli called, wanting to discuss Shelly Michael's fax about securing a loan for the embroidery machine.

"She said, 'Our finances aren't the best,'" remembered Teets. "She said, 'Maybe there is a different way you guys should go about doing it.' She wasn't mad about it. She was just giving her input."

Teets then called Shelly at Ruby Memorial, reporting back on what his wife had said.

"I told her, 'She's not mad about it,'" he said. "'She just wants to let you know that maybe there's a different way.'"

Around 10:00 a.m., Bobby Teets was back in Morgantown driving along Route 250, when he received a call from Brenda Shiflett, who was becoming more and more concerned about Jimmy.

Teets said he had just called the Michaels' landline, and it was busy. He'd also called Jimmy's cell, going straight through to voice mail.

Then Brenda asked him to stop in at Killarney Drive on his way back to the office, and check to see if Jimmy was there and if everything was all right.

Bobby Teets said he would, and on the way over called Ruby Memorial Hospital, to ask Shelly if she knew where Jimmy was. Trainee receptionist Joanna Duesenberry took his call, paging Nurse Michael, who asked her to take a message, as she was in the middle of her morning rounds.

Teets then left a message to tell Nurse Michael that her husband had not turned up for work, and nobody knew where he was.

CHAPTER 18

Flashover

If Shelly Michael hadn't shut the bedroom door on her way out after setting the fire, things might have been very different. But with all the windows closed, and limited oxygen to feed it, the fire progressed far differently than it would have otherwise.

Investigators believe that after she left the house, the fire quickly took hold, fueled by the ample bedding and other clothes around it. But within a few minutes, after consuming all the available oxygen, the flames subsided.

For the next one-and-a-half hours the bed and area around it smoldered, slowly burning Jimmy Michael's body beyond recognition. The bedroom gradually filled with thick black smoke, darkening the windows and leaving a layer of soot over everything.

Underneath Jimmy Michael's body, a pile of birthday cards and newspapers on the carpet by a nightstand near the headboard slowly burned into embers. Eventually, the embers and charcoal burned down through the three-quarter-inch floor and the half-inch plywood sub-floor. It then devoured two two-by-ten-inch joists, burning through into the drywall living room ceiling below.

Finally, the oaken headboard and nightstand collapsed on the floor. It created a pile of smoldering charcoal, eventually burning a large hole through the floor and falling down into the living room below.

This caused a sudden inrush of air, bringing the fire back to life with a vengeance. The bedroom then burst into flames, sending temperatures inside soaring to 1,200 degrees Fahrenheit. At that point there was flashover—the most dangerous phase of a fire, where everything ignites simultaneously.

Then, seconds later, at precisely 10:27 a.m., the bedroom window blew out.

A few minutes earlier, two Morgantown utility workers had driven past 545 Killarney Drive. Monty Savage II, who had spent the morning unplugging drains, noticed smoke coming out of the rafters of the house, telling his colleague Rodney Compton, who was driving.

"He didn't believe me," remembered Savage. "I told him to turn around, because I was worried there were kids or somebody in the house."

Eventually Compton turned around and saw the smoke pouring out of an upstairs window. He called his dispatcher on his two-way radio, telling her to call 911 and report the fire.

While Compton made the call, Savage ran up to the front door and pounded on it as hard as he could.

"I could hear the smoke alarm going off," he recalled. "And I looked through the window."

As he peered through a small window pane, he saw burning debris falling through a large hole in the ceiling, onto the living room floor.

"There was a line burning across the floor," remembered Savage. "And particles falling down."

Then off-duty fireman Keith Summers, who lived three houses away on Collins Ferry Road, arrived to see what was happening. He'd been told by a deliveryman that the house opposite was on fire.

"I left my house to walk down the street," he said. "There at the chimney level was white smoke pouring out of the eaves."

Summers also dialed 911 on his cell phone, asking Monty Savage, who was standing at the front door, what he knew.

"I asked him if there was anybody home," said Summers. "He didn't think so."

The firefighter tried to open the front door, but it was locked. Then he peered through the small front door window into the house, seeing the burning debris plunging through the ceiling.

"I was trying to see if anybody was in there," he said, "sleeping on the couch or something. On the left-hand side, I could see a light haze of smoke on the first floor of the residence."

Then Summers walked around the house, looking for an unlocked door. As he approached the rear, he noticed that a second-storey right-hand window, directly over where the fire appeared to be, had turned black.

"Almost limousine-tinted," he would later describe it. "That window was very darkly stained, and I assumed that was where the fire was. There was still smoke coming from the eaves."

Summers was about to break in through a set of French doors at the back of the house, when the top right-hand window suddenly shattered above him as flashover occurred.

"Flames burst from that window," he said. "Flames and smoke."

At that point, the off-duty fireman decided to wait for assistance, as he didn't have any protective clothing or proper equipment. His firefighting experience had also taught him that there had been a build-up of smoke and pressurized gases in that room, creating a very dangerous situation.

Ironically, the entire Morgantown Fire Department was about to tour the Health Sciences Building at Ruby Memorial Hospital when the first emergency call came in. Ten firemen immediately responded to 545 Killarney Drive, with three engines and a ladder truck.

At 10:32 a.m. Morgantown fireman Gary Freshour and his crew were the first to arrive.

"We had fire coming out of the upstairs window," Freshour later testified. "It appeared to be starting through the roof."

As his engine pulled past the house to start setting up equipment, Freshour jumped out and began pulling the fire hose towards the back of the house, where the fire was raging. Then, after it had been attached to the nearest fire hydrant, the water was switched on.

"It was a mistake," said Freshour. "Typically, you take the line dry to wherever you want to go and you call for water. That didn't happen this time."

This resulted in the fire hose getting "bunched up" at the door, and as another member of his crew untangled it, Freshour tried to gain entry through the back door.

"It was locked," he remembered, "and I kicked it in."

After donning protective gear, he went inside the house. He saw a light smoke on the first floor, but no signs of fire. He knew he had to get upstairs where the fire was raging, first taking a cursory walk through the first floor.

"There was a hole in the ceiling," he said, "and there was debris on the ground underneath that hole."

As another fireman straightened out the hose, Freshour started wetting down the still-smoldering piles of materials lying beneath the hole.

"I just remember hitting it with water before I did anything else," he said. "To make sure that once I went upstairs, the fire didn't get behind me. Also, while the line was still being untangled, I shot water up through the opening, hoping to dampen it down a little bit."

As the three firemen were preparing to fight the blaze inside the house, four of their colleagues climbed up a ladder truck, battling the flames from the outside.

When the hose line was finally ready, Freshour and his colleagues Andy Laskody and Chris Grabb put on breathing equipment, dragging it up the staircase and into the hallway. They noted that with the exception of light smoke, all the rooms along the hallway were undamaged, except for the last room on the right.

"It was starting out of that room," Freshour remembered. "The fire was pretty heavy. It had basically started to consume everything in that room, and it was now going to work back to the other areas of the house."

But at the door, the firefighters found it impossible to enter the burning bedroom, as the fire was just too intense.

"There was just a lot of fire," said Freshour. "It was on three sides of us—left, right and front."

So they stood at the entrance, spraying gallons of water into the burning room to "knock down" the fire, and get it under control. The smoke was so thick, the firefighters couldn't see their hands in front of their faces.

"It was hard to see," said Freshour. "Usually you can't see further than two feet in front of you, if that much. But it eases once the fire goes out, and there is a place for the smoke to go."

At that point Bobby Teets arrived, finding Killarney Drive blocked off by fire engines and other emergency vehicles. When he realized it was Jimmy Michael's house on fire, his first thought was that his friend had discovered the affair and done something terrible. He felt "a ton of guilt," believing that he had betrayed Jimmy and was responsible.

"I was pretty distraught," he later explained, "because I just had an affair with his wife. I felt pretty bad. It was a pretty good-size fire when I got there. And it was coming out of the window of the bedroom. It was pretty severe."

He parked at the end of the road, calling Brenda Shiflett on his way up to the house.

"I know why he's not answering the phone," he told her. "It's because his house is on fire."

Brenda wanted to come straight over, but Teets told her to stay where she was and he'd be in touch. He then rushed into the front yard, where Morgantown Deputy Fire Marshall Lieutenant Ken Tennant was standing with Fire Chief David Fetty and Police Sergeant Harold Sperringer.

"He grabbed me from the back," recalled Tennant. "I turned around. he was very upset and agitated, and I didn't know the guy from anybody."

"If his car is in there, he's there," Teets told them breathlessly.

And when Lieutenant Tennant asked who he was referring to, Teets emotionally spluttered, "Jimmy."

When he finally calmed down, Teets explained that his boss Jimmy Michael hadn't turned up for work that morning. So if his silver Mitsubishi car was in the garage, he was probably still inside the burning house.

Then, after ordering Teets behind a police safety barrier, Chief Fetty told Lieutenant Tennant to break into the garage.

"Both garage doors were closed," remembered Tennant. "The windows were frosted glass. You couldn't see through them."

So he picked up a crow bar, smashing one of the windows and seeing a silver car parked inside.

"I radioed the commander that there possibly could be someone inside," Tennant recalled. "So they immediately began to do a more thorough search."

Although Chief Fetty had come as an observer, he now took charge of the fire scene. When he learned there was a car in the garage, the chief's immediate reaction was that presumed owner Jimmy Michael had possibly committed suicide.

"I said, 'Check inside the car,'" said Fetty. "We checked inside the car but there was no body. So then the second thing in my thought process was, 'He's a guy who's home when he should be at work. What's he doing home?'"

At around 10:35 a.m., as he anxiously watched the firemen fight the fire from behind police tape, Bobby Teets called Shelly Michael at Ruby Memorial. When he couldn't get through, he called his wife Kelli, telling her that Jimmy's house was on fire and asking her to call Shelly, and then Rob Angus and Stephanie Estel, to ensure that none of the children were in the house.

After putting down the phone, Kelli called Ruby Memorial, asking for Shelly Michael. She was put on hold while an operator tried to contact her.

"I thought, 'Oh my gosh, she doesn't even know,'" Kelli would later testify. "When she came on the phone, I said, 'Shelly, I don't want to be the one to tell you this, but your house is on fire.'

"She said, 'What? Whatever.' And I said, 'No, seriously, there is a fire at your house right now.'"

Then Kelli explained how, when Jimmy hadn't turned up for work, Bobby had driven by the house and seen the fire trucks.

"And she went, 'Oh my God!'" remembered Kelli, "and hung up the phone."

PICU clerk Nancy Buffalo was with her when she received the call, observing Shelly's "strange" reaction upon hearing that her house was on fire.

"She took the phone call and she didn't say too much," Buffalo remembered. "And then she said, 'I have to leave. My house is on fire.'"

Shelly then went into her office, closed the door and at 10:38 a.m., left the following message on Jimmy's cell phone voice mail: "Jimmy, where are you? I just heard that our house is on fire. Where are you? Call me back."

She then came out of her office, asking Nancy Buffalo to tell Dr. Romano that she had to leave. Once again the clerk was struck by her casual manner, and how she didn't appear to be in any hurry.

"I [saw] no emotion," Buffalo later testified. "It was like she was doing her everyday thing. It struck me as strange."

At 10:45 a.m., Nurse Shelly Michael left the Pediatric Intensive Care Unit on the third floor of the hospital, wearing her white lab coat. Two minutes later, she was photographed by a video surveillance camera walking out of the hospital to her Ford Expedition in the parking lot. She then opened the hatch of her SUV and looked around inside for a few seconds, before shutting it and driving out of the parking lot.

On her way back to 545 Killarney Drive, she called Bobby Teets twice on her cell phone, at 10:48 a.m. and 10:52 a.m.

"Shelly called me on the way over," recalled Teets, "and said, 'What's going on?' I said, 'Your house is on fire.'"

When she asked where he was, her lover replied that he was at the house waiting for her.

Soon after getting the fire under control, firefighter Gary Freshour received a radio call from Chief Fetty.

"We were told that there may be a resident inside," Freshour later testified. "The fire was out in that room [but] visibility was still very minimal."

Chief Fetty instructed Freshour to continue the overhauling process, ensuring that no pockets of fire were lurking behind a wall or in an attic. Working as a team, Andy Laskody and Chris Grab then joined hands, feeling their way around the bedroom, with its near-blackout conditions, with smoke and steam from all the water that had been pumped in.

Eventually, using the hole in the floor as a reference point, they located the bed and mattress spring. Then, by feeling around, they eventually found a body, lying on what remained of the bed.

"It wasn't easy to determine," recalled Freshour, "because the fire had made the body not very distinguishable."

When they radioed their discovery to Chief Fetty, his immediate reaction was that there might be another corpse underneath.

"I said, 'Check under that body,'" he said. "Because you don't know if the guy's home having an affair or something."

Once a body had been found, everything changed. It was no longer a simple house fire, and became a death investigation for the Morgantown Police Department.

And Lieutenant Ken Tennant's role also changed. "I went into an investigator role," the 35-year-old experienced firefighter explained. "We needed to limit the damage that we do. Because basically, it's a crime scene until it's ruled not to be. At that point the victim was deceased and the number-one goal is to prevent the rest of the building from burning down."

Lieutenant Tennant then went upstairs to view the body. Fans had been set up to clear the smoke, but when he entered the bedroom, there was little visibility.

"It wasn't comfortable without breathing apparatus," he remembered. "But within fifteen minutes it was all cleared out, and you were able to see the victim."

Then he ordered the three firefighters to stop throwing pieces of charred carpet and furniture out the window, and not to move anything from now on unless they had to.

"I also told them to try and protect the body, which was severely damaged," he said, "from anything that may fall down."

When Sergeant Harold Sperringer, who was waiting downstairs, learned of the body, he immediately alerted Morgantown detectives.

"We knew we had to wait for the fire department to be done," he said. "I was calling out all the detectives, because we now had a death scene. And it was right about this time when Michelle Michael showed up."

CHAPTER 19

Detective Paul Mezzanotte

Detective Paul Mezzanotte had been working in the Detective Division at the Public Safety Building when he'd heard the first emergency radio fire call go out. Then, half-an-hour later, Lieutenant Kevin Clark told him a body had been found, ordering him to 545 Killarney Road to lead the investigation.

At 11:18 a.m. the detective drew up outside the Michael house, where there was still some smoke coming from the roof. He was escorted through the police tape to meet Sergeant Sperringer, before going into the house with Lieutenant Ken Tennant and Fire Captain Bill Graham.

"I followed the fire hose up the steps," remembered Mezzanotte. "The fire was pretty much out, but it was very smoky. I looked around at some of the fire damage and then Lieutenant Ken Tennant walked me into the bedroom. There was a hole burned through the roof, and when I arrived, the fire was venting through [it]."

Although Captain Graham told him the body was on the bed, it still took him several seconds before he could make it out.

"That's how bad it was devastated," the detective recalled. "I remember you could see his teeth very clearly. And that was how we put it together."

As the body was burned beyond recognition, Mezzanotte knew the teeth would be the only identification point. For the moment they could only presume it was Jimmy Michael.

As Lieutenant Tennant pointed out some of the fire damage, Detective Mezzanotte was immediately struck by how it was limited to the bedroom, with all the other upstairs rooms virtually untouched.

"It was remarkable to me," he explained later. "If you would have chopped the first floor off that house, it was still livable."

Then he asked the Morgantown fire investigator for his initial thoughts.

"He said that this was a very unusual fire," said Detective Mezzanotte. "There were several red flags. The position of the body was unusual for a fire inside of a bedroom. [It] looked as if he was asleep. It was like no fire damage I had ever seen on a body. Very bizarre."

It was still raining heavily when Shelly Michael parked her Ford Expedition on Eastern Avenue, as the immediate area around her house was sealed off. She then ran towards her house, first encountering Fire Captain Max Humphreys outside.

"[She was] wearing a lab coat with a name pin," recalled Humphreys, who is also a clergyman, and had been summoned to the scene to provide grief counseling for the widow. "She asked me, 'What the fuck is going on?'"

Bobby Teets then came up and hugged Shelly, escorting her out of the rain and into the back seat of Sergeant Sperringer's Durango SUV. A few seconds later his wife Kelli turned up.

"She was in the back seat of the police car with [an] officer," Kelli remembered. "Everyone was waiting to see what was going on. She was hysterical. She said, 'Find him! He has got to be in there. Maybe he went for a jog. He has got to be in there.'"

Then Rob Angus, who had heard about the fire from his close friend Lieutenant Kevin Clark, arrived.

"When I got there, Shelly was in a police cruiser," he said. "She was, I guess, out of it."

As he held his ex-wife in his arms to comfort her, Sergeant Joel Smith, a psychologist with the Morgantown Police Department, arrived with Max Humphreys to break the tragic news of Jimmy's death, finding Angus cradling his ex-wife in his arms.

"I opened the rear door," remembered Humphreys. "I then informed Ms. Michael of the serious nature of the fire and that [it] had claimed her husband's life. She did not cry, but in an agitated state she kept asking me to 'Check and make sure if he's alive.'"

Soon afterwards a breathless Jeremy Miller arrived. His wife Tara had learned of the fire and immediately called his car dealership, asking him to drive over and check.

Jeremy had then called Jimmy Michael's cell, going straight to voice mail. Then, after calling his home and getting a busy signal, he had come to Killarney Drive.

"I was expecting he was burning some leaves or something," recalled Miller. "But as soon as I drove up and saw the house in flames, I called my wife and said, 'Oh my gosh, this is bad.'"

After parking as close as he could, he rushed up to a police officer who was securing the area outside the house.

"I told him I was Jimmy's brother," said Miller. "And they sent me down to a police car. Shelly was in the back seat, squirming. She was moaning and whimpering something like, 'Go get Jimmy! Go get Jimmy!'"

He then asked Shelly if Jimmy was at work or still on his hunting trip.

"And that's when the officer looked at me and said, 'You know, he didn't make it,'" said Miller. "So I stepped out of the vehicle at that point. And I remember standing in the rain and just crying so hard."

A short time later, Shelly summoned him back into the police cruiser.

"Jeremy," she whimpered, "tell God to give Jimmy back, tell him to give Jimmy back."

Miller was lost for words, saying that, unfortunately, it didn't work that way, but she just kept apologizing to him, over and over again.

Later, Max Humphreys told Chief David Fetty about Shelly's bizarre reaction on hearing that her husband didn't make it.

"He was shaking his head," remembered Chief Fetty. "And I said, 'What's the matter, Max?' And he said, 'That was the strangest thing I've ever seen.'"

With the appalling weather conditions, Shelly Michael's neighbor Shannon Tinnell invited her to take refuge at her house on Eastern Avenue. Kelli Teets and a police medic helped Shelly over there, bringing her into the living room and laying her down on a couch, before wrapping her in a blanket. Over the next few hours, a procession of Shelly's relatives and friends arrived to comfort her there.

Rob Angus had left to collect the children from school, ensuring that they wouldn't learn about the fire from anybody else. He also started calling family members to tell them the terrible news.

At 11:23 a.m., Detective Mezzanotte interviewed Bobby Teets in the back of the police cruiser. Teets explained how he had gone to the house, after his boss Jimmy Michael had not turned up for work that morning. He'd arrived to find the house on fire, telling police to check the garage for Jimmy's car.

He told the detective that Jimmy never drank or used drugs, and never discussed having any problems.

"Robert Teets never knew Jimmy Michael to be depressed," Mezzanotte later noted in his official report. "[He] was unable to provide any additional information at this time."

One of the first people Rob Angus called was Jimmy Michael's ex-wife, Stephanie Estel, who was driving to the store to buy dog food with her husband Dan and their 4-month-old daughter Audrey.

"We received the phone call about 11:00 a.m.," she remembered. "There had been a tragedy at Jim and Shelly's. A fire, and they needed us to come over. They needed help."

As Rob Angus gave no further details, Stephanie assumed it was a minor fire, joking to Dan that they'd probably be giving Jimmy and Shelly a bed to sleep in that night. Then they debated whether to first drop off Jacie's assignment book at school, before going to Killarney Drive.

A couple of minutes later, Stephanie's best friend Kim, who also worked at Ruby Memorial, called in tears. By now news of the fire and Jimmy's death was all over the hospital.

"All she could say was, 'Stephanie, I'm so sorry. I'm so sorry. What do you know?' "

Stephanie told her that she already knew the house was on fire, and she was on her way over to help. But Kim just kept saying she was sorry.

"Kim, what's wrong?" she finally asked.

"Oh, Stephanie," Kim replied, "I'm so sorry. I'm so sorry."

"Is Shelly OK?" asked Stephanie.

"Shelly is at work."

"What about Jim?"

"Stephanie, he's dead."

"And I let out a blood-curdling scream," she remembered. "I hung up with her and I hit the button to redial Rob's number. I said, 'Rob, someone just called and told me Jim is dead.' And he said, 'I'm sorry, Stephanie. He didn't make it.' "

A few minutes earlier, Deborah Harris arrived at Shannon Tinnell's house, where Shelly was being comforted by Kelli Teets and a volunteer fire medic, who were holding a cold rag to her head.

"I went up to her and hugged her," Harris later testified, "and I said, 'Shelly, what happened?' She said, 'I don't know.' "

Then Kelli left to make some phone calls, leaving her alone with the new widow.

"So I sat down with her on the couch," Harris said. "She was just breathing in hard. I was just stroking her shoulder and said, 'Shelly, it's going to be OK. It's going to be OK.' "

Then Shelly told her friend how she had left for work at 6:30 that morning. Jimmy had been sleeping in, as he had gotten home so late the night before. She said she had called her home phone at 7:30 a.m. to check up on him, but it had rung and he hadn't answered.

"I don't understand why they can't find him," Shelly told her. "I don't know what happened."

Then a doctor arrived to treat Shelly for shock, and Harris left. On her way out she saw Jimmy Michael's ex-wife coming up the front path and running into the house.

Stephanie then dashed into the living room to find Shelly lying on a couch, with a blanket up to her chin.

"Shelly, what's going on?" Stephanie shouted. "Somebody said that Jim's dead."

Then Kelli Teets grabbed her by the shoulder, and yanked her out of the room by her jacket. She told her to be quiet, as Shelly still didn't know Jimmy was dead.

"And I just remember standing there," said Stephanie, "and Detective Mezzanotte coming up and asking me if he could ask me a couple of questions."

After interviewing Bobby Teets in his police cruiser, Detective Mezzanotte walked around the corner to the neighbors' house, where everyone had started gathering. He introduced himself to Shannon Tinnell, requesting a table and a couple of chairs to conduct some interviews out of the rain.

"There were a couple of things that struck me as odd," recalled Mezzanotte. "I was amazed at the amount of people that were coming in the house. Friends, relatives and acquaintances. There were just herds of people. That was the first clue that I got there were an ex-husband and an ex-wife, and there were children. And they all arrived at the house."

Eventually Mezzanotte asked Stephanie Estel to help him sort out who everyone was, and their relationship with each other.

"It was kind of getting confusing," he recounted. "I actually started doing a little [family] tree in my note book."

At the start of his death investigation, Detective Mezzanotte wanted to learn as much as possible about the presumed fire victim, Jimmy Michael. He knew it would be important to discover why everybody was there.

"You have to start putting a puzzle together with pieces of the victim," explained the detective. "And that would cover spouse, children, employment, friends [and] in this case church, pastors."

At 11:45 a.m., Detective Mezzanotte sat down with Jeremy Miller, who told him Jimmy's life was far from perfect. Miller said his best friend had a lot of stress in his life, with work and, especially, his wife Shelly, who had just finished school to become a nurse practitioner. "Jeremy Miller had personal observations," Mezzanotte later reported, "as to the marriage beginning to show signs of having problems in the last two months. The marriage was in trouble in his opinion."

CHAPTER 20

"I Wish I Would Have Loved Him More"

That morning, Denny Michael had been preaching at a funeral when he came home to find his wife Ruth in a terrible state.

"She was hysterical," he recalled. "She was screaming that Jimmy was in a fire."

Ruth described how Kelli Teets had called her just after 11:00 a.m., saying that Jimmy's house was on fire and they needed to come to Morgantown. At first she hadn't thought it too serious, calling Kelli back to ask if everything was OK.

"No," replied Kelli.

"What do you mean?" said Ruth. "Are the kids out? Is everybody OK?"

"No."

"Who was in the house?"

"Jimmy."

Ruth then asked if her son was all right, and Kelli Teets refused to tell her.

"And then I called her back and wanted to talk to Shelly," said Ruth. "But she wouldn't talk."

Then Denny and Ruth got in their car and drove straight to Morgantown, at high speed.

"It was raining hard that day," recalled Denny. "And we drove real fast—about ninety miles an hour."

During the hour-long drive through the Cumberland Gap, Ruth called her son Steve, who then left an anxious message at 12:09 p.m. on Jimmy's cell phone, asking him to call Mom.

And as they approached Morgantown, Ruth called Kelli Teets, asking if they should go to the hospital.

"She said, 'No, you need to come to the house,'" said Ruth. "And I knew then that Jimmy was dead."

At around 12:30 p.m., Jimmy Michael's anxious parents arrived at 545 Killarney Drive. Denny Michael marched straight up to the front door, but was stopped by Sergeant Harold Sperringer, who was securing the outside.

"He was trying to get in the house," said Sperringer. "And we couldn't allow that."

Denny demanded to know what was going on and if Jimmy was all right.

"At first I wasn't telling him," said Sperringer. "I said, 'You need to calm down.'"

When eventually told that their son hadn't made it, Ruth Michael dropped to her knees crying. Denny demanded to see his son's body, but police refused the request, saying it was a crime scene. The distraught father then attempted to run into the house, and had to be forcibly restrained.

"They wouldn't let me go in the house to see my son," said Denny. "So I got in a fight with the policeman and he gave me a black eye."

After Sperringer had calmed Denny down, he brought him and Ruth over the road to the house, where everyone had gathered. As they approached, Michael Goots came over and put his arms around Denny.

"He said, 'I hate to tell you this, but your son didn't make it,'" recalled Denny. "And then he said to me, 'Well, they'll never be able to determine what caused the fire.'"

Then Goots, a qualified electrician, rubbed two fingers together, as if they were electric wires.

"And I thought," said Denny, "'That's the dumbest thing to say to a father who's just lost a son in a fire.' It really bothered me."

Then Jimmy's parents went inside the house, where Shelly was being comforted by her sister Jennifer.

"She was just sitting there with her head back," said Jimmy's mother. "And she had a blanket on her. She wasn't crying. She wasn't saying anything. I sat down beside her."

Denny then came over and hugged Shelly, thanking her for loving his son.

"She stood up," he remembered. "She wasn't emotional. I didn't see tears. And she said one of the strangest things: 'I wish I would have loved him more.'"

Later, Denny would say that that was when he knew she had murdered Jimmy.

"I'm thinking," he explained, "I just came from her father saying they'll never be able to determine what the fire is. And now she's saying, 'I wished I loved him more.'"

"And I'm saying in my mind, 'You killed my son.'"

Across the living room, Detective Paul Mezzanotte was interviewing Rob Angus, who had just returned with the children.

"He was very helpful to me in determining the family structure," said Mezzanotte. "I was told there were four children [from] previous marriages. And I was trying to get this kind of thing organized."

Angus told the detective that he had "no issues" with either Jimmy or his ex-wife Shelly.

"He had nothing from the kids, as far as any problems in the home," the detective duly noted. "He knew that the marriage seemed to be okay."

Angus said that when he'd last talked to him the previous Sunday, Jimmy had seemed fine.

"No indication was given to him of any problems," wrote Mezzanotte, "or anything out of the ordinary."

At 1:00 p.m. he interviewed Stephanie Estel, who said her relationship with her ex-husband was "pretty good." She said they shared joint custody, admitting Jimmy was being investigated by Child Protective Services, after disciplining his son Drew with a belt.

She described Jimmy as "an excellent father," telling Mezzanotte that he always called Alec and Jacie when they were at her house, to say goodnight.

"The kids had not related anything out of the ordinary," wrote the detective in his report, "to Stephanie Estel about James Michael's relationship with Michelle Michael."

Finally, Detective Mezzanotte asked her who Jimmy's dentist was, for identification purposes.

At 1:10 p.m., the lead detective left the house to interview volunteer firefighter Shawn Alt, outside in a police cruiser. Alt explained that he and the Michaels were neighbors, and that he'd known Jimmy for years, since they were at respiratory school together.

Alt described arriving at his Killarney Drive home at just after 8:00 a.m., and smelling what he recognized as "a structure fire." He had looked around, but did not see signs of a fire. Nevertheless, he'd called a fire department colleague, to see if anything had been reported. He had then gone inside his home to change, coming out a few minutes later and still smelling the smoke.

Then he had left to drive to a fire station, where he was on call that day.

"As Shawn Alt was driving west on Killarney Drive, approaching a four-way intersection at Eastern Avenue," Mezzanotte later wrote in his report, "he advised he saw Michelle Michael backing out of her driveway. He knew positively it was Michelle Michael by the vehicle, the silver Ford Expedition. He had seen that vehicle numerous times and knew that it was operated by Michelle Michael."

Back at 545 Killarney Drive the preliminary death scene investigation was well underway, supervised by Morgantown's chief fire investigator, Lieutenant Ken Tennant. While they were waiting for State Medical Examiner John Carson to arrive, Deputy Fire Marshal Mike Bean started photographing everything.

"We started photographing the outside of the building and worked our way in," explained Lieutenant Tennant. "So you go from the least damaged to the most significant damaged."

They carefully noted where all the utilities were, looking at the electrical panel and where the power shut off, as well as what type of heating and ventilation system was in use.

"All these things had to be examined as a possible cause to the fire," explained Lieutenant Tennant. "We're looking at things like the hot water tank, the model, the serial number and what type of furnace it was. All those things had to be documented."

The fire investigators methodically worked their way upstairs to the burnt-out master bedroom, where the victim's charred body still lay on the remains of the bed.

"Everything, as far as the fire indicators we looked at," said Tennant, "pointed back to the area of the bed. We had a large hole that burned through the floor, and would later become a key part of this case. Everything was right there. The most significant damage was right around the bed. The ceiling showed that's where the fire started, so we knew that everything pointed back to the bed. An iron was found right there at the foot of the bed."

The body was so badly burned that the experienced fire investigator found it difficult to visually separate it from the charred remains of the box-spring mattress it lay on. One leg was completely missing, and other parts of limbs had been burnt away. There was a large hole on the left side of the chest near the rib cage, where the tremendous heat had caused a blowout.

Lieutenant Tennant then made a hand drawing of the bedroom, which he later scanned into a computer. He also diagrammed the entire house, as well as taking precise measurements of the body from various locations all over the bedroom. But one thing that struck Tennant from the beginning was the way the body was positioned.

"I thought it was a little peculiar," he recalled, "that the victim was still in the bed in the kind of laid-back position he was in."

He was also baffled as to why none of the muscles had contracted, as would be expected.

"In a fire, when a body is subjected to these high temperatures," he said, "the muscles contract with such force that it even breaks bones. So normally you see the arms folded up in a pugilistic stance."

Although everyone believed the victim to be Jimmy Michael, until it could be determined scientifically by the medical examiner, it would officially remain a John Doe.

At 1:42 p.m., West Virginia State Assistant Medical Examiner John Carson arrived with his team, to begin the difficult process of removing the burned remains of the victim from the bedroom. After donning protective Tyvec suits, Dr. Carson entered 545 Killarney Avenue with Detective Mezzanotte and his assistant, Detective Chris Dalton.

"We walked in through the front door," said Detective Dalton. "To our left there was a noticeable hole in the ceiling of the living room."

There was a lot of smoke damage downstairs, but no fire damage, although they could see up through the floor to the master bedroom.

As they walked through the kitchen, they found Jimmy Michael's cell phone, lying on a countertop near the back door.

Then they went upstairs to the second floor, where there was still a lot of smoke, proceeding straight to the master bedroom at the end of the corridor.

"That's where the most fire damage was," said Detective Dalton. I didn't even realize that there was a body in there, until minutes after I walked into the room. It was unrecognizable. Everything was black. You couldn't really distinguish a body from everything else that was there."

Then Dr. Carson took casts of the victim's teeth, so they could be compared to Jimmy Michael's dental records. When he had finished, Detective Dalton helped the assistant medical examiner extricate the body from the bed, so it could be taken to Charleston for autopsy.

"The body was stuck to the metal box springs of the bed," said Dalton. And it was hard to separate it. I remember we actually had to cut some of the metal box springs away and leave them attached to the body, to get it out."

At 2:50 p.m., they carried Jimmy Michael's remains downstairs in a body bag, bringing it outside to a waiting ambulance. And it was there that Denny Michael was allowed to see his son's body.

"They tried and tried to keep me from seeing him," said Denny, "because of the state he was in. He was burned up. And I said, 'It doesn't matter, I know he's burned. I want to see him.' And I said, 'Only the Lord is going to get in the way of me seeing my son's body.'

"I knew that once he went to the autopsy, I wouldn't get to see him. I needed to say goodbye."

Kerri Whitacre was at a business lunch in Cumberland, Maryland, when she received a call from a friend who worked at Ruby Memorial Hospital.

"She called to tell me there was a fire at Jimmy and Shelly's house," said Kerri. "And then she called back and said Jimmy did not make it out of the house."

Kerri immediately called her husband Seth and they drove to Morgantown, arriving at Shannon Tinnell's house by early afternoon.

"There was a little foyer area," she remembered. "And I peeked around the wall and I saw Ruthie, Denny and Shelly. There were medical personnel in there, taking Shelly's [blood pressure]. So we did not go in."

Kerri, who was still wearing her business suit, waited outside. When things quieted down, she went over to Jimmy's parents to offer her condolences.

"I just cried with them," she said. "They were very upset and we talked, and then I went back out of the room."

Once again, Kerri waited patiently outside for an opportunity to talk to Shelly.

"I remember saying to my husband, 'Gosh, I don't know

what to say to Shelly. There's nothing I can say to help the situation.' He said, 'You'll figure it out.' "

Kerri felt the whole thing "surreal," thinking it "odd" that Shelly wasn't crying, as she received a stream of visitors.

Finally, after Shelly's family left, Kerri walked over to Shelly, sitting down next to her on the couch. She was still trying to compose her thoughts about what she could possibly say at a time like this.

"And before I could even say anything," remembered Kerri, "she said to me, 'Did you get that outfit at B. Moss?'

"I looked at her and I just said, 'Yeah, Yeah.' I couldn't believe she just asked me if I got my outfit at B. Moss. I was truly dumbfounded, and so taken aback. I'm sure my facial expression showed that I was not expecting a question like that.

"I just told her, 'I don't know what to say.' And she said, 'I'm sorry. I'm so sorry.' It was a crazy, odd exchange."

Then, at a loss for words, Kerri left, returning to her husband in the foyer area. She immediately told him what Shelly had said, saying she felt something was wrong.

A few minutes later, Deborah Harris came back and asked Shelly if there was anything she could get her.

"A new husband," replied the new widow.

CHAPTER 21

"She's Not Grieving Right"

At 3:20 p.m. Detective Paul Mezzanotte walked over to Shelly Michael, sat down and introduced himself.

"The first thing out of her mouth was," said Detective Mezzanotte, "'Why are you talking to everybody else and nobody's talking to me?' I thought, 'That's fine.'"

Then, with her father and sister hovering around the couch, he asked what she had done that morning, before learning of the fire.

Jimmy had come home the previous evening from basketball practice "extremely tired," she said, before going to sleep. The last time she had seen him was at 6:00 a.m., when she gave him "a kiss on the cheek," before leaving for work.

Then she went into some detail about her patients that morning, mentioning that between 8:00 and 8:30 a.m., she had briefly left the hospital to go to her car in the staff parking lot and get her pager.

The detective listened carefully, taking notes, but never mentioning Shawn Alt's report of seeing her at her house at about 8:15 a.m.

He then asked for a detailed description of everything in the master bedroom, and its location. Among the many items she mentioned was an iron, lying on an ironing board in the corner of the room, away from the bed.

"And then I told her that in order to investigate the fire," said the detective, "we were going to go through the house and look at a variety of things, and take samples of the heating ducts, etc., to try and figure out the fire."

Shelly readily agreed to sign a consent form, allowing investigators to search her house.

After a few minutes of conversation, Detective Mezzanotte felt that Shelly's demeanor was inappropriate for such a tragic situation.

"She struck me as just very, very calm," he would later relate. "But also as very controlling."

She seemed far more interested in discussing her own medical condition than her recently deceased husband. Every time Mezzanotte asked her a specific question, she steered the conversation back to herself.

"She would say, 'I'm a nurse and I know that I'm not feeling well,'" Mezzanotte remembered. "'Is an ambulance still outside?'"

All through the interview, various people came over to see how she was, and they all appeared to be far more upset than she was.

"Oh that's my friend," she would tell the detective when someone entered. "'Come over here. Did you hear what happened?' And she was wanting everything to be centered around her."

He was also surprised at how she hardly mentioned her dead husband, except to say that she had been told there was a body in the house, but that Jimmy should not be home.

"There were some little things that just kind of bothered me," said the detective. "Just off our initial conversation. It got my attention that she's not grieving right. She doesn't seem to be asking the right questions. I had handled a lot of death investigations, and her reaction to me wasn't of normal grieving. I don't even remember seeing her cry."

At 4:00 p.m., Kathi Goots arrived at the Eastern Avenue house to see her daughter. The legal secretary had been in Huntington, West Virginia, on business, when she had received a call from Shelly's cell phone at 11:10 a.m., with Kelli Teets leaving a voice mail message.

Then she called her daughter's cell phone and Kelli answered.

"I could hear Shelly in the background, just hysterical," Kathi remembered. "And she said, 'We can't find Jimmy.'"

Ten minutes later, Kelli called back, saying Jimmy was dead.

"Shelly was very hysterical," said her mother. "She couldn't even talk on the phone. And it was Kelli who told me about it."

Shelly's mother had then driven 170 miles east to Clarksburg, before being taken to Morgantown by a friend.

"It was just horrible," she remembered. "When I walked in, Shelly was sitting on the couch, and it was just like she wasn't even there. She was just so detached."

Later that afternoon, Jimmy Michael's business partner Rich Brant offered Shelly a room at the Hotel Morgan, which he owned. He said she could stay until she sorted herself out.

"The decision was made for us," Ruth Michael recalled, "to go over and get a room at the Hotel Morgan."

Since she had arrived, Jimmy's mother had closely observed her daughter-in-law, and was surprised by her apparent lack of emotion.

"She just sat there," Ruth remembered. "She didn't cry. She just sat there. I would describe it as cold."

At 4:05 p.m., Jimmy Michael's dental records were handed to Assistant Medical Examiner Dr. John Carson. Forty minutes later, he made a preliminary identification that it was Michael's body.

At 4:55 p.m., Detective Paul Mezzanotte arrived at the Ruby Memorial Hospital morgue, to observe a brief examination of the body, before it was transported to the Office of the Chief Medical Examiner in Charleston for autopsy. "When I went to the morgue," said Detective Mezzanotte, "the position of the body started to bother me. I took some pictures and watched what the medical examiner was doing."

Dr. Carson informed him that once Jimmy Michael's body arrived in Charleston, it would be tested for carbon monoxide, to see if he had died in the fire.

After checking into Room 505 at the Hotel Morgan, Shelly Michael took to her bed, looked after by Bobby and Kelli Teets. For the rest of the evening, Shelly received various friends and relatives, who came to pay their respects.

"There was a ton of people there," Bobby Teets recalled. "Me and Kelli and the kids. I knew Jimmy's parents were there. Jimmy's brother and his wife. I mean, there was a lot of people there. Her family."

At one point, Dan Estel arrived to offer his condolences and was stunned to see Bobby Teets and Shelly lying on the bed together under a blanket, surrounded by various family members.

During his brief visit, he noticed Shelly and Kelli Teets going through Jimmy's insurance information.

After leaving the morgue, Detective Mezzanotte returned to 545 Killarney Drive, to brief his investigative team. Detectives Brian Hennessy and Chris Dalton, and Officer Bethany Kahl had all helped process the crime scene and were now completing photo and evidence logs, as well as sketches.

Detective Eric Powell, who had spent the last few hours canvassing the neighborhood, was now instructed to video the inside and outside of the house, paying particular attention to the master bedroom.

Over the next few hours, the investigators began collecting evidence from the bedroom, as well as samples of the living room carpet, wood floor and other items needed for the fire investigation.

By 9:00 p.m. the investigators had done everything they could that day. After Detective Mezzanotte checked that all the evidence collected was marked, and the chain of custody pristine, there was nothing further to be done until Jimmy Michael's autopsy, scheduled for the next morning.

But the detective was still not ready to quit that day.

"There was something that continued to bother me," he later recalled. "So I went to the Hotel Morgan to meet with Shelly Michael before I went home that night."

At 9:30 p.m., he knocked on the door of her hotel room. When he went in, he was surprised to see Bobby Teets holding the new widow on the bed, as his wife Kelli made funeral arrangements.

"I was just trying to feel her out," said Detective Mezzanotte. "I just wanted to listen to what she had to say, and get my head around this."

Once again, Shelly outlined her day, repeating that Jimmy had been OK when she'd left for work. When the detective asked again about her getting her pager, she never mentioned leaving the hospital grounds and going home.

Then he asked about Jimmy's normal sleeping positions. Shelly said he slept on his back with his hands wrapped through a pillow, which was then wrapped around his head.

"Michelle Michael described the exact body position of the deceased, as located during the initial examination of the crime scene," the detective later noted in his report.

He also asked about life insurance, and Shelly said they had a homeowner's policy and Jimmy had taken out life insurance with Northwestern Mutual soon after he'd started his business.

Detective Mezzanotte then pitched in and helped with the funeral preparations, promising to arrange for Jimmy's body to be released to the family. But the whole time, he was watching Shelly like a hawk.

"I just wanted to see her reaction," he explained. "She was more concerned with calling her friends, and telling everybody what happened. She was very indifferent about what had happened. And to me that was just completely a red flag."

He also befriended her, realizing the importance of cultivating a good relationship with a possible suspect. He warned her that things would be difficult over the next few days, saying he was the only person she should listen to.

After half-an-hour, Shelly's parents arrived, and Detective Mezzanotte used the opportunity to question Kelli Teets. She told him she had been at work when Bobby called about the fire. She had immediately called Shelly at work. At that time nobody knew Jimmy Michael was dead, although Bobby had told her that his car was still in the garage.

She also told the detective that she considered Jimmy and Shelly's marriage to be fine.

"She observed no obvious signs of problems in the marriage," Detective Mezzanotte duly noted. "And stated that it was very normal."

After leaving the Hotel Morgan at around 10:30 p.m., Detective Paul Mezzanotte drove the short distance to the Detective Division in the Public Safety Building on Spruce Street. There he met with Lieutenant Ken Tennant, Detective Chris Dalton and the rest of his team, to go over their progress, strategize and hand out assignments for the next day.

"We had no accidental causes at the end of the day," said Lieutenant Tennant. "The fire was undetermined and obviously there were some things that just were not making any sense.

"He's a thirty-three-year-old non-smoker who's always at work at seven-thirty. What's he still doing at the house this time of day?"

After everybody left, Detective Mezzanotte found himself alone in the office with Detective Chris Dalton, the second detective on the case, who he was also training.

"And I just told him, 'Chris,'" recalled Mezzanotte, "'I don't know what the autopsy's going to tell us, but we have something wrong. There's something bad with this case, and we're going to be working it.'"

That night, Ruth Michael, her son Steve and his wife Stacy stayed in the hotel room with Shelly, her daughter Kylie and Jacie. Alec and Drew were being taken care of by Rob Angus and Stephanie Estel. Shelly's parents and sister had now left, driving back to Clarksburg. And Jimmy's father had also gone home.

The television in the room was on, tuned to the local 11:00 news on channel 5, featuring the deadly Morgantown fire as its top story. When Shelly saw video of her burned-out house, she flew into a fury, picking up the phone and calling the WDTV studio to complain.

"She was upset and she was angry," said her mother-in-law. "She said it was her house and she didn't want it shown on TV."

Stacy was also shocked by Shelly's outburst.

"She called the TV station yelling," she said, "telling them not to show her house."

Then Kylie and Jacie fell asleep in a chair, while Ruth, Steve and Stacy were awake the whole night crying. Amazingly, Shelly managed to get a good night's sleep.

"It was like a nightmare," remembered Stacy. "Shelly just laid in bed sleeping and didn't make a sound. Her eyes were shut [and] she didn't move or wake up. I found it odd, because I know if it was my husband, I'd be crying all night."

That night, Reggie Ours went to Killarney Drive, to see the remains of the house himself. When he had heard about the fire earlier that day, his initial thoughts were that maybe the smoke had overcome Jimmy, and he'd fallen downstairs as he tried to escape.

"I felt terrible," he recalled. "I just rode around and around and saw it. I called my wife and said, 'There's something wrong. This is not right. His bedroom was the only thing that caught on fire. All he had to do was get out of the bedroom.'"

CHAPTER 22

Homicide

On Wednesday morning, Morgantown's *Dominion Post* newspaper ran a dramatic front-page story, headlined "Man Dies In Suncrest." While noting that police still had not positively identified the victim, it revealed that the blaze had been at the home of James and Shelly Michael, and his co-workers believed him to be the victim.

Susan Riddle was quoted, saying she had sent Bobby Teets to the house, after her partner Jimmy Michael hadn't turned up for work.

"It was highly unusual for us not to see him by 8:00 a.m.," she told *The Dominion Post*. "He always beats me into the office. So we sent Bobby over to Jim's home, because they were friends."

The story also described "an unidentified woman," crying in the back of a Morgantown police SUV and being comforted by police.

"Investigators aren't sure how the man died," read the article, "or if he was asleep when the fire started."

The Michaels' neighbor August Lucci, said he'd dashed home from work after hearing of the fire.

"What a shame," he told a reporter. "They are a very nice family."

* * *

At 9:15 a.m. Deputy Chief Medical Examiner Dr. Hamada Mahmoud, M.D., began autopsying the burned remains, now designated John Doe 115 until positive identification could take place. The body, wrapped in a white sheet and sealed in a locked body bag, had been delivered the previous night to the Jefferson Road, Charleston, Office of the Chief Medical Examiner. Along with it were two brown bags, containing assorted debris found nearby, believed to be remains of missing limbs.

The Egyptian-born medical examiner began by looking at what was left of the body, which was charred completely black.

"We could not recognize any external features," Dr. Mahmoud would later testify. "There [was] no surface of the body left. No hair, no face, no skin."

In fact the body was in such bad condition, it was impossible to know the victim's race or sex.

In life Jimmy Michael had been almost 6 feet tall, weighing 230 pounds. But Dr. Mahmoud's official autopsy report listed him as just 5' 7" and only 151 pounds, as the muscles and joints had contracted and fractured in the intense heat, and nearly a quarter of the body had burned away.

The left arm was missing from the elbow down, as was the lower right arm. The left leg and right foot from the ankle down had been lost. The abdominal wall had literally exploded, leaving a big hole, where the intestines and other internal organs were coming out.

"Here is a rupture of the abdominal wall," Dr. Mahmoud pointed out. "This is very common in severe burns."

The only remaining skin on the body was a small area on the back and upper buttocks.

"In this area, some skin was still intact," said the doctor, "and showed this person was a white person."

What remained of the limbs were flexed in a "pugilistic position," due to the muscle contraction caused by the intense heat.

"It was like a boxer," said Dr. Mahmoud. "Which is common . . . from the severe burn of the body."

Dr. Mahmoud then X-rayed the entire body, looking for any evidence of shotgun or stab wounds prior to the fire. But there was none.

Then he began the autopsy by taking a toxicology sample of Jimmy Michael's blood. "We have to determine [if] this body was alive when the fire started," explained the medical examiner, "or he was dead. A very common practice. Some people say, 'Well, I can kill this person and set the house on fire.'" The blood would be tested for carbon monoxide, which, if found in high levels, would show he'd been dead prior to the fire.

As well as testing for the presence of carbon monoxide, Dr. Mahmoud looked in the airways for soot. If a person is still breathing when the fire starts, soot will be inhaled and be seen in the upper airways.

"If we don't find this, we have a problem," explained the doctor. "That means the person was probably dead and did not inhale the soot, and we are dealing with something other than the person died from the fire."

When the doctor tested for carbon monoxide, there was no evidence of elevated levels. And there was also no soot in the victim's airways.

"We could determine immediately this person was dead when the fire started," said the doctor. "He was not alive. That was a big alarm to me."

Then the doctor took tissue and blood samples for further toxicology testing.

"Because some of the body was charred," said the doctor, "it was hard to get tissue and blood. But we succeeded and were lucky."

The liver was in good shape, so Dr. Mahmoud sliced off a piece, as well as taking some bile, the fluid inside the gall-bladder. He also collected heart blood and gastric content. Later, he sent the samples off to the Toxicology Section of the West Virginia State Police Crime Lab in Charleston to be tested for narcotics and common medicines.

As there were no hands remaining for fingerprints, Dr. Mahmoud X-rayed the oral cavity so positive identification could be made through teeth fillings. He sent the X-rays to Dr. Carson, who is also a forensic dentologist, who later confirmed that the dead man was definitely Jimmy Michael.

At 11:15 a.m., Dr. Mahmoud completed his autopsy, listing the cause of death as an undetermined homicidal act.

While her husband's autopsy was underway, Shelly Michael visited Mountaineer Home Medical. Reggie Ours, who was there, was surprised to see her. But he was shocked when she immediately offered him the job of full-time respiratory therapist, to replace Jimmy.

"And it just amazed me," said Ours. "She doesn't say, 'I miss Jimmy. I'm miserable.' She's like, 'We can't really put a value to this business unless we have a respiratory therapist working full-time. Would you be interested?' "

That morning, Rob Angus set up "The Michael Family Benefit Fund" at the First United Bank & Trust. Over the next couple of weeks there would be an outpouring of sympathy in Morgantown, generating hundreds of dollars for Shelly Michael.

Detective Paul Mezzanotte spent Wednesday afternoon at Ruby Memorial Hospital, investigating Shelly Michael's movements the morning of the fire. Before leaving, he asked Detective Chris Dalton to send some pieces of evidence taken from the fire scene to the Bureau of Alcohol, Tobacco, Firearms and Explosives (ATF) office in Wheeling, West Virginia, for hydrocarbon testing.

He was also interested to learn that the Channel 5 TV station had called, reporting Shelly Michael's angry phone call and asking about the status of the case.

He arrived at the hospital at 1:30 p.m., meeting first with head of security Dan Harris, who is married to the Michaels' neighbor Deborah Harris. The detective asked him to search yesterday morning's hospital surveillance video, to see if Shelly had left the hospital, colloborating Shawn Alt's report of seeing her around 8:20 a.m. at her home.

"I gave him some general time frames," recalled the detective, "and asked him to look through the video."

Then Detective Mezzanotte went off to interview the hospital staff who worked with Nurse Shelly Michael.

He first interviewed PICU receptionist Nancy Buffalo, who said that Shelly had left the hospital between 8:00 and 9:00 a.m. to fetch her pager, but could not remember when she had come back.

The receptionist also said that Bobby Teets had left a message for Shelly, saying they couldn't find her husband. She remembered Shelly making the comment that she wondered if they had tried Jimmy's cell phone.

Then fifteen minutes later there had been a second call, saying her house was on fire.

"Michelle Michael took the phone call," noted Detective Mezzanotte. "And then told Dr. Romano, her boss, 'I have to go, my house is on fire.' And she left the unit at 10:45 hours."

Mezzanotte next interviewed trainee receptionist Joanna Duesenberry, who had taken both calls. She told the detective that "someone in respiratory therapy" had said he'd seen Shelly Michael drive by her house yesterday morning just after 8:00 a.m.

At 3:10 p.m., he interviewed PICU director Dr. Michael Romano, who said that yesterday had been Nurse Michael's first day back, after taking several weeks' sick leave for a knee injury.

"Dr. Romano was aware that Michelle Michael had left the hospital," wrote Mezzanotte, "to go to her car prior to the morning report from 0800 to 0900 hours. Dr. Romano stated [she] was not in morning report."

Twenty minutes later, the detective had an interview with Reggie Ours that would change the course of the investigation.

"He told me that Michelle Michael had been on a trip to Chicago with Robert Teets," Detective Mezzanotte recalled. "And that Jim Michael did not make the trip. Now we have to figure out, why is there a trip to Chicago?"

Ours also said he had personal knowledge that Jimmy

and Shelly had "marital problems," describing the marriage as "not very good."

"One of the first things I told Detective Mezzanotte," said Ours. " 'You need to find out what's going on,' because I think something was happening. And I think Jimmy knew it was too."

In another part of the hospital, Security Chief Dan Harris had been busy looking through all the hospital surveillance video for Shelly Michael. There were two cameras set up monitoring each of the two front entrances, as well as other ones scanning the outside parking lots.

"I started backtracking," he said, "all the way up to . . . when I was notified about the fire."

He soon spotted Shelly Michael at 8:11 a.m., wearing a distinctive white top and skirt. She was walking through the west entrance lobby, past a cappuccino machine and out of the hospital. Another camera then tracked her leaving the hospital and going into the employee parking lot.

Fourteen minutes later, at 8:25 a.m., Shelly's silver Ford Expedition SUV showed up again on surveillance video in the parking lot, trying to find a parking space. She is then seen parking her vehicle and getting out, putting up an umbrella, and walking towards the hospital's east entrance.

At 8:27 a.m., she crosses the street outside Ruby Memorial Hospital, and a minute later another camera captures her coming through the east lobby doors, heading towards the elevators.

The final sighting of her is at 10:45 a.m., leaving the hospital after being told her house was on fire.

When Detective Mezzanotte checked back with Dan Harris after his interviews, the security chief showed him the video sightings, frame-by-frame.

"That was very significant," said Mezzanotte. "We now had direct evidence that supported Mr. Alt's statement, placing her at the scene of the fire between 8:20 and 8:30 on November 29."

Then, a few minutes later, at 4:45 p.m., Deputy Medical

Examiner Dr. John Carson called with the news that Jimmy Michael had been dead before the fire started. He informed the detective that Dr. Mahmoud had reported that toxicology tests showed no signs of carbon monoxide in the body, or soot in the victim's airways.

"The cause of death remains undetermined pending toxicology results," Mezzanotte wrote in his report. "The manner of death has been listed as homicide."

Late that afternoon, Renee and Eric Del Viscio arrived at the Morgan Hotel to comfort Shelly Michael. Michael Goots had left a message on Renee's answerphone the previous afternoon, but before she could return it, Eric called, having just heard the tragic news from Susan Riddle.

"I'm shaking," Renee told her husband, as she called Michael Goots, who told her what had happened. They then arranged for Eric's parents to babysit, and bought some clothes for Kylie and Jacie for the funeral, setting off for Morgantown the next morning.

After checking into the Morgan, they walked into Room 505, finding Shelly in bed being comforted by Bobby Teets.

"She had a glazed look over her face," remembered Renee, "almost as though she wasn't there. Then all of a sudden, when no one was around, she would go into these fits— almost like panic attacks, where she would grab her chest [because] she couldn't breathe. She would try not to do it in front of the children."

Although the heating in the hotel room was turned up high, Renee says Shelly was under a blanket, shivering.

"She was cold all the time," said Renee. "She wouldn't eat, she wouldn't drink—I would categorize it as shock."

According to Eric Del Viscio, Shelly would break down occasionally into a plaintive wail, asking what had happened and why her whole life had changed.

"It wasn't so much crying," he said. "It was just the pillow or whoever was next to her. "She said, 'my whole life has changed. What happened to it? It's all gone.'"

But Renee also sensed something was going on between

Shelly and Bobby, who seemed to be the only person she wanted to talk to.

"[It] did bother me," she remembered. "The way Bobby Teets seemed to comfort her. The way they looked at each other. He would lie down on the bed next to her and she would kind of nuzzle into his shoulder. I just thought it was odd. He was comforting her in a way that didn't fit well with me."

When Renee and Eric went back to their room, she voiced her concerns about how close Shelly and Bobby appeared to be.

"I felt very guilty," she said. "I told Eric, 'I feel bad, but there's something going on between those two.' And of course he thought I was crazy."

It was late evening when Detective Paul Mezzanotte met with his team of detectives, at the Detective Division in the Public Safety Building. Over the next month, they would meet several times a day for briefings.

"We had regular meetings with the team," explained Detective Mezzanotte, who had now been appointed lead detective, "Just to see where everyone was and go over the case."

Detective Mezzanotte informed his team that Jimmy Michael's autopsy now proved he'd been dead prior to the fire, making it a murder investigation. And he told them of the various gossip circulating about Shelly.

"We had heard a rumor about Bobby and Shelly having an affair," said the detective. "Some people had told us about a business trip that seemed a little out of place . . . a week before the fire. So that shifted our investigation towards Bobby. And we started working on the affair."

At the meeting, Mezzanotte assigned detectives to go on the Internet, checking out the various hotels around Chicago's O'Hare International Airport. "To just basically do some good old-fashioned legwork," he explained. "And get on the phone and call every hotel and see if Robert Teets or Michelle Michael had rented a room sometime in the middle of November."

He also asked Morgantown Fire Investigator Lieutenant Ken Tennant to contact the ATF's certified fire investigator, Rick Summerfield, for possible assistance and expertise.

"I was directing the investigation," said Detective Mezzanotte, "and Ken was coordinating the fire evidence."

And it was also decided to obtain a search warrant for Shelly Michael and Bobby Teets' cell phone records.

After the meeting wound up at 10:00 p.m., Detective Mezzanotte sent the Drug Enforcement Administration (DEA) a syringe that investigators had discovered in the basin of the kitchen sink. He requested latent prints and a toxicology exam.

"The syringe was out of place," he later noted. "The syringe was taken for the contents to be examined."

Ruth Michael spent another restless night with Shelly at the hotel. She could not fathom how her daughter-in-law could possibly go to sleep under the terrible circumstances.

"Shelly slept that whole night," Ruth said. "I just don't know how."

And at 5:50 a.m. the following morning, she called her son Jimmy's cell phone, just to hear his voice message, before hanging up.

CHAPTER 23

"Maybe She Drugged Him"

Early Thursday morning, December 1, Morgantown Police Chief Phil Scott called a top-level meeting in his office on the second floor of the Public Safety Building. It was attended by Monongalia Prosecutor Marcia Ashdown, her assistant Perri DeChristopher, Fire Chief David Fetty, Lieutenant Ken Tennant and Detective Paul Mezzanotte.

"They informed us that James Michael was dead prior to the fire," Lieutenant Tennant later said. "So for us, that changes everything, and the detectives immediately went into a possible murder investigation."

During the meeting, it was decided that Detective Mezzanotte would get Shelly Michael's permission to search the house again.

As Shelly Michael and Bobby Teets had become prime suspects in a possible arson/homicide, the investigation now focused on their Chicago trip.

After the meeting, Detective Mezzanotte received a phone call from Reggie Ours, who was becoming increasingly concerned about his friend's death. He repeated his suspicions that Shelly and Bobby Teets were having an affair.

He then asked if Jimmy had been beaten, stabbed or shot. When Mezzanotte said there were no signs of foul play,

Ours questioned why Jimmy couldn't have just rolled out of bed to escape.

Then Ours told the detective that he should start considering the possibility that Jimmy Michael had been drugged by his wife. So Mezzanotte asked the respiratory therapist for a list of available drugs at Ruby Memorial Hospital that she could have given him.

After hanging up, Reggie Ours called Dr. Mike Ferrebee, who also worked at Ruby, and was a good friend of Jimmy Michael.

"I said, 'What drug could have killed him?'" recalled Ours. "We went though the list and he told me all of the drugs that could have killed him, and which could do it the quickest."

One drug mentioned was vecuronium, a paralytic given to patients prior to intubation, which was readily available to Shelly in the Pediatric Intensive Care Unit.

"Anybody could have gotten it," said Ours. "It was just sitting out there."

Ours then faxed Dr. Ferrebee's list of drugs to Detective Mezzanotte, who promised to forward it to the medical examiner.

Later that day at the hospital, Reggie Ours mentioned his suspicions to nursing manager Shannon Rudy, who was Rob Angus's sister and had once supervised Nurse Shelly Michael. Rudy agreed it was a possibility that Jimmy had been poisoned with some kind of paralytic.

Then she called her brother, saying she thought the police should know that Jimmy might have been poisoned, but wanted to remain anonymous. Shelly Michael's ex-husband agreed to quietly tip off Morgantown Police Lieutenant Kevin Clark, who was a close friend of his.

That morning, Kathi Goots and Eric Del Viscio went to 545 Killarney Drive to collect clothes for the children, a computer and other personal items that Shelly had requested. A trampoline, slide and swing set still lay in the back yard next to piles of burned debris littering the driveway.

"I put a 'NO TRESPASSING' sign on the doors," recalled Del Viscio. "[We] went in and got Kylie's cheerleading uniform and also Alec's band uniform, and a box of pictures."

Tara Miller was with Shelly at the Morgan Hotel when Michael Goots entered, pushing a hotel trolley full of stuff from the house.

"Shelly had asked them to go pick up things at the house," remembered Tara, "and her father came in with her computer. I thought it was very odd and suspicious. Those were the things that she was worried about getting out of her house."

At 1:35 p.m., Detective Mezzanotte arrived at Mountaineer Home Medical, to interview Jimmy Michael's business partners Richard Brant and Susan Riddle. They told him that several months ago Jimmy had said he needed a divorce lawyer, and their corporate attorney had given him several names. They also said Jimmy had approached them about funding an embroidery business, to be run by Shelly Michael and Bobby Teets.

After spending half-an-hour interviewing them together, Detective Mezzanotte requested one-on-one interviews. First up was Richard Brant, who said that Shelly was "in charge" of the marriage.

"He sensed the marriage was not in very good order," noted Mezzanotte in his report. "The fire does not sit well with him . . . he stated that James Michael would be the last person in the world who would ever commit suicide."

Brant also told the detective that under their business agreement, the company was now obligated to purchase 55 percent of Mountaineer Home Medical, the proceeds going directly to Shelly Michael.

At 2:30 p.m., Detective Mezzanotte interviewed Susan Riddle, who felt that certain factors in Jimmy's death did not add up. He was not a "late riser," she said, and when Bobby Teets had spoken to him on the phone the night before the fire, he had been fine.

According to Riddle, Jimmy acted like he was "on egg

shells" whenever his wife was around. Riddle gave permission for the Mountaineer Home Medical laptop computer to be forensically examined.

Next, Detective Mezzanotte interviewed office manager Brenda Shiflett, who did not believe her boss's death an accident. She said that Jimmy had admitted not having a "good marriage," saying, " 'I love my wife, but she gets on my nerves.' "

At 5:30 p.m., Detective Mezzanotte met with Detectives Chris Dalton and Eric Powell at the Detective Division. By now they had spoken to the three divorce lawyers recommended to Jimmy Michael, but none had ever been contacted.

Mezzanotte also learned that the last call made on the Michaels' home phone had been to Bobby Teets, and that Shelly had called North Elementary School after the fire, checking up on her children.

At 6:35 p.m. Detective Mezzanotte drove to Hilltop Lane, Morgantown, to interview Jimmy's ex-wife Stephanie and her new husband Dan Estel.

Dan Estel described Jimmy Michael as a "good guy," although they'd had "a few arguments" in the past over Shelly and the children. He described Shelly as a "strong person" and "very manipulative."

"It was Dan Estel's opinion," Mezzanotte later wrote, "that there was a bad relationship between Michelle Michael and James Michael's kids."

Estel also said Drew and Jacie had told him how Shelly was often out over the last several months, leaving Jimmy to look after the kids.

Asked about Bobby Teets, Dan Estel described his relationship with Shelly as "very weird." He said when he had visited Shelly at the Hotel Morgan yesterday, Teets had been holding Shelly in bed.

"This was a very weird occurrence," noted the detective, "because they were surrounded completely by family, and yet Robert Teets was laying under a blanket with Michelle Michael consoling her."

Detective Mezzannote then interviewed Stephanie Estel, who described her ex-husband as a "very light sleeper," suffering from insomnia. She said when she'd lived with him, he had been an early riser, who did not need much sleep.

Asked about his sleeping habits, Stephanie said Jimmy always slept on the side of the bed towards the wall. He usually slept on his side, although sometimes on his back, constantly moving around and never staying still.

She also described him as a "very religious" person, who did not smoke, drink or use drugs.

"Stephanie Estel stated that she does not get along well with Michelle Michael," noted Mezzanotte, "but they have tolerated each other more recently for the children. She did not believe Michelle Michael was acting appropriately for someone who had just lost their husband."

She said she had also seen Shelly and Bobby Teets together on the bed, also claiming to have personally seen him visiting 545 Killarney Drive when Jimmy was out.

"She always thought that Michelle Michael would replace James Michael," wrote the detective, "just based upon past actions."

It was late afternoon when police finally released Jimmy Michael's body to the family. The Del Viscios drove Shelly Michael to Cumberland, Maryland, to discuss funeral arrangements. There they met with Jimmy's parents at the Adams Family Funeral Home, where they were later joined by Bobby and Kelli Teets.

"We were sitting around the table discussing the funeral arrangements," recalled Denny, "and Shelly came down with her best friend Renee."

On arrival, Shelly took her father-in-law to one side, asking about the condition of her husband's body.

"She asked me several times what he looked like," Denny

recalled. "And I told her he was burned up completely. She wanted to see that body in the worst way."

Then Shelly came over and sat on her mother-in-law's lap, as the meeting began with Jimmy's $500,000 life insurance policy being given to the funeral director as collateral.

During the meeting, the cost of transporting Jimmy Michael from Charleston to Cumberland was raised, with Shelly becoming very upset. Then to Jimmy's parents' amazement, she announced she would take care of it herself, to save money.

"She said she could get a van and bring the body down," said her father-in-law, "if it's going to cost that much money. She was arguing about spending money for Jimmy's funeral. It just kind of blew me away. I said, 'Well you've got five hundred thousand dollars, Shelly, I think we can afford to have them transport his body to Cumberland.'"

Then, looking hurt, Shelly claimed not to have realized Jimmy had taken out life insurance, even though she'd been present at the signing. But she assured Denny she didn't want the money, and only Jimmy back.

"Well, she knew about it," said Denny, "because I'd talked to her about it, and Jimmy had told me. Right there everything just came together. She showed no emotion whatsoever. She acted like she didn't know anything about the insurance policy. But she was *the* sole beneficiary, and she's the one that insisted he take a five hundred thousand dollar insurance policy."

On the way back to Morgantown, Shelly Michael had dinner with Eric and Renee Del Viscio and Bobby and Kelli Teets. By this time Renee was certain she had been mistaken about Shelly and Bobby.

"I even went to dinner with Bobby and his wife," she said, "and I certainly wouldn't have done that if I thought my intuition was correct."

During the meal, Kelli impressed Renee with her efficient handling of the funeral arrangements, and taking care of the good-will donations, now arriving daily at the hotel for Shelly and the children.

"Kelli really took control of the situation," remembered Renee, "and Bobby was always rubbing [Shelly's] shoulder and her head."

They all drove back to the Hotel Morgan. Soon after they arrived, Detective Paul Mezzanotte turned up unexpectedly, finding Shelly and Bobby Teets in what he considered a compromising situation.

"To be pretty blunt," the detective recalled, "they were just lying around in bed together. Like she was upset and he was consoling her. It was extremely odd."

He now befriended his two main suspects, who were completely unaware that it was now a murder investigation, enlisting their help to investigate the fire.

"I began to meet with them to talk," Mezzanotte explained. "To show up and to see what was going on. Something kept drawing me to be around her, because something never sat right with me from the beginning of the investigation."

After reviewing Shelly's stated theory that the fire could have been caused by the iron or a hair dryer, the detective had her sign a consent form, giving him access to the house the next morning, when home insurance investigators were scheduled to come.

"At the time I almost said to Shelly, 'Don't sign that,'" recalled Eric Del Viscio, who was present. "But I didn't, and she did."

When Shelly asked the detective if he knew how the fire had started yet, he said he did not. Then he requested a photograph of her husband, and Shelly took him next door to the Del Viscios' room. As he entered, he saw a large blue-green container on the floor, with various personal pictures scattered around the floor, appearing to be drying. Then Shelly showed the detective several photographs of Jimmy.

"[She] showed no signs of remorse," Detective Mezzanotte later noted. "She stated numerous times . . . 'I hope he did not suffer.'"

* * *

That night Reggie Ours received a phone call from Kelli Teets, asking him to call Shelly, as she wanted him to be a pallbearer at the funeral.

When he called Shelly, he asked if anyone would want to hurt Jimmy, and whether there was anything missing from the house. When she said no, he asked what could have caused the fire.

"And she told me that that morning she ironed her clothes," Ours said, "and that they had an iron that was faulty."

Ours then pointed out that it was an iron that would shut itself off automatically, but Shelly said hers would "kick itself" back on, saying she had also left the window open. Her concern, she told Ours, was that the iron may have blown over and started the fire.

"And she said she felt terrible about that," he said.

Then to reassure her it was not her fault, Ours speculated that if the iron had been on a metal ironing board, it would have only burned the covers, and would not have caused the fire.

She then said she had assorted clothes and towels strewn around the floor that could easily have caught fire.

"But there was no way," said Ours, "because she had terrible OCD, and that would have bothered her."

CHAPTER 24

The Grieving Widow

On Friday, December 2, Morgantown was hit by a snow-storm, as temperatures plunged. The deep freeze would remain for the next month, placing the physical investigation of the fire scene on hold.

At 8:45 a.m., Detective Paul Mezzanotte arrived at the Morgan Hotel, bearing a search warrant for him to reenter 545 Killarney Drive with the insurance investigators. After Shelly Michael signed it, he returned to the Public Safety Building to prepare another search for the Michaels' landline.

He was busy working at his desk when Lieutenant Kevin Clark informed him of a tip-off from Rob Angus, advising a toxicology check for a paralytic drug called vecuronium. Lieutenant Clark said Rob Angus would soon be in touch with more information. A few minutes later Angus called, agreeing to come in for an interview that afternoon.

Later, in the official police report, Detective Mezzanotte would write: "[I] was advised that Clark had received an anonymous call . . . that we should check the toxicology results for a drug called Vecuronium, which is a paralytic, not a narcotic, and is readily available to all persons associated with the pediatric intensive care unit."

At 10:40 a.m., the lead detective met with Jimmy Michael's friend and counselor Pastor Kevin Cain, who told him of his suspicions about Shelly.

The pastor said that Jimmy had sought marital help, complaining that Shelly had gotten drunk during the Labor Day weekend, never coming home from the Clarksburg Italian Heritage Festival.

"Pastor Cain stated that he had seen Michelle Michael at church two or three times," Detective Mezzanotte noted. "And there was never any talk of infidelity in the marriage."

At midday, the detective received a call from Medical Examiner Dr. John Carson, confirming that the body had now been positively identified as Jimmy Michael's through dental records. A few minutes later, Morgantown police called a press conference.

Sergeant George Cress told reporters that although police and fire investigators still did not know the cause of the fire, it did not appear suspicious. He appealed for anyone with any information about the fire to immediately contact Morgantown police.

A few hours earlier, Lieutenant Ken Tennant had arrived at 545 Killarney Drive, hoping to conduct a thorough examination of the burned-out master bedroom. He was joined by Morgantown Detectives Chris Dalton and Eric Powell, and State Farm Insurance fire investigator Robert Stewart, who conducted his own independent investigation.

"When we went back on Friday it was snowing, and everything had frozen," said Tennant. "So you had a layer of ice several inches thick on that bedroom floor, and it was going to be impossible to do a complete scene excavation."

But the investigators did manage to collect some electrical wiring and a ceiling fan. They also took samples of the bedroom door, to be examined for any traces of flammable liquid. A state fire marshal walked K-9 dog Brady, trained to sniff out accelerants, through the fire scene.

"The dog alerted in ten different locations," said Lieutenant Tennant. "Four in the pile of debris in the living room, and the other six in the master bedroom suite around the bed area."

The freezing conditions prevented a more thorough search. It wouldn't be until January, when the snow and ice finally thawed, that they would be able to make one.

At 12:30 p.m., Detective Paul Mezzanotte re-interviewed Jeremy Miller, who disclosed further details of Jimmy and Shelly Michael's troubled marriage. Miller said that although his best friend "tried to walk the line as a Christian," by late summer he was having serious marital problems.

Miller told the detective how Jimmy had once suspected Shelly of cheating on him, also complaining of her all-night drinking and spending too much time on the family computer.

"James Michael received a sweater in the mail that was sent to his house," Detective Mezzanotte later wrote in his report, "with a note attached to it that said, 'Keep your whore wife away from my husband.' "

Miller said he knew Jimmy had agreed to help Shelly and Bobby Teets start an embroidery business. He also knew that Shelly had flown to Chicago for training, although he did not know that Teets had accompanied her.

A nervous Bobby Teets arrived at the Public Safety Building at 1:30 p.m. for another interview with Detective Mezzanotte. He was brought up to the third-floor Detective Division, where Mezzanotte was waiting in an interview room.

At 1:50 p.m., the lead detective turned on a tape recorder, for the fourteen-minute interview.

"Bobby," he began, "you're here today to provide information about this incident. What we're going to try to do is establish a timeline."

He then methodically went through Teets' movements the day of the fire, leading up to him alerting police that Jimmy Michael might be inside the burning house.

But slowly the detective honed in on his relationship with Shelly Michael.

"Everybody's been talking about several things to us," he told Teets. "You've heard rumors."

He then asked about any business ventures outside Mountaineer Home Medical that he might be involved in with the Michaels.

"We were gonna have an embroidery business," Teets replied. "It was gonna be me and Shelly, but Jimmy was backing us. And we were gonna work it out of their basement—embroidered shirt and coats, you know, whatever customers wanted."

Then Detective Mezzanotte casually asked if he and Shelly had made any business trips together.

"We went to Chicago for a seminar," he admitted, giving the detective the flight times from Pittsburgh and the name of the hotel they had stayed at by O'Hare Airport.

Detective Mezzanotte then asked about his relationship with Jimmy Michael.

"In the last four or five months [we] have become really good friends," said Teets. "We were friends before because of football, but our friendship grew. And now he was actually my boss. So, it got to be a really good friendship."

What about his relationship with Shelly? asked the detective.

"It was pretty much the same way," he replied. "Her and my wife were probably closer than me and her, of course. They would go on biz [sic] trips to Baltimore and stuff. But our friendship was equally close."

Towards the end of the interview, Mezzanotte asked Teets for his thoughts about the fire and Jimmy's death.

"I just wish I knew answers," said Teets. "I mean, he had no enemies. I can't imagine anybody doing this to him. I can't imagine, for any reason, him doing it to himself."

Then he became very emotional, saying he hoped the fire had been an accident and Jimmy had gone peacefully.

"It bothers me every day just thinking about it," Teets said. "I would be happier to know that he didn't suffer. I would be able to sleep a lot better."

After the interview, Detective Mezzanotte confirmed

that Shelly Michael had booked a single room for November 17 at the Marriott at O'Hare Airport. And he arranged to have local Des Plaines, Illinois, police check out any available hotel surveillance tapes, at the earliest opportunity.

That afternoon, Shelly Michael went shopping at Morgantown Mall, so she could look her best at Jimmy's upcoming funeral. As she was getting ready to leave, Tara Miller walked into the hotel room with some new outfits she'd bought for Shelly.

"I mean, her house had burned down with all her clothes," said Miller. "A friend and I went shopping and took clothes to the hotel."

When Tara arrived, Shelly and Rene Del Viscio were fixing Kylie's hair.

"She was very snappy," remembered Tara. "She was trying to pick out clothes to wear, and she pulled out a pair of panties that someone had bought her. And she turned around and said, 'I don't want to offend anybody, but I can't carry on wearing these—I've got to go to Victoria's Secret.'

"And I thought, 'If my house had just burned down and all my clothes destroyed, I would be thankful to have anything to wear.'"

Then Eric Del Viscio drove Shelly, Kylie, Renee and Kelli to the mall.

"She bought a suit to wear the day of the funeral," recalled Kelli, "at Petite Sophisticate's."

At 4:30 p.m., Detective Mezzanotte interviewed Rob Angus at the Detective Division, never mentioning that Reggie Ours had already suggested testing for vecuronium. Angus told the detective how his sister Shannon Rudy had once been Shelly's nursing supervisor at Ruby Memorial.

"I received a phone call from my sister," Angus later testified, "that made reference to a drug that was used on the floor of the hospital."

She explained that vecuronium caused paralysis, and was something that police should test for. But Angus said he did not want to "drag my sister into it," asking that she remain anonymous.

"Robert Angus advised," Mezzanotte wrote, "that the nurses had told him that they [the investigators] needed to test for drugs."

After the interview, the detective called the medical examiner's office, asking that they test Jimmy Michael's remains for vecuronium.

An hour later, Reggie Ours called Mezzanotte again, reporting Shelly Michael's conversation about leaving the iron on.

"She said she ironed a shirt for work and they kept the window open all night," noted Mezzanotte. "At the time this conversation took place, Michelle Michael's demeanor was stoic, she was not upset, and did not break down while talking to Reggie Ours."

At 7:26 p.m., he returned to the Morgan Hotel, giving Shelly Michael a copy of the search warrant, and a list of evidence seized that day.

"[She] seemed very concerned and very scared," the lead detective noted in his report, "when she was presented with a copy of the warrant and the return."

CHAPTER 25

The Funeral

On Saturday, Jimmy Michael's obituary appeared in *The Dominion Post.*

"James Andrew Michael, 33, of Morgantown, W. Va., and formerly of Cumberland, Md.," it read, "went to be with his Lord on Tuesday, Nov. 29, 2005, at his home, as the result of a house fire."

The previous night, after Detective Mezzanotte's visit, Shelly Michael had driven to Cumberland to prepare for Sunday's funeral. She stayed at Ruth and Denny Michael's house, and early Saturday morning, started calling friends to invite them to Jimmy's funeral.

"She called my home," recalled Deborah Harris, "to chat a little bit about the time of the funeral and the viewing."

On the day of the fire, Harris had agreed to collect her mail, now offering to bring it to the funeral. But Shelly said her only concern was a bank card from Morgantown's First United Bank & Trust, where "The Michael Family Benefit Fund" had been set up.

"She just wanted the bank card for access to the money," said Harris. "I thought it odd she wasn't interested in any of the other mail, because she asked me to look through the mail for the card."

As she was sorting through the mail, Harris found several doctors' appointment cards for the children.

"I mentioned that," Harris said, "and she didn't seem to be even concerned about any of the other mail. Just the bank card."

That afternoon, Shelly Michael visited the Adams Family Funeral Home, where a viewing for the family and close friends was scheduled between 6:00 and 9:00 p.m. It would be a closed-casket affair, because of the state of Jimmy Michael's body.

When Shelly arrived, she asked to see the body. When the funeral director refused, saying it was in too bad a condition, she flew into a rage.

"[She had] a complete meltdown at the funeral home, wanting to see Jimmy's body," recalled Renee Del Viscio. "And they tried to deter her from that."

Then her father-in-law tried to calm her down, saying he had seen Jimmy's body and strongly advised her not to.

"She was very angry and adamant," said Denny. "She wanted to see the body.

"I said, 'There's nothing to see, Shelly.'

"'Well, how bad is he burned up?'

"And I said, 'He is burned up bad.'

"But she still wanted to see it herself."

The viewing, at the funeral home's memorial chapel, was packed with Jimmy Michael's old high school friends, many of whom had never met Shelly before.

"And they were coming up to me," said Kerri Whitacre, "and saying, 'What's the deal with his wife? She's not crying.' She just seemed cold. Flat. I mean she had no affect whatsoever. There were no tears. Nothing."

At one point, Jimmy's distraught 12-year-old son Drew climbed on top of the closed casket and began talking to it. When his mother Stephanie came over to help him, Shelly suddenly ordered everyone to leave the area around the casket, saying she needed time alone with Jimmy.

"She caused a little bit of a scene," recalled her mother-in-law. "I don't know what her reasons were. She complained about Drew, and she kept questioning things. Drew was upset."

At 9:00 p.m., as everyone was leaving, a tearful Drew remained by his father's casket, not wanting to leave it.

"[Shelly] wanted to know why Drew was still there," recalled Ruth, "and when his mother was going to get him."

And when Stephanie came to take him out of the chapel, Shelly demanded to know what they were doing.

"It was like she didn't want his mother tending to him," said Ruth.

After the viewing, Shelly asked her father-in-law if Bobby and Kelli Teets and their two children could stay at their house with her, instead of another relative's house as planned. He agreed.

"She said she wanted them to stay at our house the night before my son's funeral," recalled Denny.

Late that night, after everyone had gone to bed, Denny left the house for an errand. When he reentered through a back door into the basement, he discovered Shelly in a compromising position with Bobby Teets.

"I was coming in the back way, into the rec room," he said, "and Bobby Teets was in his pajamas, hugging Shelly and kissing her on the cheek. And when she saw me walk in, she pushed him away."

On Sunday morning, Shelly Michael spent so long preparing herself for her husband's 1:00 p.m. funeral that around noon, Denny and Ruth Michael left without her.

"She wasn't ready," said Ruth, "and she was all upset because we were going to the church first."

Shelly had previously arranged for Pastor Tim Kraynak to officiate at the funeral at the Memorial Heights Baptist Church, even though Jimmy had had little to do with him after the Marketplace Community Church closed.

"It just showed how out of touch Shelly was," said Jeremy Miller, who sang at the funeral. "I'm not so sure Jimmy would have selected Tim to do his funeral, but he did a great job."

The church was packed with mourners, and the service was highly emotional. But Shelly appeared cold and stoic, whereas Jimmy's first wife Stephanie cried throughout the service.

Stephanie, who brought Drew and Jacie, did not sit with Shelly and the family, thinking it inappropriate.

Halfway through the service, Drew suddenly broke down and started sobbing uncontrollably.

"And I heard this blood-curdling scream and crying," said Stephanie. "I thought, 'Oh, Shelly's finally breaking down.' I didn't want to look over, but when I finally did, it wasn't Shelly. It was my son. It was Drew."

Stephanie remembers feeling very uncomfortable during the funeral, for although she had moved on with her life, she still loved Jimmy.

"It was very odd," she said, "because there's a whole church full of people, and everybody was allowed to grieve except for the ex-wife."

Reggie Ours, Jeremy Miller and Bobby Teets were among the pallbearers appointed by Shelly. At the end of the funeral, several of Jimmy's close friends stood up to share some memories of him.

"After they all finished," said Denny, "I got up, and I had to say something. And Shelly grabbed Ruth and said, 'What's he going up there for?'"

At the end of the service, the mourners proceeded to the David Memorial Cemetery for the burial, followed by a dinner at a local restaurant.

And many of the mourners could not help wondering about the widow's coldness at her husband's graveside.

"Her demeanor at the funeral, in my opinion, was very odd," recalled Deborah Harris. "She didn't cry. She just sat stone-faced. Most of the people at the funeral were crying, and I did not see her cry."

* * *

At 7:35 p.m. Sunday night, Detective Paul Mezzanotte contacted Officer Mike Myers of the Des Plaines Police Department, asking him to investigate Shelly and Bobby's November 17 stay at the Marriott Courtyard hotel. Two hours later, Officer Myers faxed him a receipt of their hotel bill. It showed they had checked in at 10:06 a.m. November 17, checking out at 4:16 a.m. the following morning. And they had both stayed in a room with one king-size bed.

Officer Myers also agreed to return to the hotel the following day, to see if any video surveillance existed of them.

On Monday, December 5, Ruby Memorial Hospital granted Nurse Shelly Michael a six-month leave of absence, allowing her to get her life in order. That morning, Northwestern Mutual Life Insurance broker Eli Henderson, who had sold Jimmy Michael the $500,000 policy, visited the new widow at the Morgan Hotel.

"She looked very tired," recalled Henderson. "Like she hadn't slept in a couple of days."

After giving his condolences, Henderson handed Shelly a special kit, instructing her on how to claim the $500,000 she was now entitled to as sole beneficiary. Although she had been with Jimmy at the policy signing eight months earlier, Shelly said she was uncertain how much life insurance he had taken out.

"It was a little bit surprising to me," Henderson would later testify.

At 10:45 a.m. that morning, Detective Paul Mezzanotte called Dr. James Kraner, the chief toxicologist at the Medical Examiner's Office, who reported that toxicology and drug screens had shown no narcotics present in Jimmy Michael's blood. He agreed to send the remaining samples of liver tissue and blood to the National Medical Services (NMS) in Pennsylvania, for additional testing for vecuronium.

That afternoon, Detective Mezzanotte conducted a telephone interview with the Michaels' friend and neighbor Deborah Harris.

"She noticed Michelle Michael to be extremely controlling and obsessive," he wrote in his report. "[She] was very moody and had mood swings."

Harris had observed "severe tension" over the two sets of children, saying Shelly treated her own children far better than Drew. She also observed that "the loving family act" had disappeared by summer, and "there were no longer displays of affection."

CHAPTER 26

"More Like Lovers Than Friends"

When the idea for a Morgantown memorial service for Jimmy Michael was first suggested, his wife had been opposed to it.

"She didn't want to do it," recalled Ruth Michael. "Because of Jimmy's social standing and his business, a lot of people in Morgantown thought she needed to have something. And so it was like, 'OK, I have to do this.'"

So on Monday afternoon, Shelly Michael reluctantly called the Christian & Missionary Alliance church to arrange a memorial service for her late husband.

"She wanted to have a service the next evening," recalled the Reverend David Goodin. "I urged her, encouraged her to consider waiting at least another day."

The pastor explained that one day's notice would be insufficient time for many of the people who would wish to attend to even hear about it.

"But she strongly wanted to do it on Tuesday evening," he said. "She simply said she didn't want to wait any longer. It had been a week since the fire [and] she felt she had been through enough already."

Finally the pastor agreed, asking her to come to the church the next morning, to help him plan the service.

At 9:30 a.m., Shelly Michael arrived at the church on

Patteson Drive, Morgantown. And as Reverend Goodin brought her into his office, seating her on a sofa in his counseling area, Bobby Teets suddenly appeared.

"He immediately sat down with her," Reverend Goodin recalled. "Shelly didn't introduce me to him . . . I didn't know who he was."

The pastor speculated that Bobby was probably a close family member, as they sat so close together, holding hands the entire time.

During the conversation, he asked the new widow if she was receiving sufficient support from family and friends during this time of loss. It was only then that she introduced Bobby Teets.

"I don't know what I would have done without him and his wife," she declared.

Reverend Goodin was taken aback by her comment, thinking it "most unusual" they would be so openly affectionate with each other, although he found some "comfort" in her mentioning that he had a wife.

"I honestly felt that they behaved more like lovers than friends," he said. "I didn't want to believe that this was the case, but I thought it would be rather brazen of someone that had just lost her husband to come and speak to the minister about a memorial service, with a boyfriend with whom she was having a relationship."

He was also struck by how little input the "emotionless" widow wished to have in her husband's memorial service.

"My usual custom is to ask if there are any special requests for hymns or scripture readings," he explained, "or desire to have certain people speak to share memories of the deceased. But her desire was we would plan the service."

At 11:45 a.m., Detective Mezzanotte received the damning surveillance video from Ruby Memorial Hospital, showing Shelly Michael leaving at 8:11 a.m. the morning of the fire, and returning seventeen minutes later.

At 12 noon, Detectives Paul Mezzanotte and Chris Dalton went to Killarney Drive, where they met with Charleston-based ATF Special Agent Rick Summerfield, who had come to review the evidence.

"I examined three wall receptacles from the master bedroom of the Michael residence," said Summerfield, "and the wiring that runs between them. And I examined a ceiling fan which had been directly over the bed."

Although all heavily charred, the certified fire inspector concluded that they had not caused the fire, as no electricity had been going through them at the time.

"I was confident after my examination," he later testified, "that none of these items were the cause of the fire or in any way contributed to it."

But with the freezing conditions, it was decided that the special agent would return for a closer look at the fire scene when the weather improved.

At 5:20 p.m. Jimmy Michael's parents arrived in Morgantown for the memorial service. But they first went to the Public Safety Building, for a scheduled interview with Detective Paul Mezzanotte. Denny Michael went into the interview room first, immediately telling the detectives he suspected Shelly of murdering his son.

"I said, 'Well, she's a nurse practitioner,'" recalled Denny. "'She has access to drugs, and I feel she drugged Jimmy and then tried to burn up the evidence.'

"And he looked at me and said, 'You're kidding.' And I said I hoped I was wrong."

A little before 7:00 p.m. that night, Shelly Michael stood outside the Christian & Missionary Alliance church, greeting people as they arrived. Inside, it was packed with the popular business owner's friends, associates and members of the Little League teams he'd coached, who had all come to pay their last respects.

When Jeremy Miller arrived with his wife Tara, Shelly came over and kissed him on the cheek. She gave him a "cold, blank stare," and he says that was the moment he knew she had killed Jimmy.

"There was that awkward pause," he later explained. "You know when you look somebody in the eye and just something tells you."

Detective Paul Mezzanotte also attended and on his way in he invited Shelly to come to Morgantown Police Department for a sit-down interview the next day.

"I wanted to see the service," he explained. "It's not out of character for a detective, especially in homicide or death investigations that have become suspicious in nature, to go to these services to watch people's reactions. And that's what I did."

The detective observed his suspects closely throughout the service, as many of those closest to Jimmy delivered moving eulogies.

"That was very, very emotional," Mezzanotte recalled. "There were a lot of very reputable people in the community there."

But he was especially struck by how everyone in the church was so obviously touched by the tragedy, with the exception of the grieving widow.

"Shelly looked bothered to be there," he remembered. "She was very indifferent and wasn't emotional at all. She was more focused on just having Bobby Teets around her than she was anybody else that was there. I saw no emotion."

The ninety-minute service was conducted by Pastors David Goodin and Kevin Cain. And in a moving eulogy, Reggie Ours told how Jimmy had once made an out-of-town visit to a female patient, who needed oxygen.

"There was real bad storm and the electricity was out," he told the mourners. "And she was scared she was going to run out of oxygen. So Jimmy actually spent the night on her couch to reassure her. That's the kind of person he was. He would do whatever he could to make people's lives better."

After the memorial service, Denny Michael drove Kerri Whitacre back to Cumberland, while Ruth and her son Steve spent another night in Shelly's hotel room. During the drive back to Maryland, Kerri finally had the opportunity to discuss Jimmy's suspicious death.

"I said, 'Denny,'" she remembered, "'I don't know if this is the right time, but I feel like I need to talk to you about this.'"

Kerri told him she felt that Shelly was "hiding stuff," and Denny said he agreed, saying he had his own suspicions.

"I think she killed him," Denny told Whitacre, "if that's what you mean."

Then Kerri told him how Ruby Memorial Hospital was rife with rumors that Shelly had killed Jimmy, and was having an affair. She said people at the hospital did not like her at all.

As soon as Denny got home, he called Ruth's cell phone, telling her about their conversation.

"And I'm saying, 'Denny, I'm in this room by myself with her,'" said Ruth, "'You're scaring me to death.'"

That night, Ruth, Steve and Stacy all stayed in Shelly's hotel room.

"My son Steve actually laid on the bed with Shelly," recalled Ruth. "She never said one word all night. Not one word. She just laid there and I think she was waiting to hear what we were saying, as she wasn't asleep."

CHAPTER 27

"A String of Lies"

The following day, Detective Paul Mezzanotte had scheduled further interviews with Shelly Michael and Bobby Teets. He planned to confront them about an affair.

But first he summoned his investigative team and Monongalia Prosecutors Marcia Ashdown and Perri DeChristopher to the Public Safety Building to strategize. It was decided to interview Bobby Teets first, before interviewing Shelly Michael, who was viewed as being a far harder nut to crack.

"Well, there was a little bit of strategy with that," explained Detective Mezzanotte. "We thought that Bobby Teets was going to be somebody who was probably going to be a little bit more honest with us."

The plan was to have Teets account for his movements the morning of the fire, before confronting him about an affair with Shelly Michael.

Just after 1:30 p.m., Shelly Michael and Bobby Teets arrived at the Public Safety Building, going up to the third-floor police headquarters. The burly goateed father-of-two looked nervous and exhausted, as he sat down on a bench next to his lover.

"It was arranged that Bobby Teets would be there at the same time as Shelly," said Monongalia Assistant Prosecutor

As a small boy Jimmy Michael taught his younger brother Steve how to play football. *The Michael Family*

Jimmy Michael and his first wife Stephanie celebrate Christmas 1995 with their young son Drew.

The Michael Family

When Jimmy first met the young pediatric nurse Shelly Angus at Ruby Memorial Hospital sparks flew.

The Michael Family

Shelly's father Michael Goots with his wife Kathi (left) and daughter Jennifer (right).   *John Glatt*

Jimmy and Shelly were deeply in love when they married in May 2000.
The Michael Family

Jimmy Michael (right) with his close friends Bill Hunt (left) and Jeremy Miller (middle). *Jeremy Miller*

After starting the successful Mountaineer Home Medical company, Jimmy and Shelly Michael often attended Morgantown business functions. *The Michael Family*

Bobby Teets became close friends with Jimmy Michael, before betraying him by embarking on a torrid love affair with Shelly.

Morgantown Police Department

The burned-out remains of Jimmy and Shelly Michael's bedroom, just hours after the fire. *Morgantown Fire Department*

Morgantown Fire investigator Ken Tennant led the groundbreaking probe into what caused the highly unusual deadly fire.

John Glatt

Det. Paul Mezzanotte had Shelly under suspicion from the very beginning.

Paul Mezzanotte

West Virginia State Police Sgt. James Merrill played a cat and mouse game with Shelly Michael, during her many hours of interrogation.

John Glatt

Charismatic West Virginia defense attorney Tom Dyer fought a long determined battle on behalf of his client. *John Glatt*

Steve, Ruth and Dennis Michael at their Cumberland, Maryland home in January 2009.

John Glatt

All that is left of the Michael Family one-time dream home at 545 Killarney Drive, Morgantown. *John Glatt*

Dennis Michael's most treasured
possession is the mounted head
of the deer Jimmy killed the day
before his murder. *John Glatt*

Convicted husband-killer Shelly
Michael will be eligible for
parole in 20 years' time.
*West Virginia Division of
Corrections*

Perri DeChristopher, "so she would see that he was there, also talking to the police."

While Shelly went into one 12-foot–by–5-foot interview room with Detective Paul Mezzanotte, Teets went into an adjoining one with Detective Chris Dalton.

"It was just to break the ice," explained Dalton. "Get his information."

Although investigators believed Teets would eventually come clean about an affair, no one was prepared for how quickly he did. Dalton did not even need to confront him about the incriminating Marriott Hotel video. Teets just broke down and confessed.

"He admitted that right off the bat," remembered Detective Dalton. "It didn't take much at all. That they had had an affair and that he had slept with her on numerous occasions out there, as well as at Shelly and Jimmy's house."

Teets said he was not in love with Shelly, saying he was afraid it would break up his marriage.

"Bobby was more worried about keeping his relationship with his wife," said Detective Dalton. "That was his goal in the interview. That was his concern. We stressed to him that day that he should probably go and tell his wife about it, because it's going to come out in the investigation."

After finishing his preliminary interview, Dalton told Bobby Teets to wait outside in the hallway. Then he called Mezzanotte out of his interview with Shelly, informing him of Teets' confession.

At 1:50 p.m. Paul Mezzanotte resumed his interview with Shelly Michael, which was now being videotaped. He was going for a full confession, zeroing in on the affair and her adulterous trip to Chicago two weeks before her husband's untimely death.

For the next hour and fifty minutes, they played cat-and-mouse, as Shelly attempted to control the interview.

"I'm the only person right now that believes you," Mezzanotte began. "And I'm working for you. Because when you've had a tragedy, everybody has something they want to tell you. And until I can talk to you, I don't know what to believe. So we've got to be on the same page."

He warned her that some of his questions might be of a personal nature and appear to be prying, but they had to be asked.

"I have to make my investigation match the fire," he explained, "so just use a little bit of caution—or, as a goofy way to put it, tell me the truth."

Then Detective Mezzanotte asked about "this Chicago trip."

"We were looking into buying an embroidery machine," Shelly replied. "Just for something to do."

She said she had gone online, finding the "How To Start An Embroidery Business" seminar in Chicago.

"We thought," she said, " 'Well, that's the best way to learn about it.' "

The detective then asked her for details of the trip, and Shelly gave a blow-by-blow account, omitting any mention of having sex with Bobby Teets.

"Was there any other particular reason why you went to Chicago?" asked Mezzanotte.

"No," she replied. "No other reason."

"This will all start making sense to you," Mezzanotte continued, "as we keep going on. There are a lot of questions I have about you and Bobby, OK?"

"OK," she replied without missing a beat.

"You guys," he said, "how many rooms did you book?"

"One."

"How many beds were in the room?"

"One."

"Where did Bobby sleep?"

"On the couch out front."

"I'm not prying," said Mezzanotte. "I don't think you're a bad person, a terrible mom, nothing. I can't leave here with doubt, Shelly. What's going on with this?"

"Nothing."

"Bobby slept on the couch?"

"I slept in the bed myself."

"I am the only one in the world right now that believes you," said the detective. "Don't change that trust today."

He said that if he had gone on a trip with a friend's wife and needed to cut costs, he might stay in one room—but with two beds.

"We wouldn't stay in the same room with one king-size bed," he told her. "I have photographs of the room you stayed in, so that I had my facts together before you came in."

"Right," snapped Shelly, unfazed. "Well the reason we booked it that way was because there was a pull-out bed, and the door closed to the bedroom."

"I've got a hard time with that, OK?" replied the detective. "This relationship with you and Bobby is suspect. There is something more to this than a business partnership."

When she repeated that she had slept alone in the room, promising the detective that Bobby "was just a friend," Mezzanotte accused her of lying to him.

"I don't like to lie, sir," Shelly snapped back.

"I think there are a couple of things that you are holding back a little bit on," continued the detective. "I know this is stressful, and it's OK, but we're going to get to the bottom of it, because we have to. I want to believe in you. I want to put all these rumors to bed that I'm hearing."

Changing tack, Detective Mezzanotte moved on to the fire, informing her that police now knew it had been deliberately set.

"The death and the fire are a little bit out of the ordinary," he told her. "I don't want to say they're suspicious . . . it's a weird situation. This fire was arson."

"You're kidding me," said Shelly, sounding surprised.

"It was set."

"Oh my gosh. How?"

"I think you already know that."

"Paul, I didn't know that."

Then Mezzanotte bluffed, saying that investigators now had a timeline for the fire, and knew how it was started.

"Well," she replied, "can you tell me, please?"

Detective Mezzanotte said he was unable to divulge that

at this time, although arson could now be "forensically, scientifically" proved.

"I think you know where it started," he said. "I think you know how it started, I think you know what was used to start it. And I think you know that Jim didn't suffer when he died."

Shelly vehemently denied any knowledge of the fire, as Mezzanotte kept firing accusations at her.

"Don't have it go full circle right back to you," he cautioned. "This is why I'm talking to you first . . . before all the results and everything are in. Because I believe in you. I trust you. Don't lie to me."

For the next few minutes, the detective appealed for her to tell him exactly what had happened to Jimmy. But she refused to budge an inch, saying she had no idea what he was talking about.

"Somebody burned your house down," said Mezzanotte. "And my gut feeling, and from all the hours I've put into this case, I think you know who burned your house down."

"I promise you, Paul, I don't know," she replied. "I can't imagine. You don't understand, I have no idea."

Then Detective Mezzanotte asked if she was curious about what had been found during Jimmy's autopsy.

"Autopsy, toxicology results—you're a nurse," said Mezzanotte. "I'm not going to talk medical stuff with you. I refuse to let myself lie to you. I'm not going to do that. I'm going to tell you the truth."

He then informed her that samples of Jimmy's heart and lung tissue, as well as other preserved bodily fluids, had been sent to a laboratory for specialized testing.

"They're not testing for heroin, they're not testing for coke, they're testing for drugs," he said. "Because we pretty much have an idea from the autopsy as to how he died."

"OK," Shelly fired back, "can you tell me?"

But the detective said they had a long way to go before he felt comfortable releasing more details.

"I just need you to tell me what happened to him," she

said. "Are you telling me the fire isn't what killed him? He didn't die from the fire?"

The detective then implored her to "unload this burden," promising it would never be made public.

"Nobody else in the world," he said, "but me, you and a police report that I file with the prosecuting attorney's office, will ever know what you tell me in this room. Nothing. Can't hold anything back."

"OK."

"Start with Bobby. What's the deal? The truth."

"We're just friends."

Becoming increasingly frustrated, Mezzanotte said he had seen her on her hotel bed with Bobby Teets.

"I saw that with my own eyes," he said. "You guys, at face value, is wrong. Please don't tell me you're just friends."

"My other friends were laying there with me too," she countered.

Then Shelly agreed that her relationship with Teets could look suspicious, admitting her daughter Kylie had even questioned it.

"We were getting ready to go to Pittsburgh to look at a machine," she said, "and my daughter said, 'Is Bobby going with you?' And I said yes. She said, 'Why is Bobby going with you again?'

"It just threw up flags to me. I'm like, 'Oh gosh, that probably does look really bad.' And I even asked Jimmy, 'Does that make you feel weird? Because, you know, Bobby and I went to Chicago for the demonstration?'"

She also claimed to have asked Kelli Teets the same question, saying that she had only realized it looked "weird" after her daughter's comment. But Detective Mezzanotte said he did not believe her.

"I don't think you ever had that conversation with Jim," he said, "because there are statements that support the fact that he was very uncomfortable with you and Bobby."

"Well, then, he wasn't telling me the truth," she replied, "because I asked him about it all the time. I said, 'Does that weird you out? How do you feel about that?' And he said, 'I'm fine with it.' "

According to Shelly, his only concern about the time she would now be spending with Bobby Teets, running the embroidery business, was that it wouldn't keep them apart like the football season had.

She said she had warned Jimmy that the embroidery business would mean many evenings in the basement with Teets, getting caught up with orders.

Finally she admitted that Jimmy had initially expressed reservations about the Chicago trip, but had no problem once she told him they would be staying in a two-bedroom suite.

"Please don't lie," said Mezzanotte, "because it hurts my investigation, and that hurts you, if you lie. Tell me the truth, because this king-sized bed in Chicago with a pullout on the couch, he didn't sleep on the couch. I'll leave it at that, because there is other stuff we need to talk about. I think you know . . ."

Detective Mezzanotte then asked who would have the motive to hurt Jimmy, before setting the house ablaze.

"I don't know. There are only two people in the world," she said without elaborating. "Everybody loved him. I don't know who would want to hurt him."

"Does Bobby?" asked Mezzanotte.

"No," she said. "What would be the motive in that? I mean, it's his brand-new boss. He loved him."

"Until I believe you," replied the detective, "it's his brand-new boss [and] he's sleeping with the boss's wife."

"No," she replied, "Bobby is very happily married."

Mezzanotte then asked if it had been a one-night-stand in Chicago, after too many drinks.

"Shelly," he said, "you could have made a mistake . . . but I'm the only person in the world that really needs to hear that mistake."

"There's no way," replied Shelly. "He loves his wife. I don't know what else to say. I'm not physically attracted to him. He's not anything I would be involved with."

Detective Mezzanotte then asked about her relationship with Jimmy.

"We loved each other a lot," Shelly replied. "We fought some. I mean, I didn't think—It was nothing like we would be separated or anything."

"The last few months?" probed Mezzanotte.

"It was fine. I mean, busy. We hadn't spent a whole lot of time together, but it wasn't a major problem. Really, there wasn't anything."

He then asked if she wanted any more children, and Shelly pointed out that her husband had had a vasectomy.

"Oh, I joke about it all the time," she said. "But that's truly a joke between him and me. I know I can't because he's fixed, but if he said, 'OK, I'll get it reversed,' I'd be like, 'No, no.' But that was one of my favorite things to tease him about."

Then Mezzanotte said he had a "tough decision" to make that day, about how much to reveal about the police investigation.

"I'm still kind of fixated on this whole Bobby mess," he said. "Because it doesn't make sense to me. I'm going to go over this again, and I need to start with this trip to Chicago."

At this point, Shelly asked to telephone her mother-in-law, to arrange to pick up the children from school. And the detective stepped out of the interview for a couple of minutes to consult with the other investigators, who had been watching outside on a TV monitor.

A few minutes later, Detective Paul Mezzanotte resumed the interview, going on the offensive. He said he was "confused" about her relationship with Bobby Teets, needing the truth before sharing any further details of the investigation with her.

"If you are truly grieving for your husband," he told her, "and you want answers . . . then you've got to do some soul-searching."

Once again, Shelly agreed that her innocent relationship with Bobby Teets could be misconstrued, saying that that was the reason she'd sought Jimmy and Kelli's approval before the Chicago trip.

The detective then said he believed she controlled Bobby and Kelli Teets' lives, theorizing that they needed to be around her for "some form of comfort factor."

"They need to be controlled by you," he told her. "That's a terrible word, but they need to be comforted by you. They need to be involved in your scene, life circle. And that's just the way they appear to me at face value."

Then, once again, he asked for her movements on the morning of the fire. Shelly said she'd got up "like normal," showered and driven to Ruby Memorial Hospital for work. After receiving a status report on her patients from the resident, she began her bedside rounds.

She then went into the X-ray room, where she called Bobby Teets, asking him to bring in his tax forms. She then came back out, telling Nancy Buffalo she was going to get her pager.

"And I went and got my pager," she told Mezzanotte, "came back in, straight up to the unit and back to the X-ray room."

Shelly then described finishing her notes, before starting her rounds of patients.

"Well I was at Bed Seven," she remembered, "and they said, 'Shelly, telephone.' I said, 'Take a message.' "

After seeing several babies, she checked in at the reception, and was handed a note that Bobby Teets had called, saying he couldn't find her husband.

She then went into her office and called his cell phone, but it went straight to voice mail and she hung up.

"[I] started to work on my computer, to type in some orders for the patients," she recalled. "And then they yelled, 'Shelly, telephone.' And then that was Kelli, and she said, 'Your house is on fire.' Then I ran, grabbed my stuff on my clipboard and handed it to my boss real quick, and said, 'I gotta go,' and ran out."

Mezzanotte asked where her pager had been, and she said in the console of her SUV.

"How long did that take you?" he asked.

"I don't know," she replied. "It was raining, so I was running. But I have no idea. A few minutes."

Then Detective Mezzanotte said ATF fire experts had determined that the fire was not accidental, and had been deliberately set.

"I can't believe that," said Shelly incredulously.

"There was something used to set your house on fire."

"What?"

"I know what it was," said the detective. "I'd really like you to tell me what it was."

"I don't know, Paul. I don't know. I have no idea."

"We know where it started," he continued. "How it started, what was used. I just have a feeling . . . that you know that Jimmy didn't suffer."

"I don't know what happened," she replied. "Please just tell me. I have no idea."

"I can't get into all the details with you," he said. "I'm telling you what I can tell you, because I just don't know. I have too many unanswered questions in my mind about this fire and about how Jimmy died."

"I just can't believe someone would start a fire in the house," she said. "I just cannot believe that."

For the next half-hour, Shelly refused a give an inch, as Detective Mezzanotte kept firing question after question about Bobby Teets and the fire. Whenever Shelly demanded answers, Mezzanotte said he still had to clear up "a couple of little inconsistencies," before he could tell her more about Jimmy's autopsy results and the fire.

At the end of the interview Detective Mezzanotte impounded her cell phone for forensic examination, before appealing for her help in solving the crime.

"I'm going to give you a homework assignment," he told her. "I want you to go home, and when the kids are asleep and no friends are around, I want you to think about everything we talked about today. I want you to think about the answers you gave to me."

At their next talk, he told her, she could either tell him

that everything she had said today was the truth, and be able to prove it—"Or, the next time we talk," he told her, "I want you to say, 'I was confused. I was scared. I believe you, I trust you—this is what you need to know.'"

And he assured her that once he was satisfied she was telling the truth, he would reveal everything he knew about Jimmy's death.

"I'm going to tell you the cause of the fire," he said, "and hopefully, I'm going to arrest somebody and I'm going to say, 'This is the person that burned your house down. This is how Jimmy died. This is why. This is what we know.' And you'll get closure, and everything is going to be OK."

Finally, Shelly asked when the police would go public with it being arson.

"You'll know before anything gets to the papers," he assured her.

At 3:40 p.m., Shelly Michael walked out of the interview room and past Bobby Teets, who was still waiting for his interview with Detective Mezzanotte. Then she walked down the three flights of stairs and into the snow on Spruce Street, gathering her thoughts and planning her next move.

Back in his office, after almost two hours with Shelly Michael, Detective Mezzanotte had more questions than ever. He knew she was lying and felt "more confused" after the interview than he had before.

Then he brought Bobby Teets into the interview room, reading him his Miranda rights, before turning on the video recorder.

An emotional Bobby Teets then confessed on the record about his passionate affair with Shelly Michael. But he was adamant that it was just a fling and nothing more.

On his way out, he said he was going home to tell Kelli about the affair, and try to save his marriage.

After leaving the Public Safety Building, Shelly Michael returned to the Hotel Morgan, where her mother-in-law was waiting for her with Kylie. Shelly was furious, complaining about how detectives were treating her.

"She came home," recalled Ruth Michael, "and said, 'I can't believe they're asking me all this stuff.' "

Then Shelly left with Kylie, driving to the Teets' house, to pick up their daughter's clothes for cheerleading practice. Bobby was there when she arrived, and she started fishing for what he had told police.

"You didn't tell them our secret?" she asked him. "Why do they keep asking us about Chicago?"

Teets denied telling detectives anything.

"I actually said, 'No, I didn't,' " he later testified, "[although] I had already told Paul that I had the affair."

During their brief conversation, Shelly desperately wanted to know why police were so concerned about the Chicago trip. But Bobby Teets played dumb, saying he had no idea.

"I didn't actually talk to her after that," he said. "That was pretty much it."

After cheerleading practice, Shelly called her parents, accusing the police of trying to "scare" her. But then, with her curiosity getting the better of her, she telephoned Detective Mezzanotte, requesting another meeting as soon as possible, and even offering to take a polygraph test to prove she was telling the truth.

"She called me," said the lead detective. "She needed to know what we knew."

After putting down the phone, Detective Mezzanotte called Sergeant James Merrill, the chief polygraph examiner for the West Virginia State Police. The two law enforcement officers had worked cases together in the past, and Mezzanotte now wanted an impartial outsider to meet Shelly Michael and give his opinion.

"I wanted to have someone from another agency come in and look at the investigation," explained Mezzanotte. "Somebody that wasn't attached to the investigation . . . to just look at it with a new set of eyes."

Detective Mezzanotte also asked Sergeant Merrill to be

prepared to give Shelly a polygraph test when he had exhausted his questioning.

"Once I had gone as far as I was going to get with her," he said, "then I was going to tell her, 'Well, the only way any suspicion about you is going to be gone is if you take and pass the polygraph.' And that's why I wanted Sergeant Merrill."

Later that night, Shelly went to dinner at Bill and Tammy Hunt's new house. Also there were Jeremy and Tara Miller and their young children.

"We just wanted to find out what caused the fire," said Jeremy. "We all thought he died of carbon monoxide poisoning. He was asleep and he died that way."

After dinner, Jeremy found himself alone with Shelly at the table, and asked if the fire investigators had discovered the cause the fire.

"And she says, 'Oh yeah,'" recalled Miller. "'My dad found something wrong with the electrical outlet behind the bed.' And I thought, 'If her dad, the heating and cooling guy, can find it, why can't the fire marshal?'"

Late that night, after putting his children to bed, Bobby Teets told his wife about his affair with her best friend Shelly Michael.

"It was probably the hardest thing I ever had to tell anybody," he remembered. "She was pretty upset about it. I think she was just kind of betrayed on the fact that her and Shelly were best friends, and we had been married for ten years."

Although she was shocked and hurt by her husband's confession, Kelli would stand by him. But from then on, she rarely spoke to Shelly again.

CHAPTER 28

Seventeen Minutes

That night, West Virginia State Police Sergeant James Merrill was fully briefed on the homicide investigation by Detective Paul Mezzanotte, who sent over the case file.

And By 9:00 a.m. the next morning—December 8—when he arrived at the Public Safety Building, he was well up to speed. There he met with Detective Mezzanotte and Assistant Prosecutor Perri DeChristopher, who told him he would be giving Bobby Teets a pre-polygraph interview in the morning, and seeing Shelly Michael after lunch.

"Ultimately we were going to run Michelle, to see if she had any involvement in it," recalled Sergeant Merrill. "She said she was willing to take a polygraph."

Prior to their arrival, a closed-circuit television camera had been concealed behind a glass mirror in the tiny interview room. This would allow detectives, prosecutors and fire investigators to watch the interrogations live on a monitor only twenty feet away down a hallway. They could then suggest possible questions or different paths the interview should take.

"It was definitely a team effort," explained Assistant Prosecutor Perri DeChristopher. "It was kind of a brainstorm to decide what to do next. What questions to ask, what angle to use."

At 9:40 a.m., Bobby Teets called Detective Paul Mezzanotte, saying he had now told Kelli about the affair. He also reported how Shelly had approached him after the interviews, probing for information about what he had told them.

Now, realizing that he was a prime suspect in a murder investigation, Bobby Teets asked to take a polygraph examination to clear his good name.

And at 10:00 a.m., a shaken-looking Bobby Teets went into his pre-test polygraph interview, before the actual one now scheduled for the following day.

"Was Bobby nervous?" said Sergeant Merrill. "Well absolutely, because he knew he was in the middle of a murder investigation and it scared him. But I found Bobby to be nervous, but very forthcoming."

After signing a polygraph release form, Teets freely discussed his affair with Shelly.

"Bobby understood why he was there," said Sergeant Merrill. "And probably within the first five minutes of the interview, he talked openly about the affair. I think he understood the seriousness of being involved with a murder investigation, and wanted to be straightforward."

Teets then provided a detailed account of everything he'd done the morning of the fire, from waking up at 6:30 a.m., until checking up on the missing Jimmy Michael, and finding his house on fire.

At 12:30 p.m., Sergeant Merrill had completed the pre-interview, telling Teets to come back the following morning for the actual polygraph test.

"Then, right before he left," said Merrill, "we had him sit out in the lobby. And that's when Michelle Michael came down, and they saw each other. Then she went into the interview."

At 12:38 p.m., Detective Paul Mezzanotte sat down with Shelly Michael in the cramped interview room. A few yards away, behind a partition, watching on a monitor were Sergeant James Merrill, Detective Chris Dalton, Assistant

Prosecutor Perri DeChristopher and Fire Investigator Lieutenant Ken Tennant.

An hour earlier, Detective Mezzanotte had received the video from the Chicago Marriott hotel showing Shelly and Bobby Teets at the check-in desk, acting like teenage lovers.

The detective began by reading Shelly her Miranda rights to remain silent, which she waived. He then asked what she wanted to talk to him about.

"You told me that the fire was set, and that it wasn't an accident," she said. "I mean, it's not set in yet."

She said she had spoken to her mother-in-law and Renee Del Viscio, who both thought it "absurd" and "crazy."

"I mean, he's such a great guy," she said, "we just can't imagine it happening."

Detective Mezzanotte said he was now at liberty to disclose slightly more information than yesterday. And he would be even more forthcoming after the ATF came back with their scientific findings.

Shelly said she had lain awake all night thinking about yesterday's interview, unable to believe anyone could have deliberately set the house alight and killed Jimmy.

"I have questions," she said. "I know what's happened. I know how he died and all that. And I don't understand why. Why would he be in bed with somebody setting a fire in my house? He wouldn't do that."

"Why was he in bed?" asked the detective. "That's a question we really don't have an answer for. And that's going to come from the toxicology and autopsy report."

Then the detective asked again who would have any motive to kill Jimmy.

"I can't think of anybody," replied Shelly. "I mean, honestly, Paul, no one disliked him. I mean, not enough to do something so horrendous. I'm at a loss. I have no idea."

"Did Jim have a girlfriend?" asked Mezzanotte.

"I can't imagine that, no," she said. "He seemed pretty faithful. I never doubted his trust."

"I'm not doubting your trust, OK?" said the detective.

"Because we're at a weird state here, where we spend more time together than I do with my wife. So we're kind of married. It's all right. It's my job, and she understands that. We're married now, kind of how this is looking. If Jim wasn't unfaithful, we gotta explore this love. Is love a motive to this anywhere?"

"I can't imagine that it is," replied Shelly. "I mean, I loved him. He loved me. I mean . . ."

Then Detective Mezzanotte returned to Bobby Teets.

"We've got to go into the circle with you," he said. "We have to put you in the middle . . . and we've got to draw a circle around you, and we've gotta say, 'If love is not a key to this with Jim, is love a key to this with you?'"

"Right," replied Shelly. "There's no way. I have no feelings for anyone but my husband."

Then the detective asked about her sex life with Jimmy.

"I thought it was OK," she said. "He wanted it more often, obviously."

Moving on, Detective Mezzanotte wondered how she would financially benefit from Jimmy's death. Shelly said that their life insurance representative was at the hotel a couple of days earlier, saying Jimmy had a $500,000 life insurance policy.

"So, I mean," she said, "I guess that's a lot of money."

He then asked who else would benefit apart from her, and she said Jimmy's ex-wife Stephanie Estel, as well as their children.

"Love or money is the two motives for this crime," said the detective. "That's how it is with every fire."

He then asked if she had spoken to Bobby Teets, after yesterday's interview, and she admitted doing so while dropping Kylie off at his house.

"I told him you were asking some crazy questions about us being more than friends," she said. "And I didn't understand why."

Changing direction, Detective Mezzanotte asked about the drugs that she worked with at the hospital.

"You ever bring anything home from the hospital?" he

asked. "Because that's going to be something that they're going to ask me at the toxicology interview."

Shelly denied ever taking any drugs from Ruby Memorial, unless they had been prescribed to her.

"So," she fished, "with that toxicology stuff, are you looking to see if someone poisoned him?"

"We're just looking to see what's in his system," replied Mezzanotte, without elaborating.

He said he had interviewed "countless people" about the state of their marriage, and what could possibly have happened to him.

"What do you think I'm hearing?" he asked.

"The only thing I've really heard," she replied, "is that he might have committed suicide and set the fire, which is physically impossible, isn't it?"

She said she could never imagine Jimmy killing himself, as he was a Christian and believed that suicides go to hell.

"He is a kind of grouchy-natured guy," she said. "He'd be in a good mood with everybody, and then when he got home, whatever was wrong in his day, he'd take it out on me."

She said when she had first met Jimmy he had "frowned a lot," and although "kind of mopey," she never saw that as "a red flag."

"He just wasn't real bubbly and happy, and energetic and smiling all the time," she stated, "but I just saw that as his personality."

Now Mezzanotte decided to call in Sergeant James Merrill, who was watching on a monitor outside.

"I'm going to take a break," he announced. "I need to talk to Sergeant Merrill of the state police, because he is talking to Bobby. I need you to look me in the eyes, and I want you to tell me what your relationship is with Bobby. I don't want you to cover anything up. I don't want you to lie."

"We're just friends," she replied.

"Just friends? Period."

"Right."

Then the detective left the interview room for a couple of minutes. On his return he told her that Sergeant Merrill had put up a "Do Not Disturb" sign on the door of his interview room.

"So he must be talking to Bobby about something," Mezzanotte told her. "He'll be in in a minute."

As the West Virginia State Police's main polygraph coordinator, 42-year-old Sergeant James Merrill averages 150 interviews a year. But in his twenty years in law enforcement, he'd never come across anyone quite like Shelly Michael.

"Most of the cases I get involved with are high-profile," he said. "Murders, arsons and sexual assaults. But she was very cold. There was no reaction."

Carefully watching Paul Mezzanotte's interview outside on a monitor, Sergeant Merrill noticed how she had tried to manipulate him and control the interview.

"I could see her just trying to lean on Paul's weaknesses," he said. "Paul comes off as being a very nice country boy. Just a nice police officer. Nice guy. And she was wanting Paul to believe her so much."

It had been arranged with the prosecutors that Sergeant Merrill would give Shelly a pre-test interview, before taking the actual polygraph test. But as soon as he sat down at the small table next to Detective Mezzanotte across from her, it was obvious she now felt threatened.

"Honey, I know you're going through a hard time right now," said Merrill, "and as a polygraph examiner, I have to understand that, OK? I'm not an investigator like Paul is. I do something completely different . . . but we are able to share information back and forth."

He then told her a polygraph test was a lengthy process, and once they started, she would not be able to leave. Shelly said she was supposed to pick up the kids from school.

"I'm kind of torn," she said. "I want to stay here and do this, but at the same time, I don't want to freak out the kids."

Then Detective Mezzanotte offered to call Rob Angus to see if he could collect them, and went out, leaving her alone with Sergeant Merrill.

"What's going through your mind right now?" the polygraph examiner asked her.

"I'm just so confused," she said. "There's so much going on. Now they're trying to tell me that someone did this. That it wasn't an accident. I just can't accept that."

She said she had not been sleeping since the fire, alternating between missing Jimmy and wondering who could have killed him.

Then Mezzanotte returned, saying that Angus would collect the children. Shelly signed the polygraph release form and the pre-test began.

"The actual pre-test is not designed to get accusatory," explained Merrill. "It's to have that person tell their side of the story."

Sergeant Merrill then began by asking some general questions about her health, and anything else that might affect the test reading. She then asked why they wanted to give her a lie detector test.

"That's a good question," said Merrill. "There's a lot of information that may tend to point to you as a 'suspect,' do you understand that? So we'll do a polygraph, to try and get you eliminated from this."

"Yeah," she replied.

At 2:15 p.m., Sergeant Merrill began questioning Shelly Michael about her life history, and her relationships. For the next half-hour she answered highly personal questions about her family, her past relationships and her first marriage.

Then Sergeant Merrill asked what type of person she was.

"I value honesty a lot," she answered. "I've always tried to be very honest. You know, I always told the kids, my husband and everybody—honesty comes first."

When asked to rate her honesty on a scale of 10, she replied, "Nine out of ten—ninety-nine percent."

The sergeant then asked if she had ever lied to make herself look better or get out of trouble.

"Well, I don't know what you mean by 'lie,'" she replied. "I mean, I wear make-up, that's fake—or push-up bras."

And when he told her that he meant saying something that was untrue, she said, "No, never."

He then inquired what kind of person would do something like this, and what should their punishment be?

"A real psycho," Shelly answered. "Go to jail forever, for life. It's hard for me to say that, because I can't imagine somebody doing this to him."

"Do you understand that the police look at you as a suspect?"

"I do now," said Shelly.

He led her through her movements the morning of the fire. And she again claimed to have only gone out to her car just after 8:00 a.m. to pick up her pager, coming straight back into the hospital.

Sergeant Merrill then informed her that hospital surveillance video existed showing her car leaving the hospital parking lot.

"My car?" she replied incredulously. "I didn't leave the hospital."

Then Shelly changed her story slightly to accommodate this new information.

"It was raining hard," she explained. "So I was going to move my car to the garage."

She now claimed to have moved her Ford Expedition into the garage, when she realized she had forgotten her staff parking card. So not wanting to pay the four-dollar parking charge, she went back out to the car park.

"I thought, 'Well I'll just forget that idea,'" she told the investigators. "I went back to park, but the rain was pouring down and I couldn't find my umbrella."

Sergeant Merrill then asked what route she had taken. Shelly explained how she had returned to find her original parking place occupied, driving to another staff lot on the other side of the hospital, so she could park nearer to the entrance and avoid getting wet.

"I'd just forgot I'd even moved it," she said, explaining why she had never mentioned it before.

"Let me ask you this," inquired Sergeant Merrill. "Did you go by your house?"

Shelly shook her head, saying she was quite certain she had not.

"Could anybody have seen you go by the house?" he said. "I'm just asking."

"I didn't leave, so . . ." she replied.

He then asked about her relationship with Bobby Teets, and once again she insisted it was purely "platonic."

"Why would Bobby say that you [had an affair]?" he asked her.

"I don't know," she replied.

"You know that I just interviewed him," Sergeant Merrill continued, "and he told me a lot of things, OK? Why do you think he would say that?"

"Saying what?"

"That he had an affair with you?"

"I can't imagine him saying that . . . because it's not true."

Shelly stuck to her story, insisting that she had no idea why Teets would claim they were sexually involved. Then Merrill asked her if she remembered Bobby's visit to her house the weekend before the fire.

"Did you guys have sex?" he asked.

Shelly shook her head.

Sergeant Merrill then asked if she knew how the polygraph test worked. When she said no, he explained that it worked off the body's autonomic nervous system. He gave the example of a driver going into a bad skid in snow and ice conditions, asking what she would do and how her body would react.

"First, panic," she replied. "Grab the wheel, turn it. You get an adrenaline rush."

"Why do you think your body is going through that?"

"Stress," she answered.

He then explained how the body releases certain chemicals when a person lies, causing a chain reaction of the autonomic nervous system. The mind cannot lie, he told her, and cannot release the chemicals, if it knows it did not do something. And they will also not be released if it is unsure or does not know something.

"So if I ask you a question," he continued, "and I hate to ask you this, but did you cause the death of your husband? Your mind knows whether you've done it or you didn't do it. Do you understand that?"

Then he assured her that if she answered all his questions truthfully, she would pass the polygraph examination.

"You're extremely nervous," he observed. "That's called 'jail nerves tension' within the polygraph field."

He then suggested a ten-minute break, so she could use the restroom, and he could type out his pre-test questions.

As Shelly got up to leave the interview room, she said she felt "flustered," voicing some concerns about the results.

"I'm afraid," she said, "it'll say, 'You're lying,' and I'm not."

"Listen to me," said Sergeant Merrill. "I've never made a mistake on a polygraph examination. If I called somebody as telling the truth, it'll never come back and show that they were actually lying to me. I never made a mistake. The accuracy on a polygraph examination is actually ninety-eight percent scientifically. That's fairly high."

It was almost 4:00 p.m. when Sergeant Merrill began hooking Shelly Michael up to the polygraph machine. First he placed two tubes around her thoracic and abdominal area, to measure any changes in breathing caused by the release of chemicals. Then he put a cardio cuff around her arm, measuring blood volume, which is also affected by the chemicals.

Lastly he put on two finger attachments to measure electrical skin activity.

"By looking at these three symptoms," he told her, "I am able to tell scientifically."

After reviewing all the questions he would ask her, Sergeant Merrill ran a polygraph acquaintance test, to ensure that his equipment was working. On a sheet of paper he wrote down the numbers 1 to 10, and gave it to her. Then he asked her to pick a number without looking at him, and circle it, fold up the paper and put it in her pocket.

"I wanted her to lie to me about that number," he explained.

He told her he would read out the numbers, and to answer "No" for each of them, so she would be lying about her preselected number.

"My goal at the end of it is to tell her what number she actually picked, without me knowing," said Merrill, "just from her reaction on the polygraph."

After reading out all the numbers, he told her that she had picked the number 5 and then lied about it—and for the first time since he'd arrived, Shelly Michael looked visibly shaken.

"I basically got her number," he said. "She would not have anything to do with the polygraph at that point."

Then, as he was detaching the equipment, Shelly suddenly admitted to an affair with Bobby Teets.

"She just came out and said it," Sergeant Merrill recalled. "It was almost like one of those slips. She just says, 'Listen, I'm not taking your polygraph, but I'll be honest with you. I did have the affair.'"

But, although Shelly was unwilling to take a polygraph at that time, she did agree to stay and answer more questions.

"I said, 'Do you understand you are a person of interest in this investigation?'" said Sergeant Merrill. "And she said, 'Yes.'"

Then he left the interview room to consult with Detective Mezzanotte, Perri DeChristopher and the other investigators. They told him to go back in and try to get as many details as he could.

For the next two hours, Sergeant Merrill, who was later joined by Detective Mezzanotte, went for a full confession of guilt.

"Now she wasn't going to take a polygraph," said Sergeant Merrill. "My goal was to put her back at the house.

We knew that her husband's house was set on fire, it was arson and he had died. And we started becoming accusatory at this point."

She was then told there was an eyewitness who had seen her pull out of her driveway at 8:20 a.m. the morning of the fire. But Shelly registered absolutely no reaction to learning this.

"That caught me off guard," said Merrill. "She would look at you, but it was a cold stare. I mean, it was just weird. There was no reaction."

Shelly continued stonewalling the investigators, refusing to admit ever leaving the hospital grounds.

"OK," said Paul Mezzanotte, who had now taken over the interviewing, "how do we explain this guy that is putting you at your house?"

"I have no idea," came her icy reply.

Then Detective Mezzanotte slowly started feeding her more evidence that the police had, to try to get at the truth.

"Did I tell you I was holding back a little information?" he told her. "Jim was dead before the fire started. The CO test you asked about? It's negative. Period. No soot. No deformity in the windpipe. Nothing in the lungs. No CO in the blood."

"OK," she replied flatly, her cool demeanor even surprising the experienced West Virginia State Police officer.

"We're basically telling her we believe her husband is murdered," said Merrill. "And most people would react to that. But there was nothing."

Then Detective Mezzanotte tried another tack. He told Shelly that his professional credibility was now on the line, asking what he was going to tell the prosecutor about his progress in solving her husband's murder, and finding out who set the fire.

"[This] is probably the biggest tragedy in the city of Morgantown this year," he told her. "This fire and your husband dying. And I'm going to say, 'OK, Miss Prosecutor, here's my theory of the crime—she gets to work, and I catch her in a lie, because she says she goes out to get her pager. But I've got video of her leaving the hospital. And she goes home, because I have an eyewitness that puts her at her house.' And they're going to say, 'Oh really?'"

He then pondered the prosecutor's response, after hearing that Shelly had refused to say why she'd gone home. And then the prosecutor will learn that federal fire experts have ruled it arson, and the medical examiner has proved Jimmy was dead before the fire even started.

"So I'm going to tell them about this," he said. "And then they're going to say, 'Well, what do you think about Shelly?' And I'm supposed to tell them, 'You know what? I don't know why she went home to the house, and I don't know who started the fire. But she said she didn't.'"

He told her that the prosecutor would think him an "absolute buffoon," probably taking the case away from him and reassigning it to a state trooper from Charleston, who had never heard of Shelly Michael.

"And then you're going to have to go through this again, with somebody you don't know," he warned her. "With somebody who is going to look at you as a monster."

Suddenly Sergeant Merrill stepped in.

"Can I interrupt you for a moment," he said, "and ask you something very specific? You talked about getting in the car, and going up to the parking garage. Tell me how you did it."

Sergeant Merrill then brought out a previously prepared portfolio book, breaking down the hospital surveillance video frame-by-frame. And as Shelly attempted to demonstrate how she had moved her car from one parking lot to one on the other side of the hospital, the detectives demonstrated that it was impossible for her to have done so.

They relentlessly kept up the pressure on her to say where she had gone between 8:10 a.m. and 8:27 a.m. But Shelly stubbornly stuck to her story, maintaining that she had never left the hospital grounds.

"Seventeen minutes in an investigation of this magnitude is like seventeen hours," Mezzanotte observed.

He then asked how long it had taken her to drive home from the hospital.

"Ten minutes," she answered.

"How long?" asked Sergeant Merrill suspiciously.

"Four or five minutes," she conceded.

Then Detective Mezzanotte informed her that he had timed the journey himself just to see. He had started off from her parking spot at 8:11 a.m., arriving at 545 Killarney Drive by 8:15 a.m. He'd waited in her driveway for three or four minutes, before returning to the hospital and parking in the staff lot.

"Guess what?" said Mezzanotte. "I actually beat the seventeen minutes."

The two investigators then pondered what a jury would make of her unaccounted seventeen minutes. They speculated that it would be plenty of time for her to have gone home, set the fire and then come back to the hospital.

For the next few minutes they fired a barrage of questions at her from every angle, with Mezzanotte playing the sympathetic friend and Merrill the objective outsider.

"He's your lifeline," Merrill told her. "He wants to believe you. I've seen this guy go home after a case and literally cry."

Finally, after two hours and seventeen minutes of questioning, Shelly Michael blinked, admitting that she had left the hospital that morning.

"I drove past Suncrest," she conceded. "Every . . . On occasion in the morning, ummm, I either have to meet my ex-husband or his wife at Suncrest Middle and give Alec his homework or his backpack, or pick up Kylie and drop her off at North, or, whatever. That's the usual pattern. I totally forgot about it but, I guess, yeah, I guess, I drove past Suncrest."

And she explained that the reason she hadn't mentioned it before, was that she was scared her boss would find out and she'd get into trouble.

"Did you go into the school?" asked Detective Mezzanotte.

"No," she replied.

"So you didn't sign in?"

"No, I didn't get out of my car, I just drove by."

"Did you drive by your house?" questioned Sergeant Merrill.

"Yeah, I did," Shelly admitted.

"Why'd you stop?" asked the sergeant.

"I just realized it."

"Why'd you stop at your house?"

"I was going to get something, umm, that I needed."

"What'd you get?"

"I didn't get anything," she said coldly. "I didn't even go in. I just pulled into the driveway, Opened my door, and then shut my door and left."

Now Shelly claimed that she'd only gone home to ensure that she had everything she needed to fax for the embroidery machine application.

"Here's a question," asked Mezzanotte. "Why didn't you go in the house?"

"Because I realized I had the stuff with me," she replied. "And I keep playing over and over in my mind—did I not see smoke, or why couldn't I have gone in and checked?"

The investigators now tried to get Shelly to admit that she had gone inside the house, asking if she was afraid of what she'd seen. But she obstinately stuck to her story.

"I didn't tell you that I left the parking lot," she explained, "because I was afraid I'd get into trouble with my boss, OK? I didn't ask him if I could leave work."

"Are you afraid you're going to be arrested?" said Sergeant Merrill. "You are lying about seventeen minutes. He has told you that your husband was murdered . . . and the house was intentionally set on fire. This was no accident. You are the number-one suspect."

At 6:30 p.m., Shelly Michael left the Morgantown Detective Division after more than six hours of intense questioning over two days. She had agreed to come back the following morning at 9:00 a.m., and take a polygraph test.

"I hope I'm the first one to run over," Detective Mezzanotte told her, "and give you a hug and tell you that I'm sorry for treating you like an asshole. And that everything is OK, and you're not involved in this."

Finally on her way out, he asked if she had anything else that would make him believe her.

"I mean," she said, "the only things I held back from you was the Bobby thing, and being at the house. I guess in my mind, I was trying to comfort myself with the fact that I wasn't there. Because how could I not go in? You know, I just feel the guilt of he's in there and I don't notice anything. I don't go in and check. You know what I mean? I just . . ."

Later, investigators and prosecutors met to discuss the interview, which they had all been watching on a monitor. And no one could quite believe Shelly Michael's arrogance and ice-cool nerve.

"She seemed very cold and very calculated," said Detective Mezzanotte, "and just continued to play the game of needing to know what was going on."

Both he and Sergeant Merrill were exhausted after all the frustrating hours they'd spent interviewing her.

"It wears you out," said Merrill. "Because you are going over something over and over that just doesn't make sense. It's intense and I know it's got to be wearing her out too. I interview maybe twenty to twenty-five murderers a year, and I'd have to put her to the top of being emotionless, cold."

That night, an agitated Shelly Michael drove to her father's house in Clarksburg.

"She said, 'The police are trying to scare me,'" recalled Kathi Goots. "That's when we told her, 'Just don't talk to anybody. We need to get you an attorney.' And we got recommendations."

CHAPTER 29

"Maybe That Iron Fell Over"

Early Friday morning, Detective Paul Mezzanotte received a call from Tom Dyer, a prominent Clarksburg defense attorney. Dyer informed him that from now on he would be representing Shelly Michael, and on his advice, she would no longer be talking to the police.

"I was awfully disappointed to learn," said Dyer, "that she'd gone in and done six, seven or eight hours of interviews without counsel. I told them the polygraph is out of the question."

With over thirty years of experience in criminal law, Tom Dyer had been recommended by a Goots family member.

"I have represented triple murderers and Mafia figures," explained Dyer. "But this little girl's story kind of spooked me."

The boyish-faced, silver-haired lawyer in his late forties, runs Dyer Law with his legal partner and wife Mary, who resembles Mary Tyler Moore.

"He's tough . . . really tough," reads their double page advertisement in the Monongalia County Yellow Pages. "She's as smart as they come."

Tom Dyer proudly boasts of being the eighth generation of his family from Clarksburg. His father started an insurance business, which his twin brother Tim now runs next door to the law offices on Washington Avenue, in Clarksburg.

Growing up, Tom Dyer loved watching *Perry Mason* shows on television, and it captured his imagination.

"I thought, 'Maybe it's fun to outsmart the other side,'" he explained.

While still in high school, Dyer attended the trial of a local underworld figure, who was being defended by a friend of his father.

"He won and was found not guilty," said Dyer. "And I don't think there was any question about his guilt. I thought that was outrageously fascinating."

A few years later, while studying accounting at West Virginia University, he decided to switch to law. And after getting his law degree, he returned to Clarksburg, going to work for a law firm owned by a family friend.

"I never set out to be a criminal lawyer," he explained. "It was the only way a young lawyer, right out of law school, could get any experience in the courtroom."

Eventually he founded his own law offices, and over the years he has carved out quite a reputation for himself.

"In the northern half of West Virginia," he said, "I'm probably *the* most recognizable lawyer in the game."

And although he had defended many accused murderers and other high-profile clients, nothing would compare to the national prominence he would soon attain with Shelly Michael.

At 11:00 a.m., Friday morning, Bobby Teets was given a polygraph test by Sergeant James Merrill. After signing his Miranda rights and polygraph release forms, Teets was hooked up to the machine. He was then asked a set of relevant questions, employing the 2005 Air Force Modified General Questions Test—the standard polygraph test used by the federal government.

"Did you plan with anyone to set fire to Jimmy's residence?" asked Merrill.

"No," replied Teets.

"Did you cause the death of Jimmy?"

"No."

"Did you set fire to Jimmy's residence?"

"No."

"Do you know for sure who set fire to Jimmy's residence?"

"No."

Then, after reviewing the data from the polygraph machine, Sergeant Merrill concluded that Bobby Teets had shown signs of deception, and failed him.

"There's a [few] inconsistencies at first," recalled Sergeant Merrill, "but then we got those pretty much cleared up."

Teets was then given a post-test interview by Sergeant Merrill and Detective Mezzanotte, convincing them he was telling the truth. They concluded that the unfortunate Bobby Teets felt responsible for Jimmy's death, because of the affair. He also feared Shelly had killed Jimmy and set the fire, so they could be together.

Ultimately, after passing a further polygraph after Christmas, Bobby Teets would be officially cleared by investigators.

On Saturday, December 10, Shelly Michael ran into Kelli Teets at cheerleading practice. It was the first time the two women had seen each other since Bobby Teets had confessed.

Shelly immediately came over to her, asking what Bobby had told her. But Kelli refused to discuss it, saying that with her husband still under suspicion, she could not talk.

Soon afterwards, Shelly arrived at Mountaineer Home Medical, asking for Teets. But as soon as he heard she was there, he sneaked out to avoid seeing her.

On Monday morning, Kelli Teets called Detective Mezzanotte, reporting that Shelly had been fishing for information. The detective thanked her for telling him, warning her that Bobby must now be truthful for his own protection.

"Kelli Teets agreed that this was very important," Mezzanotte later noted. "[She] advised that she would talk with her husband, and that they wanted to do the right thing."

In Morgantown, everybody knew everybody, so it was surprising that so far nothing had leaked to the press about the fire being suspicious. On Tuesday, December 13, *The Dominion Post* carried a brief routine update, its first coverage on the fatal fire in ten days.

"The cause of the house fire last month that killed James A. Michael," read the three-paragraph story hidden away on page 11, "remains under investigation."

At the end of the story, there was an appeal to anyone with any information to contact Morgantown police.

Although Shelly Michael was under suspicion, it did not stop her visiting the burned-out remains of her house. Over the next several weeks, she entered at least three times, with her friend and neighbor Deborah Harris.

"The first time I went in with her," remembered Harris, "she just kind of looked around and said, 'Oh, I really shouldn't have come here.'"

A few days later, Shelly called to see if her husband Dan could help Mike Goots remove a large desk from the house that afternoon. A few hours later, Deborah arrived home to see Shelly's Ford Expedition and her father's vehicle parked outside 545 Killarney Drive. As her elder daughter and her boyfriend were at her house, she asked them to go across the road and help Shelly's father move the desk.

"So the three of us walked over," said Harris, "and she came bouncing out of the kitchen. 'Hey, how are you?' Like it was a summer day and nothing was wrong, and it didn't bother her to be there at all. I thought that was odd."

At 11:25 a.m. on Tuesday, December 13, Shelly Michael arrived at the State Farm Insurance office in Morgantown, for a routine interview about the fire. Jimmy had taken out a homeowner's insurance policy, and Shelly now stood to receive almost $260,000 in compensation. Eleven days earlier,

State Farm fire investigator Robert Stewart had ruled the cause undetermined, after inspecting the fire scene.

"I explained to her that we were gathering facts on the cause of the loss," said State Farm claims representative John White, who interviewed Shelly. "And just an overall of what was in the fire and what occurred at the house."

With Shelly's permission, White taped the twenty-minute interview, running through her personal details and asking what she had done the morning of the fire. Then he asked if she had been inside 545 Killarney Drive since the fire.

"I drove over to the back side of the house," she told him, "and my son and aunt went in and got a couple of things. But I haven't gone through it, no."

She said they had removed some clothing, keepsakes and trophies, as well as the home computer, which she needed for pictures of Jimmy at the funeral.

Towards the end of the interview, White asked if she had any ideas on how the fire could have started. And Shelly told him she was "worried" that her iron could have caused it, saying she'd almost written to the manufacturer in the past, as the automatic shutoff was faulty.

"You know how you have automatic shutoff?" she asked him. "Well, this one time I was up there. And I had gone downstairs to do something else. The iron was on the ironing board still, and it had shut off. And I had accidentally knocked it over, and it turned itself back on, by getting knocked or bumped . . . and it started to burn my carpet real quick, and I picked it up."

Shelly said at first she thought it was a "fluke," but since then, she'd realized it was not.

"I noticed if I'm ironing and I stop," she explained, "then I go do something else and it shuts off. All I have to do is pick it up and lay it back down on the clothes or ironing board, and it turns itself back on."

She told White she'd been "brainstorming like crazy" since the fire about it.

"That is the main thing that keeps popping into my head," she said, "is, maybe that iron fell over. It was windy that day . . . we had the window open, because it was kinda warm . . . I don't know . . . I mean, I just thought . . . I keep thinking maybe that fell over onto the bed or, I mean, the carpet or something and . . ."

White then asked if the iron had been plugged into an electrical socket, but Shelly was uncertain.

At 11:45 a.m., the interview finished and Shelly Michael returned to the Morgan Hotel with a stack of personal property inventory forms, which she would spend the next few days carefully filling out.

At 3:15 p.m., Detective Paul Mezzanotte conducted a telephone interview with Jimmy Michael's oldest friend Kerri Whitacre. She said they talked "religiously" every Tuesday, and had last spoken a week before his death.

The family counselor told the detective that Jimmy often discussed his marital problems, and she would advise him. And he had mentioned that Shelly wanted another child, although he had had a vasectomy.

"Kerri Whitacre felt this was causing problems in the marriage," Detective Mezzanotte noted. "He told her that Michelle Michael did not want to work at home at all, and that she wanted to be a stay-at-home mother."

Whitacre also described how she had dashed to Morgantown after hearing about the fire, and her astonishment when Shelly greeted her with the words, "Did you get that outfit at B. Moss?" She also remembered Shelly saying she had called her home phone at 7:30 a.m. the day of the fire, and it had been busy.

"[She] stated in her opinion as a counselor," wrote Mezzanotte in his report, "that Michelle Michael was not reacting normally to the situation. She was not grieving right and did not cry until the final gravesite service."

On Wednesday morning, Kelli Teets telephoned Detective Mezzanotte from work, asking if she and Bobby could meet him as soon as possible. At 5:00 p.m., they arrived at Morgantown Police Department.

"Robert Teets shared the following remarks," Detective Mezzanotte later noted. "Michelle Michael would often tell him she did not want to share her husband, she did not want to share Robert. And she always stated, you never know what can happen in the future."

Bobby Teets said that his first thought on reaching the fire was that Jimmy had found out about the affair and committed suicide. He also confided that prior to the fire, Shelly had never said she loved him, but expressed guilt about Kelli. He asked to take a second polygraph examination.

Earlier that day, Mezzanotte heard from the DEA Laboratory in Maryland that the syringe found in the kitchen sink at the Michaels' house contained huge amounts of ibuprofen, as well as an unidentifiable pink liquid.

When the lead detective spoke to DEA Agent Steven Demchuk, he learned that it was possible to overdose on ibuprofen, although it would take an enormous amount. Demchuk also said it was the first time he had ever seen the drug in a syringe.

CHAPTER 30

God's Way of Punishing Her

On Thursday, December 15, Shelly Michael arrived at her new attorney Tom Dyer's law office in Clarksburg. After she walked in and introduced herself, Dyer asked her to take a seat in his waiting room.

"After about five minutes, I felt kind of rude leaving her out there in the waiting area by herself," he recalled. "I said, 'Michelle, why don't you come back and sit in my comfy chair back here, and I'll join you in a few minutes?'"

Dyer had left a half-finished Coca-Cola on the table, near where she was sitting. When he walked in several minutes later, he was going to finish it.

"But I looked at her and I looked back at the Coke," he said. "I kept thinking, 'Damn it. She's been sitting in here for three or four minutes by herself. I'm not quite sure.'"

Dyer had already heard Shelly referred to as a "sociopath," and decided not to risk drinking the Coke.

"God bless," he said. "I certainly want to give this girl every benefit before I really get to know her, but I'll be damned if I pick that Coke up. It's terrible."

And that day, when he sat across the table from Shelly Michael, he thought of Charles Manson.

"The first thing that catches your attention are her Charles Manson eyes," he said. "She's the only woman I ever met in my life with absolutely black hole eyes. Look right into her eyes and tell me it doesn't send a shiver up your spine."

But over the next few weeks, he developed "a tremendously fond relationship" with his new client, who he soon discovered could be very challenging.

"Shelly is a difficult personality type to be around," he said. "She is a compulsive, driven, obsessive person. Very energetic and extremely intelligent. I don't know what her IQ is, but it's certainly greater than mine."

That week, Ruth Michael arrived from Cumberland to help her daughter-in-law find a new apartment. It had now been more than two weeks since the fire, and Shelly wanted to get her life back on track and move out of the Morgan Hotel.

"I stayed overnight," recalled Ruth. "We went to look at some apartments."

Shelly soon settled for a smart townhouse rental on Meadow Ridge Drive, in Morgantown, only five minutes away from Killarney Drive. And for a little extra spending money, Shelly sold her late husband's 1988 Ford truck to her uncle, forging Jimmy's signature to transfer the title, backdating it to November 27, 2005—two days before the fire.

On Friday, December 16, Renee Del Viscio arrived from Philadelphia.

"I went back to help her move into her new place," Renee said. "And we did some shopping to buy basic necessities—cups, plates and bowls."

One night, over dinner, the subject of Bobby Teets came up, and Shelly confessed she had slept with him.

"She did admit to me that something had happened," recalled Renee. "And that's when I told her it was obvious to me."

Shelly explained how Teets would always "flirt" with her, telling her she looked beautiful.

"This would even happen at their children's football games," said Renee. "He was just kind of a flirt. According to Shelly, nothing had happened until they went to Chicago.

There were drinks involved, there was a hot tub involved, and things progressed from there. And I was told that was the first, last and only time it happened. It was a one-time thing. They talked about it and realized it was a silly mistake, and that was it. Period. And that's what was told to me."

Shelly then questioned if the fire and Jimmy's death might have been God's way of punishing her for what she had done.

Although she thought it unconscionable, Renee never had the heart to tell her. "I felt as though she was hurting enough," she explained. "I didn't feel the need to be that harsh."

The shock of learning about Shelly's infidelity would be the first in a series of revelations Renee would soon learn about her oldest friend. It would make her wonder if she'd ever known the real Shelly Michael.

"In all of my years with her, I always thought that I knew her," said Renee. "But obviously, looking back, so many things have happened in her life that she just kept to herself, that I just never knew about or would find out about by accident after the fact."

And after that trip to Morgantown, their friendship would never be the same again.

"Once she admitted to me about the whole Bobby situation," Renee said, "I didn't know how to proceed with my relationship with her. Because I just found it to be so despicable."

The next day, after moving into the new Meadow Ridge Drive house, Shelly threw her son Alec a 13th birthday party at the Wisp ski resort in McHenry, Maryland.

Ruth and Denny Michael attended, and could not help noticing how Michael Goots was avoiding them.

"We went up and her dad was there," said Ruth. "Every time I went to sit beside her dad, he gets up to leave."

Throughout the week leading up to Christmas, the investigation into the fire and Jimmy Michael's death proceeded slowly and methodically. On Thursday, December 22,

Detective Paul Mezzanotte wrote out a search warrant affidavit, allowing police and fire investigators to return to 545 Killarney Drive to gather more evidence.

The next morning, Monongalia Prosecutors Marcia Ashdown and Perri DeChristopher joined Detective Mezzanotte for a conference call to Charleston with the state's chief medical examiner, Dr. James Kaplan; Dr. Hamada Mahmaud, who had performed the autopsy; and Chief Toxicologist Dr. James Kraner. "Detective Mezzanotte had a list of drugs . . . that [Shelly Michael] had access to," said Dr. Kraner, "and that we needed to pay special attention to." Prior to the call, Detective Mezzanotte had faxed over a nine-page list that had included the paralytic drug vecuronium, first mentioned by Rob Angus.

During the conference call, the doctors restated that Jimmy Michael had been dead before the fire, as there were no traces of carbon monoxide in the body. His heart was also in good condition, so he couldn't have died accidentally of a heart attack.

They also confirmed having Jimmy's heart and liver, as well as samples of bile, blood and vitreous fluid, which they were sending to the National Medical Services (NMS) for additional testing.

At 1:40 p.m., Detective Mezzanotte received another telephone call from Shelly Michael's new attorney Tom Dyer.

"He advised that [she] had invoked her Miranda rights," said Detective Mezzanotte. "That he wanted to meet with [me] to go over the case, and stated, 'I will point you in the right direction.'"

The following afternoon, investigators carried out a two-hour search of the fire scene. At 1:10 p.m., Detectives Mezzanotte and Dalton met Morgantown fire investigator Lieutenant Ken Tennant and ATF Agent Rick Summerfield, outside 545 Killarney Drive.

It was now three weeks since they had last been inside the fire scene, and all the accumulated snow and ice made it impossible for them to get on their hands and knees to carry out a thorough search.

"It had been snowing quite a bit," recalled Agent Summerfield, who was taking his first look at the fire scene, "and the roof was off the house at that point, because of the fire. Pretty much everything in the bedroom was ice-encrusted from the snow building up there and melting and refreezing. And we just couldn't do anything significant that day."

But they were able to find the flat iron that Shelly Michael had claimed was faulty on the bedroom floor at the foot of the burned-out bed.

"That's a heat-producing appliance, and could potentially be a fire cause," Summerfield later testified. "And it was easily retrievable. I cut the branch circuit wiring, which is the wiring in the walls . . . on either side of the receptacle that the iron was plugged into."

They carefully removed the iron, still plugged into the electric outlet with all wall wiring completely intact, for later processing by the state-of-the-art ATF Fire Research Laboratory in Beltsville, Maryland.

After inspecting the fire scene, Agent Summerfield requested further federal ATF support and expert assistance.

"The scene on Killarney was, from a fire development standpoint, really unusual," he explained. "The fire behaved strangely at that scene. It had obviously burned for a long period of time, yet it never escaped the master bedroom, at least until very late in its development."

He too thought it strange that, although the bedroom and everything in it had been completely destroyed, there was very little damage to the rest of the house.

"There was a great deal of energy released in that room," he said. "It was a pretty intense fire. But you could go down the hallway on the second floor and pretty much the only damage was smoke and soot deposits on the wall, about four or five feet off the floor.

"If that hallway had been exposed to fire very long, then it would have been severely damaged, and the house would have probably collapsed. The fire would have progressed very rapidly."

But as that had not happened, he deduced that it must have been an oxygen-deprived fire that had smoldered for a long time.

"The fire burned very completely in the master suite," he said, "but not outside it. The roof above the master suite was destroyed. The explanation for that is, the fire had to have progressed over a long period of time in a ventilation-limited manner."

Surveying the damage, Agent Summerfield realized that he was not equipped to calculate how long the fire would have smoldered before it finally found enough oxygen to re-ignite and do its real damage.

"The reason I contacted the ATF Lab," said the agent, "was to calculate the ventilation limit—that's how much the air will let the fire burn. I wanted a reliable answer, so I contacted our engineers, who are specifically trained for that."

While the investigators were inside 545 Killarney Drive, a reporter and photographer from *The Dominion Post* arrived at the scene, having been tipped off by a neighbor. Although none of the on-scene investigators there would talk to the reporter, Morgantown Fire Chief David Fetty did later.

"We're still not sure how the fire started," he said, "so they're out there trying to piece that together."

After two hours at the fire scene, the investigators abandoned the search. It would be almost a month before the weather conditions improved and they could go back and do a complete excavation.

On Friday, December 23, *The Dominion Post* printed a front-page story headlined, "Officials Return To Scene of Fatal Fire To Investigate." Accompanying the story was a large photograph of Detective Paul Mezzanotte and two other investigators, taking measurements. The story noted that although Morgantown Police Sergeant George Cress had earlier said the fire was not suspicious, he was now refusing to comment on yesterday's search.

That morning, Shelly Michael brought Alec and Kylie over to the Millers' house for a pizza lunch, and to pack Christmas presents. Before she arrived, Tara Miller had read the *Dominion Post* story, which she'd placed on top of the refrigerator.

Then, while the children were outside playing, she asked Shelly if she had seen today's newspaper. When she said she had not, Tara handed it to her.

"And Shelly flipped out," she recalled. "She was just very shocked and furious."

Shelly then demanded to know why detectives were inside her house without her permission.

"It's my house!" she raged. "They told me I could tear my house down if I wanted to. They should call me before they go in."

Tara Miller was amazed by Shelly's reaction.

"If it was my husband," she said, "I would want to know what happened to him. And I would want them to be there all the time until they found out."

Shelly Michael spent Christmas Day with her late husband's family at her new townhouse. Ruth Michael came with her son Steve and Jimmy's daughter Jacie—but Denny and Drew refused to go.

"From the day of the funeral, Drew didn't want anything to do with her," said his grandmother. "He said, 'I never want to see any of them again as long as I live.' But Jacie was younger, and still had this friendship with Kylie."

So Ruth telephoned her daughter, making an excuse that Drew needed some time alone.

"So we all went over to her townhouse with presents," said Ruth. "It was really hard. Then we went to a restaurant and she got all upset, because Denny and Drew didn't go."

Steve Michael recalls Shelly being in good spirits over Christmas dinner, although it had been barely a month since Jimmy's tragic death.

"She didn't act like she was sad," he said. "She was just bubbly Shelly."

On Thursday, December 29, Detective Mezzanotte drove to Clarksburg to interview Kathi Goots. He arrived unannounced at the law offices of Steptoe & Johnson, where she worked.

"He came to my work and interviewed me," said Kathi. "I ended up losing my job."

"Kathi Goots stated that her daughter was very upset over being accused of the crime," noted Mezzanotte in his report. "[She] loved James Michael and all the kids."

The next day, the lead detective arrived at Stephanie Estel's house in Cheat Lake, to interview 11-year-old Drew Michael. The little boy said he did not like his stepmother Shelly, because she treated him worse than her own children.

"Drew stated that he heard various arguments in the home," Detective Mezzanotte later wrote in his report, "about money, business and problems with his mom."

Drew also said that if Shelly did not get her own way, she started "crying and yelling." Then his father would give in, so she would stop.

The little boy said he believed his father had been upset over something else, causing the incident when he hit him.

"Drew stated that he knew his dad loved him," wrote Mezzanotte, "and his father was sorry and upset over the whole Child Protective Services incident."

Later police had Drew draw a detailed sketch of the master bedroom, to help ATF investigators visualize exactly where furniture and other items were located.

As the new year began, Shelly Michael was busy getting her new life together. After Christmas, she called her late husband's business partner Richard Brant, saying she wanted to begin settling Jimmy's estate and her share of Mountaineer Home Medical. Again, she called Reggie Ours, urging the licensed respiratory therapist to go full-time.

When Deborah Harris visited her new condo on Meadow Ridge Drive, Shelly was arranging the installation of a regular landline.

"She told me it was going to be the same phone number from the house," recalled Harris. "And she said, 'Did you know if you call my house, the line's busy?'"

Harris then asked why she would possibly call her house, after it was destroyed by fire.

"And she said, 'Well, when I called the home the day of the fire at seven-thirty, the phone was busy.' And she kind of went on and surmised that possibly the phone lines had been burning at the time. That's why the phone was busy."

On the day of the fire, Shelly had told her about that 7:30 a.m. phone call. Only then she'd said the phone had rung and Jimmy had not answered.

CHAPTER 31

A Deep Excavation

On January 9, 2006, Shelly Michael's attorney Tom Dyer called Detective Mezzanotte, asking if detectives required any further access to 545 Killarney Drive, saying that if not, he would authorize the State Farm Insurance company to have it destroyed. Mezzanotte told him the fire investigation of the house was far from finished.

Later that day, Shelly officially filed a $194,000 personal loss claim to State Farm Insurance.

"I am attaching an inventory," she wrote in a cover letter, "which shows in detail the quantity, description, actual cash value and the amount of loss of all personal and business property, for which a claim is being made."

After signing the letter, she sent it, along with a hand-written thirty-four-page itemized inventory, methodically listing each item, its age and replacement cost. She was claiming hundreds of items, with everything from $72 for twelve bottles of nail polish, to $40 for her framed wedding vows.

On Monday, January 23, investigators returned to 545 Killarney Drive for a thorough three-day search of the fire scene. Earlier they had obtained a search warrant from a Monongalia Circuit Court judge.

It was a well-coordinated group investigation, involving four detectives from the Morgantown Police Department, Lieutenant Ken Tennant from the City Fire Marshal's Office, and four ATF agents, including Rick Summerfield and Scott Markward, the operations manager from the Beltsville, Maryland, laboratory.

"The weather broke," explained Lieutenant Tennant. "In order to do a full-scale excavation, we had to have everything thawed out in order to sift."

The excavation started with a cursory examination of the outside of the house, checking for any dangers.

"There are a lot of potential hazards in a fire-damaged building," explained Agent Summerfield. "We tried not to get anybody hurt."

The investigators were also looking at the structure of the building, noting which windows were vented and where the electricity came into the house from the power pole. They also made sure the house was properly grounded, as well as inspecting all the electrical meters.

Then they went down into the basement to look at the furnace, removing the cover to ensure that it was functioning properly and had not caused the fire.

"There [was] no discoloration of the metal or buildup of soot anywhere in the furnace," said Summerfield. "It is apparent the furnace did not malfunction."

Also examined was the heating, ventilation and air conditioning system, as well as the ducts throughout the house. There was nothing untoward.

Then they inspected the living room, where heaps of debris from the master bedroom above had fallen through a hole in the ceiling onto the floor. Summerfield found signs of an old chimney fire in the brickwork above the chimney, covered by a drywall façade which had been torn down by the firefighters. He soon ruled out the fireplace having anything to do with the fire.

"If there had been a problem with the fireplace," said Agent Summerfield, "I would expect to see soot deposits and stains very prominently on this brickwork and on the drywall behind it. And I would also expect to see these studs burned away. I observed none of that in this scene."

Agent Summerfield then examined the joists from the bedroom floor, now clearly visible through the large hole in the living room ceiling. He noted that the bottom edge of the floor joists had absolutely no burn damage, as they were protected by the drywall ceiling underneath.

"This is a classic top-down burn," he explained. "It's virtually textbook. It means that the fire started above the floor level in the bedroom."

And it proved that the fire had burned down into the joists, and through the compartment space between the bedroom floor and the ceiling below.

The investigators then came upstairs, inspecting each of the four rooms going clockwise, until they came to the incinerated master bedroom.

They began by photographing and diagramming the bedroom, taking measurements of everything with a laser measuring device. Then they began hours of systematically sifting through the room on their hands and knees, using a simple garden trowel to scrape out the burned-out debris in the master bedroom. Every piece of debris was then put into plastic buckets, taken outside and sifted through a series of screens.

"It's a very unglamorous process," said Summerfield. "A pair of knee pads is a good idea."

The debris covering the floor was in layers, with the remains of the ceiling lower than the roofing material. So they started methodically removing the top layer of roofing material, carefully looking at everything they were scraping away.

A few hours into the excavation, Detective Chris Dalton made a significant discovery, about three or four feet from the end of the charred bed, hidden under several inches of debris.

"We were on our hands and knees sifting through the debris," recalled Detective Mezzanotte, [when] Detective Dalton yelled for us to stop for a second. And he said, 'I found this. It looks like a syringe cap to me.'"

Lieutenant Tennant then took a look and agreed, and Agent Summerfield, a former paramedic, also identified it as a hypodermic needle cap.

The orange plastic syringe cap had been protected from damage by the fallen debris on top. After being carefully diagrammed and photographed, it was sealed in an evidence bag and taken into custody.

There was great excitement after finding the syringe cap, as investigators believed it could be the smoking gun to prove that Jimmy Michael had been poisoned by his wife.

"We all talked about it," said Tennant. "We knew that he had died prior to the fire, although at that time we didn't know what caused his death. But it's a possibility that he could have been drugged. As far as developing Shelly as a suspect at this time, she's a nurse, and nurses are trained never to recap a syringe."

During the search, investigators also found birthday and gift cards, and pieces of paper buried in debris under the bed, as well as Shelly's cosmetics.

"It originally looked like this stuff was laying on top of the bed," said Lieutenant Tennant. "But when you spray water and do fire operations, sometimes things get moved around a little bit."

After completing the excavation, ATF Fire Research Engineer Stephen Hill collected samples of carpet, paint, flooring, windows and the box spring bed and mattress on which Jimmy Michael had died. These were taken to test for accelerants, and possibly to re-create an exact replica of the bedroom at the ATF's Maryland lab.

"We collected samples of those items," Hill would later testify, "to be able to make sure we understood what the materials actually were, if we decided to go ahead and re-build the bedroom . . . for a full-scale fire test."

To help diagram the master bedroom, Bobby Teets, who had been there with Shelly just two days before the fire, agreed to come in and tell investigators where everything had been positioned.

"We took Bobby into the house to help," recalled Lieutenant Tennant. "He had obviously been in the bedroom, and obviously knew his way around."

While investigators were removing windows from 545 Killarney Drive, Shelly Michael drove by to see what was happening. She stopped her Ford Expedition across the street, got out and walked up to the Morgantown Fire Marshal's van.

"She knocked on the window," recalled Lieutenant Ken Tennant, who was sitting inside with an ATF agent. "I opened the door and said, 'Can I help you?' And she said, 'I'm Shelly Michael, and I want to know what you're doing to my house.'"

After Lieutenant Tennant told her they were executing a search warrant, she demanded to know why they were taking windows out.

"And I said, 'Those are being taken as evidence,'" said Tennant. "She just said, 'OK,' nodded her head and walked away."

During the three days the ATF were inside her burned-out home, Shelly regularly telephoned her neighbor Deborah Harris, who had a clear view from her window.

"She called me every day on a fishing expedition," said Harris. "Chit-chat at first, and then she started to ask me questions of what I had seen."

On Thursday, January 26—the day after the investigators had left—Shelly called Harris, asking if she would accompany her again into the house, as she needed to retrieve a clipboard with football information out of the den.

During the three-day search, Morgantown police had secured the house day and night, but by now all the officers had left.

"I felt like she was just dying to get in there," Harris recalled. "She asked me if she came over at 4:30, would I go into the house with her? And I said, 'sure.'"

Shelly arrived at Deborah Harris's house at the appointed time, and the two women walked over to 545 Killarney Drive. First they looked at the back porch, where investigators' equipment and other things had been piled up.

"Would you look at all this mess?" Shelly said disgustedly.

Then they went into the den, where Shelly found the clipboard she wanted.

"I thought we were finished," said Harris, "and that was our only purpose there."

So she went back out through the kitchen and out the back door, but when she turned around, Shelly was gone.

"I thought she would be right behind me," said Harris. "So I stepped back into the kitchen, and heard the steps creaking upstairs. So I went up and she was standing in her bedroom, looking around."

Shelly said she couldn't believe what the police had done, asking why they would have taken out the windows and torn up all the flooring.

The next morning, *The Dominion Post* ran a story saying that police were still seeking answers about the cause of fire. Sergeant Harold Sperringer told a reporter that detectives were still awaiting lab results from the autopsy, which might take weeks.

"At this point," said Sergeant Sperringer, "I can't say if it was arson or not. But I can say there is nothing really overly suspicious."

Once again the newspaper printed a phone number for anyone to call with information about the fire.

Several days after discovering the hypodermic syringe cap in the debris beneath Jimmy Michael's bed, Detective Paul Mezzanotte visited Ruby Memorial Hospital. He had earlier asked to see all the Pediatric Intensive Care Unit records for October and November, discovering that Nurse Shelly Michael had ordered a one-millimeter Ativan syringe at 7:01 a.m. the morning of the fire.

At the hospital he viewed a sample syringe cap, photographing it before logging it into evidence, so it could later be compared to the one found under Jimmy Michael's body.

One night, Ruth and Steve Michael and Reggie Ours went inside 545 Killarney Drive to see for themselves where

Jimmy had died. It was a highly emotional occasion as they entered the house and walked into the kitchen.

"If it wasn't for the water damage," said Ours, "you could have walked in and lived there."

By now Shelly Michael had taken what she had wanted out of the house, and Reggie Ours had been told to take whatever he wanted, before it was given away to the Salvation Army. He asked for the dining room table.

At first they had all been hesitant to go upstairs, but they finally decided they had to.

"It was weird," recalled Ours. "I didn't want to go upstairs at first. But then we all walked up the stairs, which were fine."

They first went to Kylie and Jacie's bedroom, which still had the Disney Princesses wallpaper with their favorite pop star posters. Then they went into Drew's bedroom, which was also as he'd left it.

"And then we walked into the bedroom," remembered Ours. "I mean, we cried. Me and his mom cried, but Steve was stronger. I mean, it was so obvious what had happened. There was a big burn mark under the bed, and it just traveled down, down, down, until there was a little hole where it went through the floor."

Then Ours went up to the hole and jumped up and down.

"I said, 'This tells me this fire was so hot,'" he said, "'and so right on what Shelly wanted to burn.'"

On February 2, 2006, a week before the toxicology results would be ready, Detective Paul Mezzanotte quit the Morgantown Police Department. His move to Kansas City to join the U.S. Postal Service as an inspector had been months in the making. He had agreed with Monongalia prosecutors to see the Jimmy Michael investigation through to the toxicology results.

Although his protégé, Detective Chris Dalton, now took over as lead investigator, Mezzanotte continued to play a vital behind-the-scenes role.

"It was hard to walk away," he admitted. "But at that point, the case was pretty much done."

"The final tox report came back" from the Pennsylvania-based National Medical Services (NMS) Labs, said Assistant Medical Examiner Dr. John Carson, "with significant levels of rocuronium." Jimmy Michael's heart blood had contained large amounts of the paralytic drug.

It was a major break in the case, but to ensure there was no mistake, another sample of Jimmy's liver was sent for further testing.

"I felt it wise to send the liver tissue for a second analysis," said Chief Toxicologist Dr. James Kraner.

That month State Farm Insurance paid Shelly Michael and Wells Fargo, who held the mortgage on the Killarney Drive house, a total of $259,992 for the fire damage. Out of that, as her husband's estate administrator, Shelly received a payment of just over $100,000, as well as more than $40,000 to cover loss of her personal property.

The now-wealthy widow was still awaiting payment of Jimmy Michael's $500,000 life insurance policy.

CHAPTER 32

"Linear and Logical"

On Wednesday, February 8—almost two-and-a-half months after the fire—Morgantown police called a press conference, announcing that it had now been ruled arson.

"We held it undetermined for the longest time," explained Lieutenant Ken Tennant, "although we were actively working it as an arson/homicide."

A few hours later, Denny Michael escorted his granddaughter Jacie to a Father/Daughter Valentine's Party in Morgantown.

"Because Jimmy wasn't there," said Denny, "I'm going with her to be [her] father."

Also there was Kylie Angus, who was being escorted by Michael Goots, as her father was at work.

When Denny first walked in and saw Michael Goots, he went straight over and invited him to join them at a table.

And for the next two hours the two grandfathers sat together at the party, as Kylie and Jacie played together.

"And the whole time, he never asked how we were doing," recalled Denny. "Never mentioned about his daughter or the accusations going around. He never once mentioned Shelly's name. Never once said, 'Denny, I hope we find out what happened.'"

And Denny deliberately didn't bring up the subject either.

At the end of the party, Ruth arrived and Shelly's father left abruptly, without even saying goodbye.

The next morning, *The Dominion Post* printed a sensational front-page story headlined, "Fatal Fire Ruled Arson."

"We have determined that the fire was intentionally set," Morgantown Police Chief Phil Scott told a reporter. "This is not a cold case by any stretch. It's actively being worked on as we speak."

The story stated that the fire had started in the second-floor bedroom, and from the beginning the ATF had been involved in the investigation. Chief Scott said police and fire investigators had met last week to review the lab results, concluding that it had been deliberately set.

Chief Scott refused to comment on whether the victim had been dead before the fire began, or if there were any suspects in the case, saying it was too premature.

"We are looking at all avenues," he said.

Morgantown Fire Chief David Fetty was quoted, saying that since fire investigators had determined the cause of the fire, the police would take over.

"The last questions are who set it and why?" he added. "And those are police issues."

The final paragraph in the story stated that Jimmy Michael's widow Shelly could not be reached for comment.

On February 22—two days after what would have been Jimmy Michael's 34th birthday—Shelly was named executrix of his estate. Three days later, *The Dominion Post* reported that the arson and possible murder investigation was on hold, pending toxicology results, which could take weeks.

"There's nothing new on that," explained Morgantown Police Sergeant Harold Sperringer. "We are just waiting on lab results. Some are in Charleston, and some at the federal level. We hope within the next few weeks . . . we might get some results."

All the pressure of not knowing where the investigation stood was starting to wear on Shelly Michael. In the three months since the fire, she had lost thirteen pounds, complaining that she had no appetite and was unable to sleep. She was now taking 50 milligrams of the anti-depressant Zoloft, prescribed by her doctor after the fire.

"She went from shock to depression almost immediately," said her mother Kathi Goots. "And she couldn't sleep at night."

Shelly hated not being in control, and could do little except wait for detectives to make their next move.

"I was fearful that she was going to do something to herself," said Renee Del Viscio, who spoke to her regularly by phone. "I think a lot of people were at that time."

The childhood friends still spoke regularly, discussing what was going on and how Shelly was getting her life back together.

"We would just talk through things," recalled Renee. "What we thought could have happened, what she thought could have happened. Who could have done it."

Although Shelly had told her she had lied to police, Renee still had no idea that her friend was under any suspicion.

"She said she went in to talk to the police," recalled Renee, "and they got a little forceful with her. I just didn't know what to think. I wanted to be able to support her, but the only way I could do so [was] from afar."

At 9:00 a.m. on March 1, Shelly had a one-hour session with a psychotherapist. She reported that her life had fallen apart since her husband's death, describing her feelings as "sad, angry, and irritable," and saying she was unable to handle them. She also complained of headaches, a tightness in her chest and heart palpitations.

She told the therapist that she did not want to sleep, as she had recurring dreams of her life before Jimmy's death. She said she was not suicidal, but felt it would be OK if she died in an accident.

"Mrs. Michael reported an additional stressor is a police investigation into her husband's death," wrote the psychotherapist later. "She reported being shocked about the news that the fire is now considered to be the result of arson, and is very upset that she is being considered a suspect in her husband's death."

Three days later—after receiving the results of the latest round of toxicology tests—Jimmy Michael's death certificate was officially changed by the Office of the Chief Medical Examiner. The cause of death was now amended to "homicide," by being "intentionally injected by lethal dose of rocuronium by another person."

On Wednesday, March 8, Shelly reported an "episode" of seeing "black dots." Although she had not lost consciousness, it had scared Kylie and Alec, who were with her when it happened in the townhouse.

The next morning, she had a second psychotherapy session recounting the incident, as well as a three-hour crying episode earlier in the week.

"The patient acknowledged," wrote the therapist, "that she was concerned that she would end up with severe mental illness later in life."

Then the doctor gave her a pamphlet on coping with grief and bereavement, later describing her thought processes as "linear and logical."

CHAPTER 33

The Arrest

On Friday, March 10, as a result of a clerical mistake, Denny Michael received an official letter from the Morgantown Police Department, containing his son's death certificate. He opened it up and was shocked to read that the cause of death was homicide, by being "intentionally injected by lethal dose of rocuronium by another person."

So he immediately picked up the phone and called the police.

"I said, 'You can either arrest her or I'm coming in,'" remembered Denny. "'I've got proof right here in my hand about what went on.'"

The call was put through to Morgantown Police Department Detective Supervisor Sergeant Harold Sperringer, who immediately realized the dilemma, as police were in the process of deciding when to arrest Shelly Michael. But he was relieved that the letter had been sent to Jimmy's father instead of Shelly Michael, who should have received it first, as the wife.

"Well, what bothered us," Sergeant Sperringer explained, "was, Michelle, at the time, didn't know that we knew what the drug was. She had a right to the death certificate, being his wife, and if she would have seen that, we feared that she was going to take off."

So Sergeant Sperringer called prosecutor Marcia Ashdown, who ordered warrants to be drawn up immediately for Shelly Michael's immediate arrest.

Detective Chris Dalton prepared the criminal complaint, which read:

On 11-29-05 at approximately 10:30 hours, Police and Fire Fighters from the city of Morgantown responded to a structure fire at 545 Killarney Drive. The structure was owned by James and Michelle Michael. Upon fighting the fire, firefighters located a human body lying in the upstairs bedroom. The deceased was later identified as James Michael. According to investigators from the Morgantown Fire Department and the Bureau of Alcohol, Tobacco and Firearms Agency, the fire was deliberately ignited on or around the bed where the body was located. No other areas of the house sustained fire damage.

An autopsy was conducted on the body of James Michael by the West Virginia State Medical examiner's Office. The Toxicology report indicates that the victim's blood carboxyhemoglobin was within the normal range, indicating no antemortem exposure to an environment with elevated carbon monoxide. The Toxicology report also indicates that a lethal dose of a nondepolarizing neuromuscular blocking drug was present in the victim's blood, which caused the victim's death. The drug is primarily used in hospitals, and is not available to the public. Michelle Michael is a nurse practitioner in the Neonatal Intensive Care Unit at Ruby Memorial Hospital, and had access to this drug.

James Michael was accompanied only by Michelle Michael on the night before this incident as well as the morning of the incident. Michelle Michael went to work in the early morning hours on the day of the incident, and thereafter left her place of work and re-

turned to her residence prior to the fire being discovered, and then returned to work. Michelle Michael was interviewed by detectives at the Morgantown Police Department in reference to her activities on that day. Michelle Michael's statements to the detectives were proven to be inconsistent and some were proven to be false.

At midday, Shelly Michael drove to Jeremy Miller's Ford dealership to get her Expedition SUV serviced. It was the first time in weeks that she had seen Jimmy's friend, and she made small talk, asking for maintenance advice for the vehicle.

While they were talking, Miller received a phone call from Ruth Michael.

"She told me she had just gotten the death certificate in the mail," recalled Miller, "and it said 'death by lethal injection.'"

As soon as he heard the news, Miller made an excuse and walked straight out of the dealership.

"I didn't want to have to look at her," he said. "I didn't know what to do, and I just walked around until she left."

Later Shelly would remember Miller being "kind of odd and not as friendly as usual."

That afternoon, after a magistrate signed the arrest warrant and a criminal complaint, Morgantown police detectives swooped down on the Morgan Hotel, where they believed Shelly to be residing. When they discovered she had checked out, they called her ex-husband Rob Angus, who said he did not know where she was. A few minutes later he called back, saying they could find her at Meadow Ridge Drive.

But unfortunately the detective taking down the information got the house number wrong.

"We went to the wrong house first," said Sergeant Sperringer. "But then we finally went and physically arrested her."

After informing her that they had a warrant for her arrest

on suspicion of the first-degree murder of her husband, the detectives allowed her to get a coat and a pair of shoes, before handcuffing her and taking her into custody.

An hour later, Shelly Michael appeared at Morgantown Magistrate Court, where she was arraigned on charges of first-degree murder and first-degree arson by Magistrate Hershel Mullins. He granted her $100,000 bail on the arson charge, but as a magistrate, could not set bail on murder. A higher circuit court judge would have to consider bond for that at a later date.

After the hearing, Shelly Michael was transported to North Central Regional Jail by two deputies, to spend her first night behind bars.

Kathy Goots was at work that afternoon when her daughter Jennifer called, saying the police had arrested Shelly. She immediately went home and switched on the television news, to see two deputies leading her daughter out of her townhouse in shackles.

"I was totally hysterical," she recalled. "I mean, I was crying so hard, I couldn't talk. To see my daughter, handcuffed, coming out of her apartment . . . it was more than I could take."

Renee Del Viscio got a call from her sister in Clarksburg, who had just seen the arrest on the news.

"I felt absolutely awful," Renee said. "It was almost like Shelly died at that point. It was just like I had lost my sister."

The next morning *The Dominion Post* carried a front-page story with the banner headline, "Wife Charged With Murder—Shelly Michael Also Accused of Arson in Fatal Suncrest Fire."

Accompanied by a dramatic photograph of the accused murderess being escorted out of her arraignment in chains by two officers, the sensational story hit Morgantown like a bomb.

"It was just devastating," said Cookie Coombs of the

town's visitors' center. "Nothing like that had ever happened in Morgantown. She was very well known and highly respected, and had no record of any wrongdoing."

The following Tuesday, March 14, the story took on an even more macabre twist, after the criminal complaint against Shelly Michael was made public. It revealed for the first time that Jimmy Michael had been poisoned before the fire had started.

"Police: Husband Drugged to Death," trumpeted *The Dominion Post*, next to a mugshot of Shelly Michael.

"Police say Suncrest resident James Andrew Michael didn't die from fire," started off the front-page story. "He died from a lethal dose of drugs."

The story stated that as a Ruby Memorial Hospital nurse practitioner, Shelly Michael had access to the "nondepolarizing neuromuscular blocking drug," as it was referred to in the criminal complaint.

That morning, a Monongalia Circuit Court judge set $350,000 bail for the first-degree murder charge, on top of the $100,000 bond already set for the first-degree arson charge. A preliminary hearing was scheduled for the following Monday afternoon.

"If she is able to post," Assistant Prosecutor Perri De-Christopher told *The Dominion Post*, "she can be on home confinement."

On Thursday afternoon—six days after her arrest—Shelly Michael was released from North Central Regional Jail, after her parents posted a $450,000 bond. Monongalia County Chief Circuit Court Judge Russell Clawges, set bail on the condition that she remain on electronic home confinement at her father's Clarksburg house until her trial.

After posting bond, her mother collected her from jail and drove her to her father's house in Clarksburg.

After the hearing, her lawyer Tom Dyer refused to comment on how his client would plead.

"I cannot offer any other comment at this time," he told *The Dominion Post*.

Morgantown police were frustrated and surprised at the ease with which the suspected arson/killer walked out of jail.

"Not too often do you see a homicide arrestee make bond," said Detective Chris Dalton, "and be allowed to walk and be free at home. But we knew our turn was coming in court."

CHAPTER 34

"I'm Not Guilty"

The day after her release, Shelly Michael met with Annabelle Scolapio, director of the Clarksburg-based Harrison
County Community Corrections Program, who would be
supervising her home confinement. Earlier Shelly had been
fitted with an electronic ankle bracelet, so her movements
could be carefully monitored.

At the meeting, the program director presented Shelly with
a brochure, entitled, "What You Need to Know About Home
Incarceration," outlining the conditions she was required to
fulfill.

"Home Incarceration is equivalent to serving a jail sentence," it began. "Please do not do anything that you would
not be allowed to do if you were in jail."

Under the program, she would be allowed time out to
work, make doctor appointments and attend church and counseling. Occasionally, with prior permission, she would even
be allowed up to two hours' leave for personal things like
hairdressers and shopping.

She also had to pay an initial fee of $350 to cover the
monitoring costs, as well as $300 a month until her trial.

"You will be provided with a list of rules and regulations,"
stated the brochure. "Violations of these rules can ultimately

result in your arrest and your return to North Central Regional Jail."

A week into her home confinement, Shelly visited Tom Dyer's Washington Avenue law offices, before going shopping for toiletries at the Clarksburg Wal-Mart.

The Shelly Michael murder case was now garnering national attention, and a crew from CBS-TV's *48 Hours* had arrived in Morgantown, to start interviewing people close to the case.

On Thursday, March 30, Shelly Michael waived her right to a preliminary hearing, where prosecutors had been expected to lay out details of their case for the first time. She would now face a Monongalia County Grand Jury in May.

The same day, the *Pittsburgh Post-Gazette* carried a major in-depth story on the case, headlined, "In Northern W.VA., Arson-Killing Has Everyone's Attention."

"A young married couple," began the story. "A recently purchased insurance policy. A lethal dose of muscle relaxant. The death of 33-year-old Morgantown businessman James Michael and the subsequent arrest of his wife, Michelle, 34, have captivated many residents of northern West Virginia.

"Details of the case, both real and rumored, seem to contain all the dramatic elements and forensic intrigue of an episode of 'CSI.' "

Although prosecutor Marcia Ashdown refused any comment on the case, defender Tom Dyer told reporter Caitlin Cleary that the case against Shelly Michael was completely circumstantial. He described his client as very smart, very educated and weighing just 90 pounds.

"If you ever saw her," said Dyer, "you'd never presume—you'd never *dream*—she was somebody capable of the crime of which she stands accused."

The defender also ridiculed the prosecution's allegation that Shelly had taken any paralyzing drug from the hospital where she worked, saying it was kept "tighter than gold at Fort Knox."

And he refuted suggestions that Shelly was having an affair with one of her husband's employees.

"This is strictly rumor," he maintained, "absolutely, adamantly denied by Mrs. Michael. The marital relationship was fine. If there was a little fling or affair, I don't know if that constitutes motive."

And the attorney, claiming to have tried more murder cases than anyone else in the area, vowed to consult with his own team of forensic toxicologists and pathologists, and "thoroughly review" the autopsy findings.

He also announced he intended to explore the possibility that Jimmy Michael had committed suicide.

"There's got to be more to this damn story," he said. "I'm really looking forward to this . . . there's very few *CSI*-type cases. You don't get that challenge very often."

On Saturday, April 1, *The Dominion Post* ran a story with Tom Dyer proclaiming Shelly Michael's innocence.

"Michael: I'm Not Guilty," was the front-page headline.

"She's a grieving widow," Dyer told reporter Brandy Brubaker, who would now almost exclusively cover the story for *The Dominion Post*. "She's very shook up . . . and it's very difficult for her to cope with and contend with all these issues."

He repeated that the defense would explore the suicide theory, saying that they were not yet ready to concede that it was homicide.

Sergeant Harold Sperringer said police would never have arrested Michael if they had not been certain it was a homicide.

CHAPTER 35

The Media Trap

On Sunday, April 9, Morgantown's chief fire investigator Lieutenant Ken Tennant traveled to Beltsville, Maryland, for two weeks of testing at the ATF's national laboratory. It would be the first of half-a-dozen extended trips that he would make there over the next year.

The prosecutors knew their main hurdle in getting a conviction was convincing a jury that the fire could have smoldered for several hours before being reported. But through sheer good luck, two trained firemen had been on the scene as bookends: Shawn Alt, who had smelled burning and then seen Shelly at 8:15 a.m., and Keith Summers, who'd seen smoke pouring out of the rafters at 10:20 a.m., just before witnessing the flashover.

"Without establishing the timeline," said Lieutenant Tennant, "it would have been very difficult to convict her. We had an eyewitness putting her there at the scene at 8:15 a.m., but then several hours elapsed, and to the normal person, a fire is going to be discovered a lot faster. So we had to scientifically prove, not that that happened, but that it was possible."

Initially, the ATF intended to use a computer simulation of the fire scene, to scientifically determine if it was possible for a fire to have smoldered for so long.

But after inspecting the fire scene in January, ATF Agent

Rick Summerfield and his team became enthusiastic about the research possibilities this unique case offered into the nature of smoldering fires. So the federally funded organization offered to stage an elaborate series of ten test burns, building six full-scale exact replicas of the master bedroom in a huge hangar, and then setting them alight under laboratory conditions. The tests would cost an estimated $1 million.

The ATF experts spared no expense in constructing the models, utilizing materials taken from the fire scene. Then they went out furniture shopping, purchasing the exact same carpet, mattress, bed and furnishings. They even took a paint sample from the wall to duplicate it.

They also re-created the four 2-inch–by–10-inch wooden joists, the plywood sub-floor and the tongue-and-groove wooden flooring. Lastly, they simulated the heating and ventilation system.

On Monday morning, Lieutenant Tennant met Agent Summerfield and his team at the national ATF laboratory's open-air hangar, where an exact replica of the Michaels' master bedroom floor system had been constructed on a raised platform.

The first three days of tests would be for accelerants, and it had been decided to test in the open air, so oxygen would not be an issue. The rationale for this was that if they found an average time for the floor to burn through with unlimited oxygen, it would take longer in limited conditions. All the tests would be video time-stamped, with careful computer measurements of all relevant data.

"These first tests were over a two-week period," recounted Lieutenant Tennant. "We wanted to see how long it would take to start burning holes through the floors, constructed identical to the one in the Michael home, down to the type of carpet."

The first test involved pouring half-a-gallon of paint thinner over the carpet and floor assembly, before setting it on fire. The carpeting burned away where the thinner had been poured, and the wooden floor below charred, but there was no burn-through, even though there was unlimited oxygen.

The second, third and fourth tests used gasoline and different strengths of alcohol, and the results were identical to the first one, with no burn through the flooring.

For the fifth test, research engineers scattered a couple of cotton shirts and a pair of jeans on the floor—replicating what had been found at the fire scene—before dousing them in paint thinner and setting them alight. The paint thinner burned away, but there was no burn-through damage to the floor.

Each day after the testing had finished, Lieutenant Tennant called Morgantown prosecutors and detectives to brief them on the progress being made.

And while these tests were going on, engineers in another part of the laboratory were testing flat electric irons, to see if that could have caused the fire.

"They used three identical irons like the one Shelly had," explained Tennant. "They were rigged up to be set on an ironing board."

The irons were turned up high and then left on, to see if they would catch fire. The testers even disabled the tip-over switch and thermostat, simulating a failure so the iron would not automatically turn off, as Shelly had claimed hers did.

"These irons would continue to go through their heating cycle," said Tennant. "But they never got hot enough to do anything other than scorch the fabric. So the iron had nothing to do with the fire."

Ten days later, on April 22, the next series of tests began, using an exact replica of the Michaels' bed mounted on larger platforms, replicating the floor.

"We moved on at that point into testing full-scale applications using a bed," said Lieutenant Tennant. "We wanted to re-create burning that hole through the floor, because one question that had to be answered was how the large hole behind the bed got in the floor. Normally fire burns up, it doesn't burn down. The only way it can burn down is if something is laying on top of the floor for a significant amount of time, eventually causing it to go through."

The fire investigators theorized that the headboard of the bed must have caught fire, eventually collapsing and burning through the floor.

"We needed to know how long it takes to do that," said Lieutenant Tennant. "We also wanted to determine how much energy, how much radiation, heat-wise, is given off by these fires. So the laboratory is testing all this information through their computer systems."

Tests six and seven were virtually identical, using the same mattress, the only difference being that in test six, an accelerant was poured around the base of the bed. High-powered video cameras had been placed inside the four joist pockets to capture the fire's progress.

"We let the fire continue to burn," explained Lieutenant Tennant, "until ultimately the headboard collapsed and eventually burned through the floor."

And after the fire was put out, Lieutenant Tennant was amazed to see how closely it resembled the bedroom where Jimmy Michael had died, which he had observed the day of the fire.

"It was shocking," he recalled, "standing on top of this when the fire was out. It was eerie. It looks exactly like the fire scene. The dimensions of the hole that was burned through the floor were almost identical. And the bed kind of falls into the hole like it did at the scene. So we knew we were on the right track."

In the two open-air tests, the headboard took forty-three minutes and nearly fifty-seven minutes respectively to burn through the floor. Investigators now knew the time it took to achieve a full burn-through with unlimited oxygen. They were ready to move on to the next round of tests, where replicas of the master bedroom would be built for testing in an enclosed environment, where the ventilation could be regulated.

On Tuesday, April 11, Jeremy Miller was shopping with his wife and children in Lowe's on Venture Drive, Morgantown, when he saw Shelly Michael.

"She approached," said Miller, "and put her arms around me."

And when Miller looked astonished to see her, as she was supposed to be under home confinement, Shelly asked if he was "weirded out." When he said he was, she smiled, telling him he shouldn't believe what he read in the newspapers.

"I didn't want to cause any confrontation," he said, "and she didn't hang around after that, and took off."

Then Miller called Prosecutor Marcia Ashdown on his cell phone, reporting that he had just seen Shelly Michael shopping in Morgantown.

The prosecutor took immediate action, filing a motion to revoke the accused murderess's bond and return her to jail. The motion also accused her of further bond violations, including visiting Alec and Kylie at her Aunt Gina's house in Morgantown, and communicating with Drew and Jacie by sending them a saxophone and braces through the mail, without a return address.

On April 18, Shelly Michael appeared in Monongalia County Circuit Court in front of Judge Russell Clawges, wearing a pink sweater with a white shirt underneath, with matching pink shoes. She also had her engagement and wedding rings on.

Prosecutor Marcia Ashdown first called Jeremy Miller to the stand, who told the judge about their encounter at Lowe's.

"I was cordial," he said. "She looked at both of us and said, 'You fell into the trap, the media trap.'"

Then Shelly's ex-husband Rob Angus testified, saying he was "angry" that she had visited their children during her Morgantown trip, as she was only allowed to talk to them on the phone.

"I was extremely agitated that she went to see the kids without my knowledge," he said. "I was shocked when my daughter told me."

Then Dyer called Shelly Michael to the stand to account for herself. she explained that after leaving her doctor's office, she had suddenly decided to run some errands, leaving a message to that effect with her home confinement officer Annabelle Scolapio.

She had then driven to the United Bank in Morgantown to stop a $387.21 monthly standing order from her joint account with her late husband. From there she had gone to Lowe's to purchase a pest repellant plug not available in Clarksburg. That was where she had seen Jeremy Miller.

Then she had driven to her Aunt Gina Harris's house in Cheat Lake, telling the judge that she had no idea her children would be there.

"I heard, 'Mommy, Mommy,'" she testified, "and I looked over, and it was my daughter. I didn't even recognize her at first."

She had then given Alec and Kylie a "quick kiss," and told them to tell their father she had been there, before leaving.

Testifying by telephone, Scalapio denied receiving any telephone message that morning from Shelly, adding that even if she had, it still would have been a violation of Shelly's home confinement regulations.

Judge Clawges then ruled that, although Michael had technically violated the regulations, it was not serious enough to revoke her bond. But he warned her that any further violations would result in immediate imprisonment, and the end of her home confinement privileges.

"The first question you need to ask," the judge told her, "when you want to do something is, if you were at the regional jail, would you be allowed to?"

On April 26, Shelly Michael resigned as executrix of her late husband's estate, after Stephanie Estel complained that it was inappropriate for her to hold that position. A Monongalia County Commissioners' meeting agreed that Ruth Michael should take over the administration of her son's estate.

Shelly appeared with her civil attorney James Martin, who emphasized that his client was "admitting absolutely no liability or wrongdoing."

Soon afterwards she called her home confinement officer,

requesting special permission to move her monitoring bracelet from her ankle to above her knee. She explained that she
wished to wear a new dress at an upcoming court appearance, and did not want it to be seen.

"I have never had anyone ask for [that before]," said her
home confinement officer, Deputy William Sothen, "so that
she could wear a dress."

She was given permission to do so, although she had no
appearances in court scheduled at that time. But she continued to wear the monitoring transmitter above her knee, until
she was eventually discovered and ordered to return it to her
ankle.

CHAPTER 36

"Not in Morgantown"

Although the *Pittsburgh Post-Gazette* had taken an early lead in covering the Shelly Michael murder case, *Dominion Post* editor Geri Ferrara was determined to catch up. It was probably the most sensational story ever to hit Morgantown, and the townsfolk were riveted.

"Morgantown still maintains a small hometown flavor," Ferrara explained to CBS *48 Hours*. "A premeditated murder of that nature, with all the bells and whistles doesn't happen. Not in Morgantown."

Ferrara had assigned one of her best journalists, Brandy Brubaker, to the story, and Brubaker had been pestering Jeremy Miller for an exclusive interview since the arrest.

"The Brubaker girl was over here all the time," recalled Miller. "And I was always very careful about what I'd say, because I didn't want to interfere with the investigation."

But on Saturday, April 29, the newshound arrived at his home with a new line of questioning.

"She's asking me questions about Shelly being perfect, and a saint," Miller recalled. "I thought, 'I've heard enough of that.' And I basically told her, 'Listen, Jimmy did question her fidelity. I'll leave it at that.'"

On Sunday morning, Morgantown awoke to a sensational

front-page story in *The Dominion Post*, headlined, "Michael Affair Alleged."

Brandy Brubaker's exclusive revealed that Jimmy and Shelly Michael's loving public persona was far from the truth.

"If you looked at it from outside the doors," Miller was quoted as saying, "you would think they're perfect for each other, but there was a lot more than people could see," adding that although his best friend was not planning a divorce, Jimmy had been working hard to improve his marriage.

"I know he loved her," said Miller, "and he wanted a good marriage."

On page 2 there was another Brubaker story. This time a moving tribute to Jimmy Michael from Miller and Pastor Kevin Cain, who had been counseling him at the time of his death.

"I'm very sad what has happened to him," the pastor said. "It's such a tragedy. It's very difficult. Jim Michael was a guy, in my opinion, who was completely committed to his faith and family, and wanted to develop in his godly character every day he lived. Most people aren't willing to take a constant inventory of their life, but Jim was constantly willing to do that."

That morning, when Jeremy Miller saw the front page about the alleged affair, he was livid.

"I thought, 'Oh no, what have I done?'" he recalled. "I felt terrible, because I always tried to go through Jimmy's mom and dad before I would talk to anybody, so I wouldn't jeopardize their feeling or stir their emotions."

The second week of May, Shelly Michael was indicted on charges of first-degree arson and murder by a Monongalia County Grand Jury. She now faced spending the rest of her life in prison.

On Thursday, May 18, she was arraigned in front of Monongalia County Circuit Court Judge Robert Stone, pleading not guilty to both charges. Judge Stone set her trial for July 11.

Attending the hearing were several members of the Michael family, including Jimmy's 86-year-old grandmother Isobel Stimson.

"She sat on a bench in the hallways of the courthouse," recalled Jimmy's uncle, James Stimson. "She didn't want to be in the courtroom."

After the hearing, Tom Dyer escorted his client through the court, out to the hallway and past her late husband's grandmother.

"I'm sorry," said Shelly, as she passed Jimmy's grandmother. Then Dyer led her away, instructing her not to talk to anyone.

After the grand jury indictment, Dyer started planning Shelly's defense strategy. He came up with a year-long timeline, and several times a week Shelly would make the ten-minute drive to Dyer's Washington Avenue office in Clarksburg, to work on her defense.

"She was in the middle of everything," said Dyer. "She served as assistant private investigator, assistant paralegal—I mean, dear God, she was out working like no other person, in assisting in the development of her own defense. And because of her medical training, she did extensive research of her own on the toxicology issues."

But before long, her need to be in total control led to bitter disagreements with Dyer and a Morgantown attorney named James Zimarowski, who was now on board with the defense team.

"She wanted to direct and control," said Dyer. "She was helpful, but always right under your feet. And of course, her idea and opinion of relevance, or just materiality of certain information, did not coincide with mine or Zimarowski's. And that would lead to a little bit of conflict."

Her sister Jennifer Barker believes that Shelly kept her sanity by totally immersing herself in the case.

"I mean, that was her life," said Jennifer. "She kept herself really busy working on the case. She knew it better than her attorneys knew it."

Over the next few months, Shelly Michael compiled a

highly detailed character analysis of many of Jimmy Michael's family and friends who could be expected to testify against her. She summarized her relationship with each, pointing out their weaknesses and suggesting strategic questions for her attorneys to ask them at trial.

She also embarked on a thirty-five-page, single-spaced typed autobiography, entitled, *Presumed Guilty Until Proven Innocent—The Untold Story*, complete with pages of family photographs from every stage of her life.

"My philosophies in life," she stated in it, "focus on being kind and compassionate, generous and giving, honest and trustworthy positive thinking and appreciative, and genuine in character."

She also gave a new version of the last time she had seen Jimmy Michael, the morning of the fire.

"All I remember is waking up to Jimmy," she wrote, "with his manly parts poking me in the back. It was about 4:00 a.m. He did that on occasion, wake up in the middle of the night horny and wanting to get frisky. I pushed him away because I was sleeping and had to get up for work shortly. He whispered to me, 'Come on Shel, just one last time for me'. I gave in and let him have his fun. We both fell back to sleep and my alarm went off at 4:45 a.m. I got up, took my shower, and got ready for work. Jimmy was sound asleep, so I gently kissed him goodbye on his forehead, and left for work."

On May 1, the West Virginia Board of Examiners for Registered Professional Nurses received a letter from Shelly Michael, responding to a move to take her nursing license away after her arrest for arson and murder.

"I am not at liberty to discuss any details that pertain to the charges brought against me by the State of West Virginia," Shelly wrote. "I can assure you that the allegations are false. I am in no way responsible for the death of my husband, nor am I guilty of any of the allegations surrounding the case."

* * *

That summer, Shelly settled into a routine. With the permission of her home confinement officer, she got a part-time job painting her sister Jennifer's house. She applied for a nursing position at a Clarksburg hospital, but was turned down.

Every day she went swimming in her father's outdoor pool, followed by an hour of jogging. She was also allowed to attend church for two hours and ten minutes every Sunday.

On Sunday afternoons, Rob Angus would bring Alec and Kylie to Clarksburg to spend two hours with their mother. The ex-spouses had always had a difficult relationship, and there was great tension during the visits. But one high point for Shelly that summer was when Kylie performed her first back-handspring.

"She had good days and bad days," recalled her sister Jennifer, who would see her every day. "Some days she would feel good about it and be working diligently on whatever she needed to work on. And then sometimes she'd have a bad day and just cry."

Since being placed on home confinement, Monongalia prosecutors received numerous calls from local residents claiming to have seen Shelly all over Morgantown, forty miles away from her father's house. There would also be numerous suspicious incidents of her electronic ankle bracelet malfunctioning.

"We called them 'Shelly sightings,'" recalled Assistant Prosecutor Perri DeChristopher. "We had lots of folks calling us to say, 'We've seen her here. She's doing this, or she's doing that.'"

Most of the callers wished to remain anonymous, but the prosecutors started compiling a list, with a view to getting Shelly's bail revoked.

On Friday, June 2, at 6:47 p.m., one of Shelly's old Killarney Drive neighbors claimed to have seen her driving past the burned-out ruins of her old house, and immediately contacted the prosecutors' office, as well as *The Dominion Post*.

A week later, the newspaper published a front-page story, headlined, "Neighbor: Michael Broke Home Confinement."

The story said that yet another report of a "suspected violation had surfaced," with the unnamed neighbor being 99.9 percent positive that she'd seen Shelly Michael. Monongalia Prosecutor Marcia Ashdown confirmed that her office was investigating.

The Dominion Post now put Shelly Michael on its front page as often as possible, as it ensured high circulation.

"Our readers wanted every single detail," explained editor Geri Ferrara. "Our single-copy sales were phenomenal."

On June 19, Shelly Michael was back in court, after prosecutors filed a motion to clarify the terms of her home confinement.

Prosecutor Ashdown told Judge Stone that she felt it important that the terms be reviewed, in the light of numerous reports her office had received about Shelly being seen all over Morgantown.

Tom Dyer then stood up, attacking *The Dominion Post* for printing "completely unconfirmed and uncorroborated reports" about his client.

"I certainly understand and appreciate the concern of some of these individuals," he told the judge. "But it has risen to the point where it is almost a type of hysteria."

After the hearing, Judge Stone ruled that from that point on, Shelly must work at a job that provided an official paycheck, and all her jogging must be within her father's property.

She soon found a part-time job on the check-out counter at a Clarksburg mall.

On June 30, Shelly Michael's trial was postponed after Tom Dyer filed a motion complaining that the case discovery was incomplete. It was now almost seven months after the fire, and Jimmy Michael's autopsy report was still not finished.

"Things have slowed down in the case," said Dyer, "because of a lack of an autopsy report."

West Virginia Chief Medical Examiner Dr. James Kaplan told *the Dominion Post* that this was not the "typical" murder case.

Prosecutor Marcia Ashdown did not object to postponing the trial, which Judge Stone delayed until October 31.

Six weeks later, on Friday, August 11, 2006, there was a pre-trial hearing in Monongalia County Circuit Court to discuss a defense motion demanding full access to Bobby Teets' half-hour-long videotaped statement in which he admitted an affair with Shelly Michael.

Going on the attack, defenders Tom Dyer and James Zimarowski portrayed Bobby Teets as a murder suspect. During the hearing, Teets would only be referred to as "R.T." to protect his identity, although several times the defenders slipped, mentioning him by name.

"The statement of R.T.," declared Tom Dyer, "has extraordinary significance . . . to the preparation of our defense. There's no mistaking who this individual is, and his significance to this case."

Dyer argued that if the Morgantown police considered Shelly Michael suspect number 1, Bobby Teets was certainly suspect number 1a.

"This R.T. is the presumed or alleged paramour/boyfriend, if you will, of the defendant," said Dyer, "and is an integral part of the State's theory of motive. He is one of the first observers to the fire. He is an integral part of nearly every aspect of this investigation."

Assistant Prosecuting Attorney Perri DeChristopher argued that there was no reason for the State to provide Teets' testimony to the defense, as he was not on the State's witness list.

"The State's position," she told Judge Robert Stone, "is that it is not exculpatory, not relevant and the State is not required to provide it."

But Judge Stone deferred his ruling on the defense motion, saying he first wanted to review the interrogation and other police reports before making up his mind.

"You have represented to me," the judge told Dyer, "that from the police report or whatever, R.T. [is]—What is that term they have developed recently?—a 'person of interest.' All of a sudden you hear that all across the country now.

"I don't know what the police report says about Mr. R.T. I'm kind of in the dark . . . which makes it difficult for me to make a decision."

A few days later, Bobby Teets was fired from Mountaineer Home Medical, where he had become an increasing embarrassment. His new bosses, Rich Brant and Susan Riddle, told him that in the light of all the "rumors," it would be better if he found a new job.

"I mean, Rich hit it on the head," Teets later admitted. "He said that Jimmy would probably not approve of us paying [you] if the rumors were true."

On Friday, August 18, Shelly Michael's kid brother Matt got married. Despite her busy schedule, the accused murderess still found time to organize every single detail of the wedding, from sending out the invitations to table placings for the seventy-five guests.

"Our son Matt got married at the house, while Shelly was under house arrest," said her mother. "She was the wedding planner, and she organized that from beginning to end. She did everything from decorations inside and outside the house, bridesmaids' bouquets and how much food we were going to have."

Then a couple of weeks later, she organized a children's birthday party at her father's house.

"We had helium balloons," remembered Kathi Goots, "and she put her name and [Jimmy's] on one of them. And then she let the balloon go, saying that she hoped that the balloon would carry up to heaven, so Jimmy could see it."

On Friday, September 15, burn testing resumed at the ATF laboratory in Maryland. As lead fire investigator, Lieutenant Ken Tennant had again relocated to Beltsville for the duration of the next round of tests.

"I was there to serve two functions," he explained. "Number one, I was the representative from the investigation. Basically, since this all turned out to be evidence, I had to be the person to observe it and mark it as evidence, and maintain a custody of documentation."

In the weeks leading up to the new tests, ATF engineers had built two identical replicas of the Michaels' master bedroom side-by-side in its medium laboratory burn facility, complete with en-suite bathroom, closets and furniture. There was an identical bed, chest-of-drawers, wall curtains and even nightstands.

The two full-scale models also included energized electrical systems with wall outlets, heating and ventilation systems and roof insulation. Once inside, with the door closed, it was impossible to tell them from the real thing.

And after each test burn, the two identical models had to be completely rebuilt for the next one.

"That's what took so long," said Lieutenant Tennant. "That's why we were here in September, November, February and then in April 2007."

In the first test the bedroom was set alight with no additional ventilation sources, with the windows and door closed, and the heating and ventilation systems turned off.

"We set the fire on the bed," said Tennant. "Fifteen minutes later, it's out. It simply consumes all the oxygen available. There's hardly any damage to the room."

The second test had the ventilation system turned on continuously. On site, investigators had already determined that the thermostat in the Michaels' home had been set at 78 to 80 degrees, so during the fire, the ventilation would have been coming on and off.

"In the second test we had it on all the time," said Lieutenant Tennant. "The vents in the room are always blowing air. But when that happens, the fire gets out of control. It burns through the ceiling and continues on its own, and you're not matching the timeline of the fire."

And it would take the ATF engineers another two months to rebuild the two bedroom mock-ups, in readiness for the next round of testing, when they would try cycling the heating and ventilation systems.

CHAPTER 37

Razed to the Ground

On Friday, October 6, the remains of 545 Killarney Drive were finally demolished. A week earlier two backhoes and other heavy equipment had arrived at the house to start preparing to raze the Michael house.

Then a John Deere backhoe loader moved in, tearing down the two-storey home and taking away the debris. All that remained of Shelly Michael's one-time dream house was a shed and pieces of outdoor furniture strewn across what remained of the back yard.

Ten days later, Tom Dyer filed a motion to delay the trial. He warned that it might have to be moved out of Morgantown, as all the negative publicity made it impossible for his client to get a fair trial.

At a special hearing on Monday, October 23, the defense attorney told Judge Stone that he had still not received the full toxicology results.

Prosecutor Ashdown agreed to a postponement, saying she was still awaiting the final results from the National Medical Services Labs.

"We are trying to move on our side as fast as we can," she said, "and we have run into obstacles as well."

Judge Stone agreed to delay the trial until early next year, to allow Assistant Prosecutor Perri DeChristopher, who was pregnant, time to give birth.

At the end of the hearing, Dyer told the judge that his client was now broke. "She is out of money," he told the judge, "and we have tapped out available resources within the family and we are here to ask the court to intervene." He said that a $45,000 loan from Michael Goots towards her defense had now run out. He asked the court to appoint him and James Zimarowski to her defense, thereby making them eligible for court subsidies.

Prosecutor Ashdown strongly objected, warning that it could set a precedent for defendants selecting their own attorneys, and then having the State pay, as they could no longer afford them.

Judge Stone refused to commit himself, saying he wanted to take *advice on* the matter under advisement.

On Wednesday, November 29, 2006—the first anniversary of Jimmy Michael's death—a new round of ATF testing began, to determine what had caused the fire.

"The next series of tests used cycling of the HVAC [heating, ventilation and air conditioning] systems," said Lieutenant Tennant. "We know that the heat would have had to come on and go off."

Earlier, ATF engineers had consulted with the manufacturer of the Michaels' furnace, determining that the heat would have been on approximately a quarter of the time.

"So we had to try and re-create a twenty-five percent duty cycle," explained Tennant. "During the time the fire's going, the computer would tell us when to turn the ventilation on and when to turn it off."

During these tests, which would last through February, investigators discovered that the fire would either extinguish itself or blaze out of control, depending on whether the ventilation was on or off.

"There were six tests using the identical structures," explained Tennant. "We would go over for a week, burn one, study the data for a day or two and then burn the next one. Then they would have to rebuild them both, so we'd come back in a couple of months."

These tests all demonstrated that the fire's progress was directly related to the heating system going on and off. Therefore, if the furnace had not been working at the Michaels' house, the fire would have soon gone out. And if it had been turned up too high, it would have raged out of control within half-an-hour.

It would be another four months before the ATF engineers finally found the correct ventilation cycle, mirroring exactly what had happened the day of the fatal fire.

At 7:30 p.m. on the first anniversary of Jimmy Michael's murder, thirty people gathered outside what had once been 545 Killarney Drive for a candlelight vigil. A simple cross stood on the site of the house, and a memorial plaque lay on a small table in the driveway, alongside nine candles marked with images of the saints.

The memorial had been organized by Reggie and Chris Ours, who handed out "Justice For Jimmy" badges as people arrived.

"We said, 'This time next year we will have justice for Jimmy,' " recalled Denny Michael.

Then everyone stood in a circle holding lighted candles, as Jimmy Michael's father addressed them, saying that he had often been called upon to comfort the bereaved, in his days as a pastor.

"I never presumed," he said, "to understand what they were going through."

He then spoke movingly about the hunting trip he and Jimmy had taken the day before the fire.

"I didn't have him to go with this year," he told them. "Matter of fact, the last day he was alive, I spent hunting with him."

Reggie Ours also spoke, remembering his friend's goodness and generosity of spirit.

"We don't want the crime to eclipse the person Jimmy was," he told the crowd.

Forty miles away in Clarksburg, Shelly Michael and Tom Dyer were working hard on her defense. The attorney was now focusing on having the trial moved out of Morgantown, commissioning a polling company to conduct a telephone survey, gauging local awareness of the high-profile case.

"Shelly and the case both commanded a lot of attention," Dyer explained. "You couldn't run into anybody in a hundred-mile radius that didn't know the last little procedural nuance in the development of the case."

Every week, Dyer and his client spent many hours together at his law offices, drafting a defense campaign. But Shelly's obsessive eye for detail caused problems.

"I paint with a broad brush," explained the defender, "and she's got one you can't see the point of. She's going to kill you with all the details."

The attorney felt he'd wasted valuable time trying to persuade her that no jury would be interested in the complex scientific toxicological minutiae she wanted presented.

"She's extremely intelligent," he said. "And that was part of the problem. She was always second-guessing. A couple of times, I lost patience."

To illustrate her innocence, she drew an elaborate series of jigsaw puzzles, highlighting the major flaws in the State's case against her.

Shelly even mapped out in great detail the closing argument she suggested he deliver to the jury.

"As you start to deliberate on this case," she wrote, "you <u>must</u> begin by assuming Shelly is innocent."

But the document she gave Dyer bore little or no resemblance to the closing ultimately made.

"It drove Tom crazy," recalled Renee Del Viscio. "She spent a lot of time researching and coming up with theories."

Once thing Shelly and her attorney did agree about was her taking the stand to testify.

"And I told Shelly all along," Dyer said, " 'We've got to be prepared to testify.' I've always been of the opinion in my entire career, that the defendant who does not testify is placing himself in tremendous jeopardy. It's a right he or she has, but the twelve people on the jury don't give a shit—their immediate reaction is, 'Son of a bitch, this person's got something to hide.' "

Shelly spent many weeks rehearsing to take the stand, using a thirty-two-page detailed Q & A she had written, which was critiqued by Tom Dyer.

Where she had written how she and Bobby Teets had both discussed loving their spouses, and not wanting to leave them, Dyer changed it to "a stupid one night stand—period."

On January 9, 2007, Tom Dyer filed a motion to move the trial out of Morgantown. His ammunition was what he called a "most alarming" defense survey, showing that three out of four Monongalia County residents questioned already had a negative opinion of his client.

In his motion he accused *The Dominion Post* of "persistent and continuing sensationalistic and tabloid coverage," creating an "unfair image" of Shelly Michael as a "rule breaker."

The defense poll showed that out of eighty-two Monongalia residents questioned who were aware of the case, sixty-two of them had negative feelings towards Shelly Michael.

Ten days later, Judge Robert Stone held a pre-trial hearing to decide the matter.

Tom Dyer told the court that the "sociological survey" had been executed by an outside company, who found that out of people surveyed, 75 percent were aware of the Michael case.

"I don't know that I ever recall seeing the media attention for any one case on trial," said Dyer, "that this one has garnered. I contend it created an unfair perception of this young lady."

Judge Stone then observed how most of the publicity had been generated by the defense feeding information to the media.

"Every time you talk to someone or you go on TV," said the judge, "that is simply an invitation to put in the press what you said."

But the defender denied giving the media stories, saying they were going to run with or without his input.

Prosecutor Marcia Ashdown argued against a change of venue, saying that just because people knew about the case, it didn't mean they had already formed an opinion. She was certain an "unbiased jury" could be found, though conceding it might require calling an above-average number of potentials for questioning.

Then, in a dramatic victory for the defense, Judge Stone agreed to move the trial to another county, the first time in his twenty-one years on the bench that he had ever taken such action.

"After very serious consideration of this motion," the judge said, "because it is very serious, with far-reaching consequences, the court is of the opinion to grant the motion of change of venue. I think it's necessary in this case. I think it's the right thing to do."

On January 24, *The Dominion Post* ran a hard-hitting editorial attacking Judge Stone's decision to move the Michael murder trial, describing his ruling as an "injustice."

"If sensationalism of this case refers to reporting developments in it," read the editorial, "then we plead guilty. However, we maintain that we have reported this case: like any alleged homicide or any other story we publish. That is, in a balanced, accurate, responsible and fair manner."

The editorial then suggested that the Michael defense team had mounted its own media campaign to move the trial, accusing Tom Dyer of granting exclusive interviews to its main competitors, the *Pittsburgh Post-Gazette* and local television stations.

"We are mindful of these circumstances," it read. "This decision on a change of venue not only displays a total lack of faith in the county's residents, but also penalizes them for the added costs without cause. Judges are no gods . . . yet in this case, our faith in one jurist's wisdom has been shaken."

Two weeks later, Shelly Michael's murder trial was officially moved to the state capital, Charleston, with the state supreme court appointing Judge Stone to preside. A new trial date of July 5, 2007, was also set, with pre-trial motions for early April.

On Tuesday, April 3, the ATF carried out the sixth and final full-scale burn test. Two months earlier, testers had unsuccessfully tried another variant of cycling the ventilation on–off. With the trial just three months away, time was running out for the prosecution to scientifically prove its theory of how Shelly Michael had started the fire.

Before the sixth test, ATF lab workers were polled about the average air cycle of their home HVAC systems. As a result, it was decided to use a cycle of ten minutes on and fifteen minutes off.

"That seemed to be realistic," explained ATF fire investigator Brian Grove, who supervised the test. "They are round figures."

Once again the head of the bed was set alight, and an engineer started continuously turning the fan on for ten minutes, and then and off for fifteen.

"At just over an hour," said Grove, "we began to get an orange glow and small flames in the southeast corner of that bedroom. And then at about an hour and eighteen minutes into the test, we saw hot gases in the joist pocket."

Finally, at two hours and ten minutes, the nightstand and part of the headboard collapsed, burning through the floor.

Morgantown Fire Investigator Lieutenant Ken Tennant, who observed the test, described it as a eureka moment, scientifically proving that the fire that killed Jimmy Michael could have been set several hours before it was discovered.

"I reported back to Marcia," said Tennant, "that test number six has, within five or ten minutes, matched the timeline that we think really happened. And the engineers are going to be able to say that that's not what happened, but it's possible that it could have happened. They were glad to hear that."

CHAPTER 38

Indignant

On Monday, April 9, Shelly Michael was back in Monongalia County Circuit Court for a crucial pre-trial hearing, to discuss eleven defense motions. Tom Dyer was now attempting to block key elements of the State's case, asking Judge Stone to disallow any mention of Jimmy Michael's toxicology results. He also wanted to stop the jury being told that the state had now eliminated all accidental causes of the fire.

But most important of all, he wanted the judge to ban any mention of his client's "adulterous affair."

"We fear that if the State starts off from the opening statements," Dyer told the court, "with a presentation to the jury that there is some casual connection between this evidence and the State's theory in this case, that we will be so far behind the eightball . . . we won't be able to recover."

Prosecutor Marcia Ashdown countered, saying that Michael's affair with Bobby Teets was "clearly relevant," and therefore admissible. She said the State might call Teets as a witness, although he was not considered a co-conspirator.

"We believe that the fact that the evidence shows," she said, "that the defendant was involved in an illicit affair with another individual only days before the death of the victim and the arson occurred, is certainly relevant. And it becomes,

I think, even more relevant because Ms. Michael chose to misrepresent it and lie to the police about that."

Ashdown said that Shelly Michael's "illicit love affair" clearly went to show "potential motive" for murdering her husband.

Judge Stone agreed, ruling that the affair had "significant relevance," saying he found it to be "evident and obvious."

In other defeats for the defense, Judge Stone ruled that the State's fire experts could tell the jury that the fire could not have started accidentally, and that the toxicology results proved that Jimmy Michael's body had contained rocuronium, freely available at Ruby Memorial Hospital.

The only two defense motions granted by the judge were that a forensic accountant could discuss the Michaels' family finances, and that videotaped test runs from the hospital to 545 Killarney Drive and back could be used.

The following morning, *The Dominion Post* named Bobby Teets as Shelly Michael's adulterous lover.

"Michael Admits Affair," was the front-page headline over the latest sensational story twist.

"Teets also admitted to the affair," read the story below. "Teets was employed at Mountaineer Home Medical—the business co-owned by James Michael at the time of his death. Although it had long been rumored that Michael was having an affair prior to her husband's death, that information had not been confirmed by investigators until Monday."

After reading the story, the Reverend David Goodin sat down and wrote a letter to Prosecutor Marcia Ashdown.

Dear Ms. Ashdown:

This letter is in regard to the Michelle Michael trial and is provoked by the article in yesterday's The Dominion Post. *Specifically I am writing to communicate information that might be of importance in light of her admission of an affair with Robert Teets.*

Michelle and her late husband had been attending our church, and we hosted a memorial service for him in Mor-

gantown. After the fire, I spoke with Michelle (Shelley) [sic]
on the phone and she indicated a desire to have a service
here even though the funeral itself was to be out of town. She
made an appointment to come and see me to discuss details.

When she came, Mr. Teets showed up as well. They sat
very close on the sofa in my office and held hands through-
out the entire time. She did not at first introduce him. I
thought he might be a family member. When I subsequently
learned that he was not, I told my wife that their behavior
with one another seemed more like lovers than friends.

Of course, I cannot speculate on any detail of their rela-
tionship, nor do I have any added knowledge that would
speak to the question of her possible guilt or motive. Never-
theless I feel some obligation to report this encounter to you
in light of the latest revelations that they were, in fact, hav-
ing an affair.

Sincerely,
Rev. David Goodin.

In late May, with the pressure of her upcoming trial building, doctors increased Shelly's Zoloft dosage from 50 milligrams to 75. Tom Dyer had started rehearsing her testimony
in a Harrison County courtroom in Clarksburg. Shelly would
take the witness chair, as Dyer and his private investigator
Gina Lopez fired questions at her, and then critiqued her
answers.

"We had targeted that we needed sixty to ninety hours of
preparations," said Dyer. "That was going to be our plan,
because you've got to balance the principle of recent memory, and the need to be able to respond to all contingencies
that come up during cross-examination."

In the weeks before her trial, Shelly Michael appeared
confident, saying she was convinced that a jury would find
her not guilty. And she felt certain she would impress the
jury when she took the stand.

She carefully prepared her answers, tailored towards the
inevitable questions about her lies to police, during the two
videotaped interviews.

"Although I did not admit to sleeping with Bobby at first," she noted in a one-page, four-point document she compiled entitled *Video Notes*, "I tried very hard not to lie to Paul."

She had insisted in the interview that she and Bobby Teets were just friends and nothing more, because she did not consider it any of Detective Paul Mezzanotte's business, or pertinent to the fire. She also did not want to "ruin" Kelli's life by revealing "our Chicago incident.

"As weird as it may sound," she wrote, "I must have completely shut off the 'affair' from my memory. It sounds quite sick, given the fact that Bobby was a pawbear [sic] and stayed with us at Jimmy's parents' house for the funeral."

She had only come clean about the affair during her pre-polygraph examination, as she did not want to be "hiding" anything in the test.

She realized that the different stories she had told police about leaving the hospital significantly damaged her credibility, but explained that she was still in denial.

"Everything was like a big blur," she wrote, "as if I was in a cloud or having some kind of outer [sic] body experience."

She claimed that if she had earlier accepted the police "theory" of murder and arson, with her as the prime suspect, she would have told the truth about Bobby Teets and leaving work.

Her oldest friend Renee Del Viscio thought Shelly too complacent, not fully appreciating the gravity of her situation.

"She was very optimistic," said Renee. "I mean, there were times I would talk to her [where] she'd be in her swimming pool or out jogging, as if life was going on as normal. That sometimes bothered me a little bit. I thought maybe that could be a bit delusional."

On Monday, June 4, Shelly Michael faxed her weekly schedule to her home confinement officer. A few minutes later, she telephoned him to confirm receipt, asking for a one-hour extension that evening, saying she had to work late at the mall.

"It was a very busy day," recalled Home Confinement Supervisor Annabelle Scolapio, "and I did not make a note of what specifically she asked the extension for."

At 6:00 p.m., after finishing work, Shelly visited L.A. Nails for a one-hour beauty treatment. While there having her nails done, Shelly was recognized by someone, who immediately alerted the Monongalia County Prosecuting Attorney's Office.

The following day, her home confinement officer, Deputy William Sothen, visited L.A. Nails, confirming that she had been there for a pedicure, under her maiden name of S. Goots. That evening Deputy Sothen went to her father's house to confront her.

"First she denied being at the nail center," said Sothen. "[Then] I told her that somebody had seen her there and she told me that she had."

The deputy then checked her ankle monitoring bracelet, discovering it had been tampered with.

"When I checked Michelle's [bracelet], the clip on it was broken," he said, "and had been taped back together . . . black electrical tape, I believe it was."

Before leaving his office, Sothen had checked the computer, which showed the monitoring equipment had been working. It had recorded her being at her father's house when she had been at the beauty parlor.

When he asked when the ankle clip had broken, Shelly said that day, at 2:00 p.m., although she had not reported it. Deputy Sothen then drove Shelly to the Home Incarceration Office, where a new bracelet was fitted.

The next morning, Sothen wrote a letter to Assistant Prosecuting Attorney Perri DeChristopher, informing her of Michael's latest home confinement violation.

Two days later, on June 8, Judge Robert Stone signed an order for the immediate arrest and imprisonment of Shelly Michael, for violating the terms and conditions of her pre-trial release.

But as officers were on the way to her father's house to arrest her, Shelly crashed her car by the Stonewood Exit on Interstate 79, and was rushed by ambulance to the United Hospital Center in Clarksburg for treatment. Later that day she was released to police, who, after citing her for failure to yield and having no proof of insurance, took her to jail.

When Tom Dyer heard she was back in jail after being caught having her nails done, he was speechless.

"I cringed," he remembered. "She's indignant that she's on home confinement. She just lacked a lot of common sense, which was rather startling, because she was a very intelligent young lady."

On Wednesday, June 13, Shelly Michael appeared before Judge Robert Stone, after Monongalia prosecutors filed a motion to revoke her bond, keeping her in jail until the trial. With her hair newly braided, she appeared in court manacled and dressed in orange jail garb and flip-flops, sitting impassively in the dock throughout the hearing.

Home Incarceration Officer Sothen told the judge that Shelly Michael's ankle bracelet had been tampered with on at least six occasions.

"Normally," he said, "we have people complete a full term, six months to a year without any problem."

He also told the judge how he had gone to question Michael after she had been seen at L.A. Nails, saying she had first lied about being there, before admitting it.

Marcia Ashdown asked the judge to revoke Michael's bond, saying she was "not to be trusted" on home confinement.

"She has been tampering with or breaking her equipment," the prosecutor told the judge. "She has shown time and again that she absolutely refuses to follow the restrictions that have been imposed by the court. And that in the face of having been admonished two times by circuit court judges."

Defense attorney Tom Dyer appealed to the judge not to revoke her bond, saying she was not a flight risk.

"She is guilty of nothing," he said, "absolutely nothing

[other] than possibly gross stupidity and arrogance of these particular rules."

He maintained that imprisonment would put her at a disadvantage, in helping him prepare a "fair and adequate" defense.

Judge Stone pointed out that she was charged with first-degree murder and arson. "The allegations in this case," he said, "are just diabolical in nature."

He was also concerned about the six known cases of her monitoring equipment being tampered with, and the previous two occasions that she had appeared in front of a judge for bond violations.

"I am disturbed enough by this," he told her. "It's the 'third-time-you're-out' kind of situation. I remand [you] to the custody of the North Central Regional Jail."

CHAPTER 39

The Trial Begins

On Monday, July 2, 2007, Prosecutors Marcia Ashdown, Perri DeChristopher and two staff members relocated to Charleston for the duration of the trial, now expected to last two weeks. It was a two-and-a-half-hour drive from Morgantown, and they would all stay over during the week, going home to their families on weekends.

The two seasoned prosecutors were relieved to be able to concentrate on the trial without having to worry about any distracting family obligations.

"Charleston was probably a godsend," explained Assistant Prosecutor DeChristopher, who was a new mother. "We would be in trial all day, and our assistants would have dinner ready for us. And then we would have witness meetings late into the evening. It was truly all day and late into the evening, every evening, which made it perfect."

The prosecution team set up an office at the Embassy Suites Hotel, where they were joined by Detective Paul Mezzanotte, now working for the U.S. Postal Service, based in Kansas City, and Lieutenant Ken Tennant of the Morgantown Fire Department.

"It was an undertaking for us," recalled DeChristopher. "We set up an entire office down there with our staff. We boxed up every single piece of paper that had to do with that case. We took a computer. We took a printer. We took Post-it Notes and staplers and pens and pencils."

Attorneys for both sides, as well as Judge Stone, were all staying at the Embassy Suites Hotel. Most evenings during the trial, they all met for cocktails in the bar, to unwind before working late into the night.

Shelly Michael was also in Charleston, being held in Southern Regional Jail. In the final days before the trial, Tom Dyer carefully rehearsed her testimony.

"We spent thirty hours in just complete solitude," he said, "in a tiny six-feet–by–eight-feet conference room at the jail, preparing."

From the jail, Shelly, at this point weighing just 95 pounds, was trying to point the finger at Jimmy Michael's ex-wife Stephanie. In a letter to Dyer, she claimed that prior to the fire, Dan Estel had been "bragging" at the hospital that Stephanie would be quitting work, as they would soon be getting enough money so she could retire.

She also now claimed that she never would have left the hospital if she had been guilty, as she was fully aware of the surveillance camera at each exit.

But her biggest concern was being incarcerated during the trial.

"Don't forget," she wrote Dyer. "Ask Judge Stone to let me out on bond July 5. Tell him I'll be under direct supervision of you and Gina [Lopez], or we'll hire a guard! Please try and get me out of here!!!"

With the prospect of a high-profile murder trial in Charleston, Kanawha County officials brought an old ceremonial courtroom out of retirement. Built in 1892, the historic gothic brick building at 409 Virginia Street, Charleston, was spared in 1921 when the state capital building burned down. Most legal proceedings are held across Virginia Street in the County Judicial Building, and the large old Courtroom Number Four is only used on special occasions.

But it would be the only courtroom big enough to house all the media expected, including a full crew from CBS *48*

Hours, who planned to record the entire trial gavel-to-gavel, using special cameras hidden in large cabinets.

Ironically, Kanawha County officials had only just approved a $100,000 renovation project for it, but it would not be ready for the Michael trial.

And over the course of the trial, the old stately courtroom's terrible acoustics would prove very trying.

At 9:00 a.m. on Friday, July 6, almost twenty months after the fire, jury selection began for the Shelly Michael trial. Judge Robert Stone was now sitting as a specially assigned judge to Kanawha County for the duration of the trial.

The defense had hired a professional jury consultant named Patricia Smith, to help in selecting the jury. All through the trial, the 64-year-old grandmother, who had helped pick two hundred juries, sat directly behind Shelly Michael at the defense bench, offering support and encouragement. She even dispensed fashion advice on what outfit she should wear each day of the trial.

"She was much more than a jury consultant," enthused Dyer. "She was like an old English nanny . . . and she was there to help assist with the PR aspect of this."

As jury selection began, Smith concentrated on helping the defense weed out the jurors to Shelly Michael's advantage.

Nearly fifty Kanawha County residents had been called for jury duty. When Judge Robert Stone asked how many knew of the Shelly Michael case, about half raised their hands. Then, after dismissing around fifteen, the judge read the prospective jurors the names of more than fifty witnesses expected to be called to the stand, including Bobby Teets.

The defense and prosecuting attorneys then began questioning the remaining thirty-four individually. Tom Dyer probed them about their knowledge of house fires, and whether they had ever been involved in one. He also asked about their favorite television crime shows, as well as if any were Rush Limbaugh fans.

"Did you like to start campfires when you were a child?" Dyer asked one potential female juror.

"I don't like camping," she replied.

"Have you ever injected anybody with anything?" he continued.

"No."

Eventually the woman was selected as a juror.

By late Friday evening, Judge Stone had seated twelve jurors and two alternates, altogether comprised of seven men and seven women. After warning the jurors not to discuss the case with anyone, and to avoid any media coverage, he ordered them to return to Courtroom Four at 9:00 a.m. Monday, for opening statements.

On Friday, June 22, Tom Dyer had subpoenaed Rob Angus's friend, Morgantown Police Lieutenant Kevin Clark, as a possible defense witness. Dyer was now concentrating on Shelly Michael's ex-husband's tip-off to the police, suggesting they search Jimmy Michael's remains for a paralytic drug. The defense also planned to make a big deal of Detective Paul Mezzanotte logging Rob Angus's call (which Clark had passed on to Mezzanotte) as an anonymous phone call in his official report.

But when the defender asked him about it, Clark said he could not recall receiving any anonymous call.

CHAPTER 40

"A Death Without Mercy"

At 8:45 a.m. on Monday, July 9, a confident Shelly Michael breezed into the Kanawha County courtroom, giving a thumbs-up sign. It was captured by a *Dominion Post* news photographer, and would soon come back to haunt her.

It was standing room only in the large courtroom, and the press gallery was packed. The technical crew from *48 Hours* had set up several cameras around the court, providing feeds to the local West Virginia TV stations throughout the trial.

To the left of the court lay the defense bench, where Shelly Michael sat, wearing a low-cut pink V-neck shirt from B. Moss. She had gotten special permission from the court to flat-iron her hair during the trial.

She was flanked by her attorneys James Zimarowski and Tom Dyer, alongside jury consultant Patricia Smith and private investigator Gina Lopez. Directly behind them sat Michael and Kathi Goots, and their daughter Jennifer Barker.

To their right, at the prosecution table, sat Detective Paul Mezzanotte with Perri DeChristopher and Marcia Ashdown. Behind them were Denny and Ruth Michael, their son Steve and his wife Stacy. Alongside them were Stephanie Estel, with Jimmy Michael's two children, Drew and Jacie.

Before the jury was summoned, James Zimarowski, who would be presenting the defense's opening statement, asked Judge Stone to exclude a one-hour-and-fifty-minute edited video of Shelly Michael's damning December 8, 2005, interview with police.

"I am concerned about the context," he explained. "I am concerned about the questions by police officers."

But Judge Stone shot down the defense motion, ruling that the tape could be played for the jury. Then, in the interests of completeness, Zimarowski demanded the entire six-hour-plus interview be played. The judge said he would consider it, although doubtful that he would expose the jury to it.

The jury was then called in, and once they took their place in the box, Assistant Prosecutor Perri DeChristopher stood up to deliver her opening statement.

"Ladies and gentlemen of the jury," she began. "This is a case about death, destruction and deceit. Death—more accurately, the murder of James Michael. The destruction—more accurately, the attempted destruction of the evidence of that murder. And deceit—more accurately, the lies and continued lies of the defendant, Michelle Michael, in her attempt to cover up her murder of her husband, James Michael."

Then, as Shelly Michael took notes at the prosecution table, DeChristopher told the jury about the fire, and how the defendant's husband's body had been found after firefighters had put it out.

"The body of James Michael destroyed," she said, "or so the defendant had wished. The fire did not cause [his] death. He was dead before the fire."

She told the jury that a subsequent police investigation had uncovered the defendant's affair with Bobby Teets, which had started during a trip to Chicago together.

"The deceit of the defendant is at the heart of this case," said the prosecutor. "Of course, after learning of the affair with Bobby Teets, the defendant became a person of interest."

DeChristopher told the jury that the nurse practitioner

wanted to quit her job, and in order to do so, she needed money.

"Several months before the fire," she said, "James Michael obtained an insurance policy. And if [he] died in a fire, Northwestern Mutual Life would write a check to Michelle Michael for half-a-million dollars."

If the Michael home were "consumed by a fire," State Farm Insurance would write the defendant another check for $500,000.

The assistant prosecutor told the jury how Shelly Michael had repeatedly lied to police, denying an affair with Teets, before finally admitting it. She had also kept changing her story about her movements during the morning of the fire, leaving seventeen minutes unaccounted for.

DeChristopher said James Michael had died of the muscle-paralyzing drug rocuronium, which was freely available as a floor drug at the hospital where Shelly worked.

"It actually paralyzes the body muscle by muscle," she said. "You will hear testimony . . . there was about nine minutes of air in the lungs, and the body is attempting to get air from somewhere, and then nothing, irreversible brain damage and death. And that's the death that James Michael suffered—a death without mercy."

Winding up, the assistant prosecutor told the jury that Shelly Michael was responsible for her husband's death, before burning her house down to try to destroy all evidence of his murder.

"And, ladies and gentlemen," she said, "at the end of this trial, we will ask you to tell the defendant that the deceit stops here. And we will ask you to find her guilty of both of those charges included in the indictment, the arson and the murder in the first degree of James Michael."

After a ten-minute break, James Zimarowski strolled over to the jury box to deliver the defense's opening statement.

"I'm Jim Zimarowski and I'm from Morgantown," declared the white-suited, bearded defender, introducing himself to the jury. "And just to understand how this combination works, Tom Dyer over there—he's the one that's a little gray. I have kind of earned my gray hair. I am a little bit more senior than Tom."

In his folksy manner, Zimarowski warned the jury that they were going to be "hip deep in gossip and innuendo," as the State's case was entirely circumstantial.

"First off," he said, "this is a whodunit. In a lot of cases of this nature, major murder cases, it's never who done it. It's always *why* they did it. But in this case, it is a whodunit."

He told the jury that they would hear from a lot of witnesses who were biased against Shelly Michael.

"[She] is not the easiest personality to deal with," he admitted. "You are going to hear a lot about her personality. She is smart, aggressive, pushy. A lot of people don't like her."

He told the jury that she had an "alibi," because at 10:20 a.m., when the fire was discovered, she was at work, and had been for several hours.

"There are lots of inconvenient facts," he said. "That's why the State has to adjust the facts to conform with their theory that she did it."

Zimarowski accused detectives of a rush to judgment, by ignoring all other suspects and shoddy police work.

"Detective Mezzanotte didn't conduct the investigation," he said, "as much as he conducted an inquisition."

At that point Perri DeChristopher stood up to make an objection, and the judge sustained it, warning the defense attorney not to be argumentative.

Then Zimarowski told the jury that Michael had fully cooperated with police, and "submitted" to the police interviews.

"She wanted answers," he said. "Her house burned down. Her husband is dead. Does that pass the smell test? Evidence will show that it does."

He acknowledged that she had concealed "embarrassing information," reminding the jury that she was not charged with infidelity.

He pointed the finger at Stephanie Estel, saying that any

"reasonable investigator" would have concentrated on her, as Jimmy Michael's ex-wife.

"Evidence will show that they had, by all definitions, an incredibly messy divorce," he told the jury. "And the ex-wife blamed Shelly Michael for the break-up. One of the reasons for the divorce, as is oftentimes the case, was financial. The ex-wife never met a credit card she didn't like."

And when he questioned whether Estel had had financial difficulties, DeChristopher once again objected, leading the judge to issue a stern warning to Zimarowski for being argumentative.

"What else is unique about the ex-wife?" continued the defense attorney. "She is a respiratory therapist. She had access to rocuronium. Her current husband is a nurse and deals with syringes."

Finally, Zimarowski reminded the jury that the case against Michael depended upon circumstantial evidence, pointing in many different directions.

"At the conclusion of this case," he said, "I am not going to ask you whether or not Shelly Michael is guilty of lying. I am not going to ask you whether or not Shelly Michael is guilty of aspiring to be a full-time mother. I am not going to ask you if Shelly Michael is guilty of infidelity.

"We are going to ask you if you think Shelly Michael is guilty of death and destruction, murder and arson. And I believe all the evidence is going to be that you are going to have to return a not guilty verdict on both counts . . . because you are not going to make your decisions based on innuendo and personalities."

The defender sat down at 12:15 p.m., and the judge took a one-hour lunch recess, before the State called its first witness.

Ruth Michael was so nervous about testifying, she had taken a Xanax to steady her nerves. In emotional testimony, she told the jury how her son Jimmy Michael's marriage had changed in the months before his death.

"I noticed it was different," she said. "It was strained and stressed."

That last summer, Shelly's attitude to her had also changed, becoming less friendly and cold.

After first learning of the fire from Kelli Teets, Ruth said she and Jimmy's father had immediately set out for Morgantown. They had arrived to find Shelly at a neighbor's house, being comforted by her sister Jennifer.

"She really didn't say too much," Ruth remembered. "She was just sitting there with her head back. She had a blanket on. She wasn't crying. I would describe it as 'cold.'"

That night at the Hotel Morgan, her daughter-in-law finally displayed some emotion during a local television news report on the fire.

"She got very upset," said Ruth. "Like she was angry."

Over the next few days, Shelly's behavior became stranger, as she seemed more concerned about the cost of funeral arrangements than losing her husband.

"Well, she still wasn't upset as far as crying or anything," Ruth testified. "And she questioned the price of a few things."

Under Tom Dyer's cross-examination, Ruth agreed that following Jimmy's death, she had attended Alec's birthday party, as well as spending Christmas with her daughter-in-law and exchanging presents.

Dyer then asked about any rumors she had heard regarding Shelly's affair with Bobby Teets.

"I don't believe the name was mentioned," Ruth replied, "but it was mentioned she was having an affair."

"What else did you hear?" asked Dyer.

"She was supposed to have had an abortion," said Ruth. "I don't know if you wanted me to say that or not."

The next witness was Denny Michael, who testified how Shelly had wanted to transport Jimmy's body to Cumberland herself for burial, to cut costs.

"She was upset," he told the jury. "It was all about money."

Then, in riveting testimony, he described the night before the funeral, when Shelly had requested that Bobby and Kelli Teets stay over at his house. He'd left to run an errand, before returning through a back door, to discover his daughter-in-law in a compromising position with one of his son's employees.

"Bobby Teets was in his pajamas," Denny testified, "an
he had his arms around Shelly and [was] kissing her on th
cheek. She immediately shoved him away when I walked i
They were like two teenagers in love, and this was the nigh
before the funeral."

Tom Dyer had no questions for Denny Michael, who wa
then dismissed.

For the rest of the day, the State focused on the fata
November 29, 2005, fire, calling a succession of witnesse
to chronologically illustrate what had happened that mornin

First up was respiratory therapist and volunteer firefighte
Shawn Alt, who told the jury he had returned home to Killar
ney Drive at around 8:00 a.m., after working a shift at Rub
Memorial, and smelled burning building materials.

After seeing no signs of a fire in the "drizzly, rainy an
overcast" conditions, he had called a fellow firefighter t
check if anything had been reported, leaving a message.

Alt had then gone inside his house to change clothes, bu
ten minutes later, when he came out, there was still the smel
of burning.

He then pulled out of his driveway, proceeding to th
stop sign at Killarney Drive and Eastern Avenue, seeing hi
neighbor Shelly Michael parked in her driveway.

"I saw a silver Expedition which looked like the one Shelly
drove," he testified, "backing out of the driveway."

And without paying too much attention, he waved to hi
neighbor and hospital colleague, but she ignored him, driv
ing straight past towards the hospital.

In his cross-examination, Tom Dyer asked if he had looke
at the Michael residence, a block away from his house, an
seen any smoke.

"No," replied Alt.

"Did you walk any closer to their residence, Mr. Alt?"

"No."

The next witness was Morgantown Utility Board worke
Monty Savage II, who drove past 545 Killarney Drive a
about 10:15 a.m., seeing smoke coming from the rafters
Under Perri DeChristopher's direct questioning, Savage

described how his colleague Rodney Compton had made the 911 call, while Monty repeatedly knocked on the door. When he'd looked through a side window in the door, he'd seen a line of burning across the upstairs floor.

"I do remember seeing flames falling," he said. "There were particles falling down and laying on the floor."

Then about five or six minutes after Compton's 911 call, the first fire engines arrived.

The State next called Morgantown firefighter Keith Summers, whose Collins Ferry Road house faced Killarney Drive. That morning, he'd been at home waiting for a new refrigerator to arrive, when the delivery driver told him about a fire several houses down.

"I left my house and proceeded to walk down the street," he told Assistant Prosecutor Perri DeChristopher. "The house did have smoke coming from the eaves, so I contacted 911 and reported the fire."

He'd then gone to the front door of the Michael house, encountering Savage and Compton. Finding it locked, he'd gone to the back, looking for an open door. He'd noticed that the top-floor window was very darkly smoke-stained, like the glass of a limousine.

Then he'd tried to gain access through the rear French doors.

"As I approached the doors," he told the jury, "the top right-hand side shattered and flames burst from that window. There [was] absolutely no visible fire until the window broke."

Morgantown firefighter Gary Freshour next testified that his crew, with three engines and a ladder truck, had raced to the scene.

"We had fire coming out of the upstairs bedroom," he told the jury. "The fire was out the windows and appeared to be starting through the roof."

In dramatic testimony, Freshour described for the jury how he had entered the house, seeing a large hole in the ceiling, and piles of fallen smoldering debris on the floor below. He had then gone upstairs, where there was light smoke and

all the rooms were intact, except the last one on the righ
which was ablaze.

"It was starting out of that room," he said. "It had basi
cally started to consume everything."

After the fire had been put out, word came over the radi
that there might be a resident inside. Later, after Jimmy Mi
chael's body had been found on the bed, Freshour went bac
inside the bedroom.

"The occupant was on the remains of the bed, layin
down," he said.

Once again Tom Dyer had no questions for the witness.

The State's final witness that day was Morgantown Fir
Department's chief fire investigator, Lieutenant Ken Ten
nant. For the rest of the day and the following morning, h
would methodically describe his findings for the jury.

He had arrived at 545 Killarney Drive to help out the fir
crews. But about fifteen minutes after he got there, an emo
tional Bobby Teets had come up behind him, saying that i
there was a car in the garage, his boss Jimmy Michael wa
inside the house.

"I took a tool and broke the window of the garage," Ten
nant testified. "And there was a car inside, a silver sedan
The information was relayed to the personnel inside fightin;
the fire, to free up a couple of people to search for a possibl
victim."

At about 11:00 a.m., Lieutenant Tennant received a cal
that a victim had been discovered in the bedroom, and a
that point, he took over the fire investigation.

"I went to the second floor," he said, "and told people i
the area to stop throwing things out of the window."

After contacting Morgantown Police Department, to re
port an "unattended death" at 545 Killarney Drive, Lieuten
ant Tennant had inspected the appliances in the basemen
utility room, checking the circuit breakers for the master bed
room, which had not been tripped by an overload.

Then, using photographs projected on a large screen to
the left of the courtroom, he led the jury on a tour of the
house the morning of the fire.

"As I came out of the hallway, looking at the kitchen," he said, "you couldn't even tell that a fire occurred upstairs, other than the front door is open or there is a hose coming through [it]."

With a laser pointer, he showed the jury the scene in the living room, with a large rectangular hole running from wall to wall.

"When I looked up through this hole," he said, "you could actually see the top of the bed frame. The headboard had already been consumed by fire, but you could see the bed itself kind of hanging down into this hole."

Then, in a well-planned strategic move, previously agreed upon with prosecutors, Lieutenant Tennant displayed a photograph of the undamaged living room fireplace.

"The fireplace had decorative walls on it, and a white birch decorative log," said Tennant, looking straight at Tom Dyer for his reaction. "There was no evidence of ashes in the bottom of the box . . . so obviously there was no fire in this fireplace at the time of this incident."

This single photograph would neutralize the defense's much-vaunted fire expert Patrick McGinley, whose report had found that the fire could have started in the fireplace. Ultimately the defense never called McGinley to the stand to testify.

At this point, Judge Stone recessed for the first day, instructing the jury to be back in their room at 9:00 the next morning.

CHAPTER 41
Cold

The next morning, prosecutors Marcia Ashdown and Perri DeChristopher were coming out of the elevator at the Embassy Suites, when they saw the front page of *The Dominion Post* in the hotel shop.

"And there's a picture of Shelly standing there giving the thumbs-up," recalled DeChristopher, who had not witnessed the incident. "It was shocking, and we're like, 'What in the world is that?'"

"And of course," added Ashdown, "the local populace was appalled."

That front page crystallized public opinion against Shelly Michael, as no one could quite believe her insensitivity at her own murder trial.

"People look at her as a cool cucumber," *Dominion Post* editor Geri Ferrara later told *48 Hours*. "That's the word around town, is that they thought she was so cold. You'd think that her attorney would have warned her not to do that."

That morning, Lieutenant Ken Tennant retook the stand, describing to the jury in harrowing detail the terrible state of Jimmy Michael's burned body. Ruth and Denny Michael sobbed continuously when the series of graphic photographs of their son's remains were projected on a large screen in front of the jury. But Shelly Michael, wearing a khaki dress suit, had no reaction.

"That's one of the most difficult things I've ever had to do," recalled Lieutenant Tennant. "And I found myself deliberately making eye contact with Shelly. She had absolutely no emotion on seeing the condition of her husband's body. Taking notes. Cold."

In cross-examination, Tom Dyer used a copy of the *National Fire Protection Association Handbook*, to pick holes in the fire investigation. He tried to get the lead fire investigator to admit that the fire had only been ruled arson after the medical examiner had ruled Jimmy Michael's death a homicide.

"Are you saying, Lieutenant," asked the defense attorney 'that your finding that this is an arson is because there's an apparent victim of a homicide?"

"It is a significant portion of the investigation," replied Tennant.

"Lieutenant," continued Dyer, "the fire determines the fire, not the fact that there is a victim, right? I mean, State Farm doesn't pay, two, three, four hundred thousand bucks lightly. Why wouldn't they have waited? They are playing by the same rules?"

At that point Marcia Ashdown objected, and Judge Stone sustained her, saying that the question called for speculation.

For the rest of the morning, Tom Dyer hammered away at the elaborate ATF fire investigation, comparing the results to "trying to squeeze a square peg into a round hole."

"They just keep tinkering with these variables?" he said.

"I don't think there was anything to tinker with," Tennant replied. "I think they may find exception to your description."

After the lunch recess, West Virginia Deputy Chief Medical Examiner Dr. Hamada Mahmoud told the jury about Jimmy Michael's November 30 autopsy in Charleston.

"Would you describe the condition of the external parts of the body?" asked Prosecutor Marcia Ashdown.

"Mr. Michael was in a state of severe charring of the

body," said Dr. Mahmoud. "Everything was gone—facial features, the neck, scars, toes, clothing. The whole charred body is charred black and [in] some areas, the skin didn't look like skin."

He described how the body was in a "pugilistic attitude," commonly found in severe burn victims, because of muscle contraction in high temperatures.

He had then checked for carbon monoxide and soot deposits, to discover whether Jimmy Michael had been alive when the fire started. There were no soot deposits in the airways or evidence of carbon monoxide, proving that he was dead prior to the fire.

As identification was impossible from the condition of the remains, the doctor X-rayed the jaw, so the teeth could later be compared to previous dental records.

But many of Jimmy Michael's internal body organs were in good condition, allowing him to take samples for toxicology testing.

"We were lucky in this case," Dr. Mahmoud explained. "The liver was intact and we took a piece and some gastric content and bile."

Months later the results came back, showing rocuronium in the body, allowing Dr. Mahmoud to complete the death certificate.

"Rocuronium overdose," he testified. "That's the main cause of death, which caused respiratory paralysis and stopping of the breathing."

On cross, James Zimarowski questioned Dr. Mahmoud about defensive wounds. He suggested that as both Jimmy Michael's hands and feet were missing, it was impossible to know if he had been defending himself.

"Well, I look at the parts that are missing," said Zimarowksi, "and I would note that [these are] the parts that we would likely find defensive wounds?"

"That's correct," admitted the doctor, adding that all the fractures shown by X-rays were fire-related.

"There are no puncture wounds, no stab wounds," noted Zimarowski, "but you couldn't tell about a nightstick?"

"Talk about bruises or abrasions or lacerations," replied the doctor. "There was no way we could find that."

The next witness was the State's chief toxicologist, Dr. James Kraner, who testified that Detective Paul Mezzanotte had sent him a nine-page fax, listing various drugs that the defendant had access to.

With this in mind he had commissioned National Medical Services to test for nonpolarizing neuromuscular blocking agents.

"Did you subsequently receive the results back from the third submission of the liver tissue?" asked Perri DeChristopher.

"Yes," said Dr. Kraner. "The liver showed a significant concentration of the drug rocuronium."

Following the afternoon recess, Jimmy Michael's life-long friend Kerri Whitacre took the stand. Under Ashdown's questioning, she told of her strange meeting with Shelly Michael, on the afternoon of the fire.

"Shelly wasn't crying," Whitacre said. "I thought that was odd. I sat on the couch beside her and I was getting ready to say something, and she said, 'Did you get that outfit at B. Moss?' "

A few days later, Whitacre had attended the funeral service in Cumberland, having the opportunity to observe her friend's widow.

"She did not appear to be grieving," Whitacre testified. "She had a very flat affect. I realize people grieve in different ways, but I did not see any outward grieving."

In his cross-examination, Tom Dyer asked if it would be fair to characterize Shelly as being in "emotional shock," after the fire which had killed her husband.

"I think that would be fair," Whitacre replied, "if there were no other conversations going on. But it appeared that she was able to . . . focus enough that my pants would match the pants from B. Moss."

"That struck you as very odd?" asked the defense attorney.

"That struck me as extremely odd," she replied.

Dyer then asked Whitacre if she was aware that Jimmy Michael had been under investigation for hitting Drew. When she said she was, Dyer asked if he had been "angry and upset" with his ex-wife Stephanie.

"Not necessarily," said Whitacre. "He said, 'It is what it is.'"

The final witness of the day was the Michael family's former pastor, the Reverend David Goodin, who had written to Marcia Ashdown a few weeks earlier about his strange meeting with Shelly and Bobby Teets.

Reverend Goodin said Shelly had insisted that the memorial service be held as quickly as possible, despite his protestations that one day's notice was not enough time.

He testified that she'd come to his office accompanied by Bobby Teets, holding his hand the entire time.

They "behaved more like lovers than friends," he told the jury, describing the recently widowed woman's behavior as "rather brazen."

In cross-examination Tom Dyer asked why Goodin had written the letter to Marcia Ashdown.

"When the newspaper reported that they had admitted to an affair," he replied, "I thought the encounter perhaps had some weight in terms of a trial. I felt a civic responsibility. It did seem unusual to me . . . that someone who is planning a memorial service for her deceased husband would bring with her a person she was having an affair with. So I felt I should inform the prosecutor."

Judge Stone then recessed for the day, warning the jury to avoid all the heavy media coverage of the case.

CHAPTER 42

"I Made a Huge Mistake"

On Wednesday morning—day three of the trial—the State called Bobby Teets. There had been much anticipation about Shelly Michael's lover taking the stand to explain himself, and the ceremonial courtroom was packed.

Under Marcia Ashdown's direct questioning, Teets said that he and Jimmy Michael had first become friends in 2000, when they'd coached their sons in Little League. His wife Kelli also befriended Shelly, as they were both coaching their daughters in cheerleading.

"We all became very good friends," he told the jury, as Shelly sat at the defense table, avoiding his gaze.

Teets said that a few days after he started working for Mountaineer Home Medical, he and Shelly had visited Chicago to attend an embroidery seminar, to help with their new business. While there, they'd had sex for the first time in a hotel room.

"We both slept in the bed," a blushing Teets told the jury. "It just happened."

"And so," asked Ashdown, "I am going to take it that you had sexual relations?"

"Correct," replied Teets uncomfortably, as Shelly looked away.

After leaving early the next morning to return to Morgantown, he'd had little contact with Shelly until the Saturday of the Thanksgiving weekend.

"Jimmy was out of town hunting that day," testified Teets. "I stopped over there early in the morning. I guess [to be] intimate with her."

And with their two daughters, Regan and Kylie, sleeping next door, they made love again in Jimmy Michael's bed.

"What kind of conversations did you and Shelly Michael have during these rendezvous that you were having?" asked the prosecutor.

"It's kind of like a high-school flirty crush thing," Teets answered nervously. "We would ask each other if we felt bad. I know her and Jimmy weren't very intimate."

"And what did she tell you about her and her relations with Jim and their times of intimacy?" asked Ashdown.

"She just said they didn't have sex very often," he replied. "Jimmy would get mad because he wanted to have sex and she didn't."

Then the prosecutor asked if Shelly had ever discussed how she wanted their relationship to progress.

"We both had said it would need to be kept a secret," he said. "I had a lot at stake."

Teets testified that sometimes "in the heat of the moment," Shelly would tell him she wanted to hold him forever. But he maintained that he'd always told her that he would never leave Kelli, because of the children.

Just three days later, when he arrived at Killarney Drive and saw Jimmy Michael's house on fire, his initial thought was that he had discovered the affair.

"I felt a ton of guilt," he told the jury. "Well, he had found out about the affair and this is what happened."

In the days after the fire, Teets had comforted Shelly in her hotel room, maintaining that nothing improper had ever happened.

"I would sit in the bed with her and hold her," he said. "I mean, her husband had just died. Believe it or not . . . after that last time, there was never ever a time when we were ever like that again."

Then Ashdown asked about the night before the funeral, and being alone with the defendant at Jimmy's father's house.

"I don't know if we were totally alone," he replied. "There were probably times when I hugged her and made sure she was OK. But, like I said, her husband just died. I probably hugged a lot of people I didn't know."

Asked about the meeting to discuss the memorial service in Reverend Goodin's office, Teets admitted holding hands with her.

"I was probably comforting her," he explained.

Finally, Ashdown asked him what, with hindsight, he felt about the affair.

"I wish I could take it back," he replied. "I mean, I made a huge mistake . . . that I should never have made."

Then Marcia Ashdown walked back to the prosecutors' table, and Tom Dyer had no questions for Bobby Teets.

Earlier in the day, the State had called a succession of highly damaging witnesses to the defense. The Michaels' former friend and neighbor Deborah Harris testified about Shelly's mercurial nature, and her obsessive need to control. She also observed how their marriage had deteriorated the summer before Jimmy's death.

"It seemed like they were not quite as together," she said, "like they always used to be."

She also testified about Shelly's strange behavior after the fire.

"[Once] I said, 'Is there anything I can get for you?'" she recalled. "And she said, 'A new husband.'"

When Harris had offered to bring her mail to the funeral, Shelly only appeared interested in getting a new bank card she'd been expecting, for access to the trust fund money.

Harris also testified that in January 2006, during the three days the ATF investigators were inside her house,

Shelly had repeatedly telephoned her on a "fishing expedition."

"Chit-chat at first," she said, "and then she started asking questions about what I had seen."

In his cross-examination, Tom Dyer asked if Harris was aware that Shelly had lost everything in the fire. When she said she was not, he asked why she had thought it "awfully curious" that she would want to access a fund set up to help her family.

"I thought it odd she wasn't interested in any of the other mail," replied Harris. "I noticed as I was looking through, that the children were receiving doctor appointment cards. And I mentioned that and she didn't seem to even be concerned. Just the bank card."

Still more damaging testimony came from her husband's two best friends, Jeremy Miller and Reggie Ours. Miller testified that Jimmy Michael had confided to him that he suspected Shelly of being unfaithful.

"She stayed all night at the Italian Festival," said Miller. "I asked him if he thought she was cheating on him, and he said he didn't know."

Miller testified that in the weeks before his death, Jimmy was receiving marriage counseling from Pastor Cain.

"Jimmy did not want a divorce," he told the jury. "He had already experienced divorce once, and he was trying to do the biblical and godly things."

Miller said that in the aftermath of the fire and Jimmy's death, Shelly seemed cold and emotionless.

"I've never seen her shed a tear," he said. "Honestly."

In his cross, Tom Dyer asked if Jimmy had had issues with his ex-wife, after she contacted Child Protective Services about him beating Drew.

"That was some of it, yes," said Miller.

Reggie Ours then testified that in the fall of 2005, Jimmy often discussed the state of his marriage.

"He was having so many problems at home," Ours told the jury.

On the morning of the fire, the respiratory therapist had

been working alongside Shelly Michael, at the Ruby Memorial Hospital Pediatric Intensive Care Unit.

"Shelly came up," he said, "and actually goosed me in the butt. I thought that was very odd."

He also testified that a few days after the fire, he had asked Shelly who would want to harm Jimmy, and if anything was missing from the house.

"And she said no," testified Ours. "I then asked, what could have caused the fire? And she told me that that morning she ironed her clothes, and that they had an iron that was faulty. She was concerned that the iron may have fallen over, and actually started the fire. She felt terrible about that."

Ours was then excused, as Tom Dyer had no questions for him.

Then Deborah Harris's husband Dan took the stand, in his capacity as Ruby Memorial's head of security. He testified that several days after the fire, Detective Paul Mezzanotte had come to the hospital, asking him to check video surveillance tapes, to see if Shelly had left the hospital the morning of the fire.

Then, projecting excerpts from the video onto a screen for the jury, Harris used a laser pointer to illustrate Shelly Michael exiting through the west lobby at 8:11 a.m. on November 29. The next excerpt was at 8:25:11, showing her Ford Explorer going past the hospital. Twenty-nine seconds later the SUV is seen searching for a parking space. She is then seen parking her vehicle, getting out and putting up an umbrella, before walking back into the hospital through the east lobby doors at 8:28:37.

The next video screened for the jury was time-stamped 10:45:49. It showed Shelly heading to her vehicle to drive home, after learning of the fire.

In his cross, Dyer attempted to show that the surveillance video proved nothing.

"OK," he said. "She leaves somewhere. She exits the hospital and walks to a point outside the hospital, as, I guess, is all you would know?"

"That's all I would know," admitted Dan Harris.

"You worked with Detective Mezzanotte in reviewing these videos, correct?" asked the defense attorney.

"I reviewed it first," said Harris, "and then told him I had it, and he reviewed it."

The next witness was Rob Angus, who was closely questioned by Marcia Ashdown about whether Shelly Michael ever left work to see her children before school while he had custody. Angus testified that he would routinely drop Alec off at school, before taking Kylie to Burger King for breakfast.

"Were there times when your ex-wife would show up?" asked Ashdown.

"Yes, sometimes," said Angus.

"Do you know if she was coming from work on those days?"

"Again, I never really kept track," said Angus. "Sometimes she would show up in dress clothes, and I assumed she was either going to or coming from [work]."

Angus also said he had first tipped off detectives, that they should be testing for a paralytic drug, after receiving a call from his sister Shannon Rudy, who worked at the hospital and was Shelly's one-time boss.

"She just briefly explained that there was a drug they used that caused paralysis," Angus testified. "And it wasn't considered a narcotic, and that she didn't know if it was something that would be tested for. She didn't make any implications as to who may have administered the drug, but she said that I may want to call and tell them."

So Angus had then telephoned his friend and Morgantown police officer Lieutenant Kevin Clark, who then put him in contact with Detective Paul Mezzanotte.

"I told him that I really didn't want to drag my sister into it," said Angus. "I would rather it be anonymous. That he could do with it what he would."

In cross-examination, Tom Dyer asked how Angus's ex-wife was as a mother.

"She was a good mother to the kids," he replied. "I can't

deny that. She was very involved. Helped my daughter coach cheerleading."

On day four of the trial—Thursday, July 12—Stephanie Estel told the jury that Shelly Michael had broken up her marriage.

"She was chasing after my husband," Estel testified, "prior to our divorce."

"How long after your marriage did she become engaged to Jimmy?" asked Perri DeChristopher.

"I believe a couple of weeks."

Preempting the defense, DeChristopher questioned her about calling in the police during "disagreements" with Jimmy. Estel acknowledged it had happened twice, with charges being filed. But eventually they had come to an understanding, after Jimmy had apologized.

She also testified that everything concerning the children had had to go through Shelly, as Estel was "not permitted" to call her ex-husband's cell phone.

"I had to call Shelly," she said. "I had to tell Shelly what the issue was. She would call Jim and then call me back with a response."

She said that after her ex-husband had beaten Drew and been so contrite, they had come to an understanding, drastically improving her and Jimmy's relationship.

Questioned about the morning of the fire, Stephanie said she had been home with her new-born baby until 10:45 a.m., when she left with her husband Dan to run errands.

In cross-examination, James Zimarowski immediately asked the nurse if she had ever worked with rocuronium.

"No, sir," she replied.

"You have never been present when it has been administered to any patient for intubations?"

"Excuse me," she asked, "you mean in a patient?"

"I'm sorry," said the defense attorney. "Whatever, correct me on the terminology. Have you ever been present when the drug was administered?"

Estel said she had been present several times when ro-curonium had been used on patients.

"You know Rob Angus, don't you?" Zimarowski continued.

"Yes," she replied.

"In fact," said Zimarowski, "you dated him for a while, didn't you?"

"Yes."

"And that was after he divorced Shelly Michael and after James Michael divorced you?"

"Yes."

"So you two got to be very close, because you had a common interest, in that your ex-spouses had left you two for another person—for each other?"

"Yes."

Then Stephanie said she no longer had any contact with Angus, and had only briefly spoken to him the morning of the fire and not since.

"Let's look at your relationship with James Michael," said Zimarowski. "You had a kind of love/hate relationship with him?"

"Yes."

"You were rather obsessed with him over a period of time?"

"No," she replied.

Then Zimarowski suggested that on occasion, she'd stalked her ex-husband, keeping watch on the Killarney Drive house. He asked if she had told Detective Mezzanotte that she had seen Bobby Teets' car parked outside while Jimmy was out.

"That's correct," she answered.

"So," asked Zimarowski, "is that just gossip, or you just happened to be in the neighborhood, watching the Michael house when you saw the Teetses' car at the house?"

"No," she replied firmly, "I was picking up Kylie Angus to take her to a church youth group."

The defender then asked if she was familiar with the inside of 545 Killarney Drive, and had ever been upstairs.

"No," she replied.

In redirect, Perri DeChristopher asked if there was a time when she had discovered that Shelly was physically disciplining Drew.

"Yes," she replied.

"How did you become aware of that?" DeChristopher followed up.

"There was a mark on my son. I asked that she not strike my children."

That afternoon, Detective Paul Mezzanotte took the stand, to tell the jury about his investigation. He was also there to set the stage for the two lengthy videotapes of Shelly's December 8 interview, to be screened for the jury later.

The detective described arriving at 545 Killarney Drive in the wake of the fire, and interviewing people close to Jimmy Michael. He said he was soon concentrating on the recently widowed Shelly Michael, after learning that the marriage was in trouble.

By the time of his first interview with the defendant, he knew fire marshals were already suspicious of the "very unusual" fire. He had also interviewed Shawn Alt, who'd claimed to have seen Michael at the house several hours before the fire was reported.

"She gave a timeframe when she arrived at the hospital," he told the jury. "She said that between eight o'clock a.m. and eight-thirty, she had left the hospital to go out to her car and get her pager."

"Did she ever tell you that she went back to her house?" asked Prosecutor DeChristopher.

"No," he replied, saying that that had caused him "concern."

Detective Mezzanotte had gone to Ruby Memorial the next day, asking Security Manager Dan Harris to look through surveillance video for any sightings of Shelly Michael. Later that day, he'd viewed the video, clearly showing Michael leaving the hospital at 8:11 a.m. and then returning seventeen minutes later.

"We now had physical or direct evidence," the detective told the jury, "that supported Mr. Alt's statement, placing her at the scene of the fire between eight-twenty and eight-thirty."

Later that day, he had learned from Reggie Ours that shortly before the fire Michael, had stayed overnight in a Chicago hotel with Bobby Teets.

"Jim Michael didn't make the trip," said Mezzanotte, "so that was another point of concern."

Things were moving fast, and then he had received a call from Medical Examiner Dr. John Carson, saying that Jimmy Michael had been dead before the fire had started.

"They were going to rule that death as a homicide," he said, "by unknown violent acts."

The detective said that after locating the hotel and the room they'd stayed in, Teets was re-interviewed on December 7, readily admitting the affair. Straight after the interview, Detective Mezzanotte had conducted a lengthy interview with Shelly Michael.

"To be honest with you," he told the jury, "I was a little more confused when she left than I was when she got there. It was just a string of inconsistencies. A string of lies."

Shelly had then requested a second interview for the following day, and Mezzanotte asked Sergeant James Merrill to sit in and give an objective opinion.

At that point, the two edited videos of the marathon six-hour-and-forty-minute interview were played on a large television monitor in front of the jury.

Over the next several hours the jury watched in rapt attention, as Shelly Michael repeatedly changed her story about Bobby Teets and going home the morning of the fire, as she was confronted with more and more damning evidence.

After the video was shown, Perri DeChristopher asked the detective how many times he had asked Michael at the first December 7 interview about having an affair with Teets.

"Too many to count," he replied, adding that she had finally admitted it several hours into the December 8 interview.

"How long into that interview," asked DeChristopher, "did the defendant admit going to her house?"

"Again, it was very late in the interview," he said. "After several hours."

In cross-examination, James Zimarowski went on the attack, asking the detective whether he had interviewed other potential suspects, like the ex-spouses Stephanie Estel and Rob Angus. He replied that he had spoken to both of them, but there was no evidence against either.

"So it was not relevant," continued the defense attorney, "when Stephanie Estel was working in the same units and having the same access to the same medications and drugs?"

"Correct," replied Mezzanotte.

"How many other people had access to those drugs at the hospital prior to November twenty-nine, 2005?"

"Not to be facetious," said the detective, "but probably everybody but the kitchen staff."

Zimarowski then asked if he had checked out Stephanie and Dan Estel's alibis for the morning of the fire, and the detective said he had.

"And you took them at their word?" asked the defense attorney.

"Why wouldn't I take them at their word?" replied Mezzanotte.

"Why wouldn't you take Michelle Michael at her word?" Zimarowski demanded to know.

"Because every time we gave her the opportunity to do that, she lied," he replied.

"Is she charged with lying?" asked Zimarowski.

"No, sir."

"Is she charged with infidelity?"

"No, sir."

"Is she charged with leaving hospital grounds without permission, which could result in termination of her employment?"

"No, sir."

For the rest of the day, Zimarowski sparred with Mezzanotte, tenaciously attacking his investigation from all angles.

"What I am asking you for the thirteenth time is," said Zimarowski, losing patience, "did you require of anyone on the hospital staff to get the records of rocuronium or any other drug on the unit, compare the inventories at a given date to another given date, minus what was administered to patients?"

"And I will answer it for you for the thirteenth time," replied Mezzanotte coolly. "No."

Finally, midway through Zimarowski's cross-examination, Judge Stone adjourned for the day, telling the jury that he now expected the trial to finish at the end of next week.

That night from her Southern Regional Jail cell, Shelly Michael wrote a letter to defense attorney James Zimarowski, firing him.

Dear Jim,
Thank you for everything you've done for my case up to this point. I have decided, however, that I would prefer that you have no further involvement in my defense—effective immediately. I want Mr. Dyer to resume the cross-examination of Detective Mezzanotte in the morning, and take care of everything else from that point forward. Thanks again,

Sincerely
Michelle L. Michael

Late that night, Judge Robert Stone held an urgent meeting in his Embassy Suites Hotel room, to decide the best way of handling Zimarowski's dismissal.

"It was certainly unusual," Tom Dyer would later say. "Shelly wanted to direct and control every single thought that Mr. Zimarowski or I had about this case. And it started to ultimately wear on Mr. Zimarowski a lot more than it did me. And that played into the ultimate decision on her part to let him go."

The next morning, before court began, there was a further meeting in the judge's chambers, attended by Shelly

Michael and attorneys from both sides. Tom Dyer began by saying that his client had not changed her mind about dismissing his co-counsel.

"Your Honor," said Zimarowski, "I would add that we also discussed the strategic implications of how that would affect witness presentation, and Ms. Michael recognizes these issues."

Judge Stone observed there was "nothing wrong" with the defendant changing her attorney in the middle of a cross-examination.

"It's just obviously very unusual," he said. "You never know what a jury might imply, or infer."

Then the judge asked Michael on the record if there had been any "pressure, threats or intimidation" on her decision.

"No, sir," she replied.

"Would you describe this as your decision?" asked the judge.

"Yes, sir. And my family," she replied.

Tom Dyer then suggested that the jury be told that Zimarowski would be unable to further participate in the trial, without elaborating any further. The judge agreed.

Then Marcia Ashdown said that word of Zimarowski's dismissal had already spread to the Morgantown Police Department.

"Somebody is already spreading the rumor and innuendos," she told the judge. "It wasn't any of us."

A few minutes later, the trial resumed for the fifth day, with Judge Stone making a brief address to the jury.

"Good morning," he said. "We are ready to continue. I need to advise you, Mr. Zimarowski is unable to participate any further in the defense of this case, so Mr. Dyer will conclude the cross-examination of the witness, who is on the stand."

"Detective," Dyer began confrontationally, "how does all this stuff happen? You're the lead investigator. Can you tell this jury? The State has called this a murder and an arson. How do these things happen?"

"I don't understand your question," replied Detective Mezzanotte.

"How is the victim killed?"

"The victim was killed by a lethal injection of a drug called rocuronium," stated Mezzanotte.

"Do you have a theory about how the accused has done this?"

"We do. Our theory of the case is that Ms. Michael, having access to rocuronium in her capacity as nurse practitioner, [and] the instability of the marriage . . . She used the drugs stolen from Ruby Hospital to inject and to kill her husband, and used the fire to cover up the crime scene and to conceal [it] and cover up evidence."

For the next few minutes Tom Dyer retraced Zimarowski's questioning from the previous day, before sarcastically dismissing the State's case.

"She has access to the drug, mechanism of death," declared Dyer. "She is the man's wife. She has been on a road trip and had a fling—committed adultery—fairly recently to his death. There is a life insurance policy. She is the beneficiary. What have I missed?"

"That she continued to pull herself into the middle of this investigation," replied Mezzanotte, "due to the constant lies that she told us and the inconsistencies in her statements."

"She has lied and been inconsistent," said Dyer. "She lied about the affair, the jaunt to Chicago, and she lied about leaving the hospital?"

"Correct," replied the detective.

"What else?" asked Dyer. "Is that it?"

"Those are two of the most important lies that we needed to cover," said Mezzanotte. "The affair led to the motive in the investigation. And the coming back to the house, you have got to account for that. And those are lies that you can't overlook when you are investigating, you know, a homicide, where the spouse is putting herself in the circle. We didn't build the investigation around her. She led us to this investigation. They are not small lies."

In redirect, Perri DeChristopher asked the detective how

the defendant's lies had altered during the course of the interview.

"When you confront Miss Michael with a fact," he explained, "the story would change until she presented an answer that would be the least damaging for her. It changed from, 'I didn't leave the hospital' [to] 'I didn't leave the hospital, I drove around the parking lot.' It just would get wider and wider and wider until you established the truth. And that happened with several topics throughout our interview."

Then DeChristopher asked where Jimmy Michael's cell phone had been found after the fire. Mezzanotte replied that it had been lying on a kitchen countertop. He said that police were surprised to find it, as several witnesses, including Shelly Michael, had said he always kept it on the nightstand by his side of the bed.

"When you retrieved that cell phone," asked the prosecutor, "you found a message from the defendant?"

"Yes, we did," said Mezzanotte.

"At what time?"

"Approximately 7:27 a.m. on the twenty-ninth," replied the detective.

On Monday, July 16—the sixth day of the trial—the State called Dr. Robert Johnstone to the stand. The Morgantown-based professor of anesthesiology at West Virginia University, was there to explain the effect of rocuronium to the jury.

"Rocuronium is a neuromuscular blocker," said Dr. Johnstone. "It's a drug that paralyzes skeletal muscles [used] frequently in the operating room and occasionally in critical care units."

He explained that the powerful drug would be standard within the stock supplies of nursing stations.

"It's widely available," said the doctor, "if you know where to find it."

And Dr. Johnstone observed the similarities between rocuronium and pancuronium, the drug used on death row for lethal injections—although out of human kindness, inmates would first be sedated, as the drug has no effect on awareness.

"So the drug should only be given to patients," he said, "who are sedated or unconscious."

The doctor told the jury that rocuronium is never given to a patient while conscious, and never used without artificial ventilation, as once it takes effect, breathing is impossible.

The anesthesiologist then gave the jury a horrific timeline of how the drug would have first paralyzed and then killed Jimmy Michael.

Standing at the witness stand he plunged a syringe full of rocuronium into a grapefruit, saying that the defendant would have needed no more than a second to administer a fatal dose.

A minute later, said Dr. Johnstone, he would have started feeling the effects, with weakness in his major muscles. Three minutes later he would be unable to stand up, and four minutes after that he would be unable to breathe, as his respiratory muscles and tongue became paralyzed.

Fully aware of his situation, and with vision and hearing intact, Jimmy Michael would have fought to survive, struggling to breathe for two or three minutes, before the oxygen in his blood was used up.

Then several agonizing minutes after that, he would have slipped into unconsciousness, before becoming brain-dead.

"What do you believe the total time would be," asked Prosecutor Marcia Ashdown, "during which James Michael would have been still conscious?"

"From injection to unconsciousness," estimated Dr. Johnstone, "would be about twelve to thirteen minutes. You would start getting progressive brain death, and death would occur within about five minutes after unconsciousness. You would be fully awake until you lost consciousness, and fully thinking."

During the doctor's harrowing account of her son's torturous death, his mother started to sob. She dropped her head into her hands, as Denny and other family members put their arms around her. Perhaps the only person in the courtroom who seemed unaffected was the defendant, who carefully took notes on a yellow legal pad.

In his cross-examination, Tom Dyer asked the doctor if he was aware if rocuronium could be bought over the Internet, without a prescription.

"I would think that no is the answer," replied the doctor.

Then the State rested its case against Shelly Michael, and Judge Stone adjourned for lunch, ordering the jury to return at 1:15 p.m., when the defense would call its first witness.

After the jury had filed out of the courtroom, Tom Dyer moved to acquit Shelly Michael on all charges. Opposing the motion, Marcia Ashdown maintained the State had submitted evidence that the defendant had had opportunity to kill her husband and set the fire.

"She had access to the victim," argued the prosecutor, "and she had special access to the very unusual murder weapon in this case."

Judge Stone dismissed the motion, finding that there was certainly sufficient evidence for the jury to believe, beyond a reasonable doubt, each of the elements necessary for the first-degree murder and arson offenses.

"The motion for judgment of acquittal is denied," he ruled.

CHAPTER 43

The Defense

For months now the two Monongalia County prosecutors had prepared for their cross-examination of the defense's fire expert, Patrick J. McGinley of Pennsylvania. Six months earlier, the highly respected and costly arson expert, who claims to have personally investigated 4,000 fire-related incidents, had submitted his report into the possible causes of the fire.

And since the beginning of the trial, Marcia Ashdown, who would be conducting his cross-examination, had spent hours preparing for it.

"He was supposed to be my witness," said Ashdown. "So I worried and fretted. We had spent tons of time with our experts as to how to ask him questions and where to go with cross-examination."

But Tom Dyer had already decided not to call McGinley to the stand, in light of some of the State's expert evidence that would have nullified his report. He was especially concerned that one of the jurors was an engineer.

"And that sucked bad," explained the defense attorney, "because that scared me more than having McGinley testify. I'm thinking, 'For God's sake, here's a guy who's going to understand that some of these theories are a bit of a stretch.'"

Dyer says there were also some very fundamental problems with his expert's testimony, and he became "horribly concerned and petrified" of what might happen under cross-examination, if he took the stand.

"In the end, Pat McGinley himself was in complete agreement," said Dyer. "I had to write a check for him. It wasn't a matter of money."

When Dyer told his client he had changed his mind about calling their fire expert, she was livid.

"Michelle and her family never quite understood," Dyer said. "Although when I ultimately took an hour-and-a-half to explain that to her one night in jail, I thought that she completely understood, and agreed with the explanation."

On Monday afternoon, Tom Dyer called his first witness, Eli Henderson of Northwestern Mutual—the agent who had sold Jimmy Michael a $500,000 life insurance policy in March 2005. The defense attorney was trying to show the jury that his client was unaware of the policy.

"Was Mrs. Michael present at any stage of the decision-making?" asked Dyer.

"No," replied Henderson, who said he later sold her a $200,000 policy.

Dyer then asked about his meeting with the defendant at the Hotel Morgan after the fire.

"Could you describe her appearance to this jury?" said Dyer.

"She looked very tired," he replied, "like she hadn't slept in a couple of days."

"Describe her level of interest in learning of this insurance-related information?"

"I would say minimal," said Henderson.

"Do you recall any conversation about the face amount of the policy at the Hotel Morgan?" asked Dyer.

"The thing I do recall," said Henderson, "is, Mrs. Michael was unsure of how much insurance Jim had."

In her cross, prosecutor Ashdown pointed out that Shelly

had been with her husband when they signed the policy forms, as well as receiving a policy delivery acknowledgment outlining all terms.

"So eight months after all this had transpired," asked Ashdown, "didn't you think it was strange that she didn't know how much coverage there was?"

"It was a little bit surprising to me," acknowledged the insurance salesman.

Late Monday afternoon, Tom Dyer called Kelli Teets to the stand, putting her through the humiliation of having to testify as a defense witness about her husband's betrayal with her best friend. At one point she broke down in tears.

The State had also considered calling the young mother, but finally decided against it, never thinking the defense would do so.

"We felt pretty bad for Kelli," recalled Marcia Ashdown. "That was the saddest thing, putting her through that."

In direct, Dyer asked her about the embroidery business, and Bobby and Shelly's fact-finding trip to Chicago.

"What was the purpose of that trip?" asked the defender.

"It was basically a seminar," replied Kelli, "about embroidery and the embroidery business."

"Were there discussions that there would only be one room reserved at the hotel?" asked Dyer.

"After the hotel was researched," she said. "The price, yes. It was a suite with a bedroom and another room."

"That, as you know," asked Dyer, "led to some type of affair?"

"Yes," she replied almost inaudibly.

"If you will, between your husband and Mrs. Michael, correct?"

"Yes."

"And I do apologize for bringing this up."

"That's OK."

"I need to ask you," said Dyer. "When did you learn about that affair?"

"The day after he was questioned by the detective about it," she replied.

The defender then asked if she'd had any communication with Shelly after learning of the affair? Kelli said that Shelly had called her soon afterwards, but there was little conversation. Shelly had also dropped off a letter of apology at Kelli's workplace.

"I would presume you were very hurt and upset by those circumstances?" asked Dyer.

"Yes," she replied.

In cross-examination, Perri DeChristopher asked if her husband Bobby had confessed to the affair before his December 7, 2005, interview with Detective Mezzanotte. Kelli said he had not.

"Did Bobby relay to you that that event took place twice?" asked the assistant prosecutor.

"Yes," Kelli replied.

"Once in Chicago and once at the defendant's house?"

"Yes."

"In the defendant's bedroom?"

"I was told it was in the downstairs of the house," she said, with more than a hint of anger.

Then DeChristopher asked if she had lunched with Shelly Michael a few hours after the last "sexual encounter" with her husband.

"I believe so," Kelli replied.

"It would be fair to say to you," said DeChristopher, "that you're not a very good judge of the sincerity of Michelle Michael?"

"Yes," she agreed.

The defense next called Renee and Eric Del Viscio, and it was the first time they had seen Shelly since the funeral. They waved to her at the defense table, but did not visit her in jail.

Renee told the jury that she and Eric had seen Shelly and Jimmy Michael an average of twice a year, staying in each other's homes in Morgantown and Philadelphia.

"It was a wonderful blended family," said Renee. "Shelly treated Drew and Jacie as if they were her own."

When Tom Dyer asked about the allegations that Shelly

had stayed out all night after the Italian Heritage Festival, Renee vehemently denied it.

"We were there until it closed," she testified, "at which point Shelly drove us back to Morgantown."

Renee testified that over that Labor Day weekend, Shelly had discussed her love life with Jimmy.

"At one point we were talking about the relationship," she said, "and discussed the fact that at that point in time they were not having an intimate relationship, and that was becoming more and more of an issue for Jimmy."

"Did it appear to you from these conversations that this marriage was in any kind of desperate situation?"

"I would not categorize it as desperate, no," she replied.

Then Dyer asked her to describe Shelly's demeanor in the days after the fire.

"When I arrived and I saw her," Renee recalled, "she appeared simply to be in shock. Just shock. She wasn't crying. It was almost as if there was just a void over her. That she wasn't there."

"You have been around her her whole life, correct?" asked the defender.

"I have, yes," she replied.

"Seen her experience a lot of different emotions, correct?"

"Correct."

"Have you seen her cry very much in her lifetime?"

"No," said Renee, "I have not."

In cross-examination, Marcia Ashdown asked if Shelly had confided in her about her affair with Bobby Teets.

"No," said Renee, "that is not something she would share. I don't think most people would."

"Some secret things people just don't share," said Ashdown. "Do you agree?"

"Right," she replied, "I mean, there are certain appearances she wanted to keep with me, and that's not something she would share with me under any circumstances."

In re-direct, Tom Dyer asked if Shelly Michael ever had any trouble walking away from boyfriends or her first husband.

"No," said Renee. "She has walked away from many men in her life."

The final witness of the day was Charles Bramble, a Clarksburg-based private investigator, who the defense had hired to time how long it took to drive from Ruby Memorial Hospital to the Michaels' home. The retired West Virginia State Trooper had made a total of six test runs over a three-day period, using two different routes. The runs, which began in the Ruby Hospital lobby just after 8:00 in the morning as the defendant's had, had been videotaped by another investigator.

The jury was shown a video of one test run, made on November 29, 2006—exactly one year after the fire. Just like Shelly had done, Bramble began at 8:11 a.m. in the lobby at Ruby Memorial. But unlike the defendant, the elderly private eye had a pronounced limp from a knee injury, taking three minutes to cross the parking lot and get into his vehicle.

The jury then watched as he drove out of the hospital, reaching Killarney Drive at around 8:19 a.m. He pulled into the empty space that had been 545 Killarney Drive, stopping for thirty-five seconds. Then he reversed out, retracing his route back to the hospital parking lot, which he reached at 8:25 a.m.—twenty seconds longer than it had taken Michelle the previous year.

Then he parked and walked back into the lobby, taking a total of seventeen minutes and fifty-three seconds.

In a rare bit of comic relief at the trial, the witness's often muddled testimony and use of the video to illustrate the various routes and timings even confused the defense attorney, as the jury looked on with amusement.

Finally, Dyer threw up his hands to stop his witness.

"Charlie, wait a minute," said Dyer. "You are already confusing me."

Finally, Judge Stone called a halt, adjourning for the day and ordering Bramble to return on Tuesday morning and complete his testimony.

* * *

On Monday night, with Shelly Michael scheduled to take the stand the following day, Perri DeChristopher and Detective Paul Mezzanotte stayed up late, painstakingly sifting through her two police interviews and counting the exact number of lies she had told, so the prosecutor could confront her with them in cross-examination.

Although Tom Dyer had spent weeks preparing her for this moment, he was now having second thoughts.

"Frankly," he explained, "after the cross-examination of Mezzanotte and the cross of the arson experts and the rest of those people, I wasn't certain. I told her, 'You're going to be surprised by this, but I'm not certain that it's necessary for you to testify. I think the *jury* will understand there's a justification in your case for possibly not wanting to testify.'"

Later, Shelly would maintain that Tom Dyer had given her no choice in the matter.

"He said unless I took the stand and testified," she said, "I would be found guilty."

CHAPTER 44

"'I Value Honesty'"

At 8:30 a.m. on Tuesday, July 17—the seventh day of the trial—the ceremonial courtroom was packed with media and curiosity-seekers, who had all come to see Shelly Michael take the stand. More than fifty people sat in the public gallery, including Shelly and Jimmy's respective friends and extended families.

With the defense's case in big trouble, everything now depended on whether she could convince the jury that she was a totally innocent victim, or would appear to be an unimaginably cruel psychopath.

But first, the defense's private investigator, Charles Bramble, returned to the stand to complete his testimony.

"Charlie, I'm going to put this picture back here," said Tom Dyer, "and we'll start back in and see if we can be a little less confused about this."

After a few minutes spent setting up the video of another of the six test routes he'd made back to the house, there was further misunderstanding.

"This is not the starting point," said Dyer testily. "Well, where are we on the video?"

"I'm not sure which route it was," admitted Bramble, "but we need to go back—I had this set up, but obviously the machine malfunctioned."

"Well," sighed the defense attorney, "before we waste a bunch of time, do you think you can rewind this to the point where we would show them one trip of Route One on the video?"

"We can try," said the witness.

In her cross, Marcia Ashdown observed that, as Bramble did not live in Morgantown, he was unacquainted with the area.

"So your only association with making these drives back and forth," she asked, "is in conjunction with working with Mr. Dyer in this case?"

"That's true," he admitted.

Ashdown also noted that his timings could be off, due to many variables he had not taken into account.

"Now," she said, "when you came out here, you observed all the stop signs and the traffic controls, right?"

"Yes, ma'am."

"And you were driving at the lawful rate of speed?"

"I tried to do it as quickly and as safely as possible," he replied.

"You weren't able to walk real fast?" she said.

"No, ma'am."

"Because you have a problem with your knee, right?"

"Yes, ma'am. I shattered it about a year-and-a-half ago."

"OK," said the prosecutor. "And actually, the day that Michelle Michael left the hospital, at that eight o'clock hour, it was raining hard. Someone might be in kind of a hurry to get to their car, and they might even run?"

"That's a possibility," admitted Bramble.

After morning recess, Tom Dyer called Shelly Michael to the stand. All eyes were on the defense table, as the petite defendant, dressed in a conservative black business suit with a light blue shirt and gold charm necklace, slowly stood up, walked across the court and entered the witness box.

"Michelle," he asked, "can you identify yourself for the record, please?"

"Michelle Michael," she replied softly.

"You are going to have to really speak up," said her attorney.

For the next hour, the experienced defense attorney attempted to paint a sympathetic portrait of his client for the jury. Through gentle questioning, she told the jury about her upbringing in Clarksburg, her college years and getting pregnant with Alec at the age of 20.

In a soft, often inaudible voice, she spoke of her first marriage to Rob Angus in July 1993, and the birth of their daughter Kylie.

"I know I had a hard time hearing that," said Dyer. "Are we still hearing all right? Can you guys hear?"

"The jury is shaking their heads," observed Judge Stone.

"Just try to keep your voice up," Dyer told her. "This is difficult."

"You can face the jury if you want," said the judge. "If they see you talking, they are going to be able to understand."

Then she described the breakdown of the marriage, saying there were "a couple of instances of abuse, but nothing big.

"We were arguing too much in front of the children, and couldn't seem to break the cycle."

Dyer then asked how she had met Jimmy Michael.

"Well I knew him through work for a couple of years," she said. "And then in the winter of '98, '99, we became pretty good buddies."

"You were seeing Mr. Michael before you had a final divorce from Mr. Angus?" asked Dyer.

"Yes."

"When did you and Mr. Michael get married?"

"May twenty-sixth, 2000," answered Shelly, looking down at her wedding ring, which she had worn throughout the trial.

"There was mention earlier in this trial of rumors that you had had an abortion," Dyer non-segued. "Let me ask you first, have you in your lifetime had an abortion?"

"I had one, yes," she replied.

"When was that?"

"Several years ago, at least 1993, I think it was."

Returning to Jimmy Michael, Dyer asked about their early life together, blending their respective children into a family.

"Me and my children moved into his home," said Shelly, "that he had already purchased, where he was living with his two children."

She said Jacie and Kylie were "inseparable," but her son Alec picked on Drew.

"That would upset Drew," she said. "But there weren't a lot of fights. They got along very well."

Then she told the jury how in May 2002, she and Jimmy had bought 545 Killarney Drive.

"It was a really nice house," she said. "We really loved it."

By 2005, she said, their lives were going well. She had just qualified as a nurse practitioner, and Jimmy was starting his own home medical business. They both had demanding coaching and church commitments, meaning they were out almost every night of the week, as well as weekends.

"Tell us a little about your activities." Dyer prompted.

"Just typical parent volunteer stuff," she said. "I was coaching my daughter's cheerleading squad, two of them actually. And then volunteering at school, read aloud, office assistant, my son's band, football. Wherever they needed help, I tried to help."

"Did Jimmy participate in these types of activities as well?"

"Oh, yes," she replied.

Moving ahead to November 28, 2005, the night before the fire, Dyer asked if it had been a "typical evening at home?"

"Uh-huh," she replied.

"Do you recall any conversation that you had that evening?"

"When I got home from cheerleading practice, he was laying on the couch," she said, "and I just remember asking him about hunting. I asked him if he had got a deer that day.

And Jimmy had a reputation of not being very successful getting a buck, so I had to do my typical tease about getting a doe. And then we talked about the embroidery business."

Dyer then asked if there had been anything "unusual" the next morning, before she left for work.

"No," she replied.

She then described her morning at Ruby Memorial, seeing patients and gathering information to present to the doctor.

Then Dyer projected a still photograph from the first hospital surveillance, showing her by the cappuccino machine at 8:11:58, on her way out of the hospital.

"Where are you going at this time of the morning?" he asked.

"Over to Alec's school," she replied. "My son Alec, in Suncrest."

She told the jury that she typically left work to "sneak a kiss" with Alec and give him lunch, most Tuesdays, Wednesdays and the occasional Monday, when her ex-husband had custody.

"That's just the way we had done it for a couple of years," she said. "I hated not being there for them since the divorce every morning."

"Michelle," asked Dyer, "are you specifically authorized to leave the hospital like this a couple of days a week?"

"No," she replied. "When everyone else was taking their smoke break, I ran out to the school."

Dyer then asked what she had told the hospital front desk clerk Nancy Buffalo.

"I told her I was going to my car to get my pager," she said.

"Is that the truth?"

"Not completely, no," she admitted.

With the judge's permission, Dyer then had Shelly step out of the witness box, to show the jury the route she'd taken on a large map. Using a pointer, she said she'd gone straight to her Ford Expedition, gotten inside and left the parking lot.

Then using the map, she sketched the route she had driven to Suncrest Middle School, where, she said, Rob Angus and her children had usually waited out in front.

"I looked down the street," she told the jury. "I did not see my ex-husband's truck."

She had then continued past the school, deciding to stop home at Killarney Drive.

"Why did you go to your house?" asked Dyer.

"Well," she explained, "I was in the neighborhood anyway, so I remembered I needed part of the embroidery papers that we were going to fax that day."

"Did you go up to the house?"

"No. When I was driving down the road," she said, "I looked over in the car seat and saw the business license application that I had to mail that day. So I grabbed it to throw in the mailbox, and under it was the form I was looking for, so I didn't need to go in."

"Did you put anything in the mailbox?" asked her attorney.

"Yes," she said, "I put the business application in the mail."

"How long were you at the house?"

"A couple of seconds. Long enough to jump out of the car and run to the mailbox . . . on the edge of the driveway."

This was an entirely new version of her movements that morning, and the first time she had ever mentioned posting anything in her mailbox.

After lunch, Tom Dyer resumed his direct examination. His biggest hurdle would be overcoming the negative police video interview, showing his client constantly lying. Now confronting this head-on, he sympathetically questioned her about why she'd lied to the police.

"Michelle," he began, "were you asked at this meeting with Detective Mezzanotte and Trooper Merrill about leaving the hospital?"

"I was," she replied.

"What did you tell them?"

"I said, 'No, I just went to my car to get the pager and went back up to the unit.'"

"And you didn't tell them the truth?"

"No."

"Why did you not tell them the truth about leaving the hospital that morning?"

"I didn't want my boss to find out I left," she told the jury. "I didn't want to get fired."

She said she'd finally admitted she had left the hospital, several hours into the interview, after realizing she was the number-one suspect in her husband's murder.

"Was there another matter you were not truthful about?" chided her attorney.

"Yes," she replied.

"What was that about?"

"Sleeping with Bobby Teets on our trip to Chicago."

"Did you lie to him on more than one occasion about having done that?"

"I did."

"And why did you lie to him about that?"

"I was ashamed of myself," she explained, her voice betraying little emotion. "I just cheated on my husband. I wanted to keep it secret and I didn't want to hurt Kelli any more. Everybody was already in so much pain, Jimmy's parents and my parents and my family and everybody. I didn't want to cause any more pain, make it worse."

"Michelle," asked Dyer, "did you tell Jimmy about this affair with Bobby?"

"No."

"Do you know if he knew, or if he suspected?"

"I don't know. I hope not."

Tom Dyer then projected a happy family photograph of her and Jimmy taken in July 2000, asking her to describe her late husband to the jury.

"Jimmy was very kind and loving, very giving," she said. "His children were the most important thing to him in the world, which I admired so much. And actually he was very handsome. And very spiritual. He loved the Lord."

Her attorney then asked if Jimmy had many stresses in his life.

"Yes," she replied. "I was one of them. I was a nag, and we weren't intimate very often, and that was frustrating for him."

"What about his ex-wife?" asked Dyer. "Was that a continuing source of problems and stress for him?"

"Jimmy had ongoing problems with his ex-wife," she replied. "There was always continued stress with that."

He then asked her about Stephanie Estel's testimony that her relationship with Jimmy had improved before his death.

"No, sir, I don't think so," said Shelly resolutely.

Finally, Dyer asked point blank if she'd had anything to do with the death of her husband.

"No, I did not," she replied.

"How about the fire at your house?"

"No, I did not."

"Do you have any idea of who had something to do with it?"

"Are you asking me to think of people?"

"Do you know?"

"No, I do not know."

"Do you know who may have killed your husband?"

"I don't know that."

"Do you know who may have burned the house down?"

"I don't know."

"Your Honor," said Dyer, "that's all the questions we have."

Then Perri DeChristopher stood up to cross-examine the defendant, immediately going on the attack.

"Ms. Michael," she began, "do you agree with me that, in fact, your husband was murdered?"

"I guess so," replied Shelly defiantly. "I mean, that's what the evidence shows. That's what the toxicology results showed. So."

"So you agree that Jim Michael was murdered?" the assistant prosecutor repeated.

"I don't know what happened to my husband."

Then DeChristopher asked about the rocuronium found

in Jimmy's remains, noting that the drug is fatal without some type of breathing assistance.

"Yes," she agreed, "I know what happens with rocuronium."

"So you agree that Jim Michael was murdered?" she asked again.

Then Tom Dyer stood up, objecting to the form of the question.

"What's wrong with the form of the question?" asked DeChristopher.

"It excludes suicide," said Dyer.

After the judge overruled the objection, Michael said she couldn't agree or disagree that Jimmy was murdered, because she didn't know.

"Based upon Mr. Dyer's objection," asked the assistant prosecutor, "do you think Jim Michael killed himself?"

"Not in my heart, no," she replied.

"Well, in mind, do you think that?"

"I don't think he would have killed himself, no."

Then DeChristopher asked if she agreed that the fire at her house was arson.

"If that's what you guys are saying," she replied glibly. "So, sure."

"So you believe everything we're saying?" the prosecutor said.

"I'm not a fire expert," she said, taking a few sips of water from a glass. "I have to go by what you're saying. I don't know."

"Well, do you think it was an accidental fire?"

"For a long time I did, yes," Shelly replied.

DeChristopher then told the jury that the defendant was "desperate" to have everyone believe it was an accidental fire, so she could collect half-a-million dollars in Jimmy's life insurance, as well as several hundred thousand dollars from fire insurance.

"You agree that five hundred thousand dollars is an awful lot of money?" asked DeChristopher.

"Not necessarily," Shelly replied.

The prosecutor then produced Shelly's thirty-five-page personal loss claim for just under $194,000, which she had submitted to State Farm Insurance on January 9, 2006.

"Is that your signature on the document?" she asked.

"Yes," affirmed the defendant.

"And you would agree with me that no item was too small to claim a value?" noted DeChristopher.

"I was going through the house trying to remember everything."

"You claimed reimbursement for twelve bottles of nail polish, totaling seventy-two dollars?"

"I had a big basket," replied Michael, unfazed. "It was an understatement."

"You requested reimbursement for the value of Jim's dress socks—thirty pair totaling two hundred and forty dollars. Is that right?"

"I guess so, if it's on there."

"You put a price on your framed wedding vows: forty dollars?"

"It was a Michaels frame," she explained. "Yes."

Then, turning to Shelly's adulterous relationship, DeChristopher began questioning her about the trip to Chicago.

"How would you describe your relationship with Bobby Teets in November of 2005?"

"The beginning of November, it was just friends," Shelly replied.

"How would you describe your relationship changing?"

"It changed in that we were intimate twice," she said.

DeChristopher then asked why she had packed a swim suit for the Chicago business trip.

"You went swimming," she said. "Went to the hot tub. So it certainly wasn't going to be all business when you got there?"

"I figured there would be time after the seminar to swim a little," Michael replied. "Yes."

"You had sex with Bobby Teets in Chicago?" asked DeChristopher. "Is that right?"

"That's right," replied Shelly, matter-of-factly.

"And when you came back to Morgantown, did you disclose that to your husband?"

"No."

"Your friendship with Kelli Teets continued on its regular path?"

"It did."

"You were able to hide and conceal that from two people that were very, very close to you, right?"

"I don't know if I was hiding it and concealing it very well. I just didn't say anything."

"Three days before Jim's murder, you had sex with Bobby Teets. Is that right?"

"Yes."

"In your own home?"

"Yes."

"In your own bedroom?"

"Yes."

"In Jim Michael's bed?"

"In Jimmy and [my] bed, yes."

"The same bed in which his body was found just three days later?"

"Yes."

"And you tell this jury that you loved Jimmy Michael and he was a wonderful person?"

"Yes."

The prosecutor then asked about dinner that night at a restaurant with Jimmy and Kelli Teets, after they had all attended a Mountaineers game.

"I said to myself, 'What the heck am I doing? This is crazy.'"

"But that must have been really quietly," DeChristopher told her, "because you sure didn't say it to Bobby, and you sure didn't say it to Kelli, and you sure didn't say it to Jimmy."

"I did say it to Bobby," Shelly countered, "but I did not say it to Jimmy or Kelli."

Noting that Kelli Teets had considered her her best friend, the prosecutor accused Shelly of having no consideration for her feelings.

"I considered her feelings very much," she replied.

"Well did you think you would be able to keep that a secret forever?"

"I didn't want to deceive my husband forever."

"Well, if he had not been murdered on November twenty-ninth, did you have plans to tell him?"

"Actually, yes, I did."

DeChristopher then asked why the defense had subpoenaed Kelli Teets as a witness.

"Above and beyond the humiliation and publicity of the affair," said the prosecutor, "you sat here and watched Kelli Teets subpoenaed to testify on your behalf, correct?"

"I did," said Shelly, as some of the jurors looked on in numbed disbelief.

"Because she was the only person that could come in and testify about your demeanor at the fire scene, correct?"

"Incorrect."

"The only witness that was put on by the defense."

"Kelli was the best witness."

Then, DeChristopher turned to her December 8, 2005, police interview, asking what her reply had been when Sergeant James Merrill asked what she stood for.

" 'I value honesty,' " she declared.

"Would that still be your answer today?" asked DeChristopher.

"Yes, ma'am."

"I'm sorry, I didn't hear that," said the assistant prosecutor, with more than a hint of sarcasm.

"Yes, ma'am."

"On the scale of one to ten, you would rate yourself a nine. Is that still true today?"

"That's what I want to be, yes," said Shelly resolutely.

Then, when confronted with her persistent lying to detectives, Michael confirmed that she had been untruthful with them, but suddenly became combative by splitting hairs.

"You lied to Nancy Buffalo when you said you were going out to get your pager?"

"I wasn't completely," she said. "Yes, I lied to her."

"Yes, you lied to her," said DeChristopher. "Was that a yes?"

"I did need to get my pager," Shelly insisted. "But I did not tell her I was leaving so, yes, I lied."

"In your interviews with Detective Mezzanotte, you lied to him over a hundred times, correct?"

"I lied a lot," she conceded.

"Well, would you doubt that it was over a hundred times?"

"Yes, ma'am, I actually counted."

"Well, so did I," said DeChristopher, "Fifty-two times on December eighth, regarding the car, correct?"

"Probably."

"You lied five times on December seventh about moving your car? Does that sound about right?"

"Probably."

"You lied twenty-eight times on December seventh regarding the affair, correct?"

"Probably."

"You lied twenty times on December eighth about the affair. Does that sound about right?"

"Sure."

"That adds up to over a hundred."

"OK," she conceded.

DeChristopher followed up, asking if Shelly agreed that her lies regarding the pager had been "pretty detailed."

"It's just a lie," she replied.

Then Perri DeChristopher confronted her with the State's theory of how she had murdered her husband, and then set her house on fire.

"You left that iron plugged in on HIGH at your house on its face," accused the prosecutor, "hoping it would start the fire, when you left at 6:30 in the morning. Isn't that right?"

"Not hardly," she replied.

"And when you didn't get that call, you went home to check to see why there wasn't a fire yet. Is that right?"

"No."

"And, in fact, that's when you took flame to the bed where Jim's body lay, already dead, correct?"

"No."

"Are you familiar with the drug rocuronium?"

"Yes, ma'am."

"Tell us how?"

"I work with it in the Pediatric ICU."

"I'm sorry. I can't hear you."

"I work with it in the Pediatric ICU."

"You have administered it?"

"Yes."

"You have seen it administered?"

"Yes."

"You have used it in settings in the hospital, specifically, the Pediatric Intensive Care Unit?"

"Yes."

"You know its capabilities?"

"I do."

"You agree that a person will become paralyzed without someone actually breathing for them, without ventilation. Do you agree with that?"

"Yes."

"Do you agree that paralysis comes with the person continuing to be completely aware of their surroundings?"

"Yes."

"You are aware that they know that they are paralyzed, but that they cannot breathe on their own?"

"Yes."

"You agree that during that state of paralysis, a person would be hungering for air. Do you agree with that?"

"Probably so, yes."

"You agree that that would be a very gruesome, gruesome death?"

"It would be horrible."

Then DeChristopher asked her why she displayed "absolutely no emotion," as she'd described seeing her husband alive for the last time to police.

"When I did what?" Michael asked incredulously.

"Described the last time you claim you saw your husband alive."

"I had no emotion?" she asked.

"You weren't crying," continued DeChristopher.

"I guess I wasn't crying in the interview, no."

"And he asked you what you did in that bedroom as you left, do you remember that?"

"No."

"Sergeant Merrill asked if he were alive, and your response was, 'Well, he was warm.'"

"I gave him a kiss on his forehead, yes."

"And Sergeant Merrill asked if he moved or if he was alive or if he was dead. And your only response in describing the last time that you claimed to have seen your husband alive was, 'He was warm.'"

"No."

Finally, the assistant prosecutor questioned her latest claim on the stand, of putting items in her mailbox after returning home the morning of the fire.

"And you got to your house and you got out of your car?"

"Yes," she replied.

"And walked to your mailbox?"

"Yes."

"And put a flag on your mailbox?"

"I think so."

"Put items in your mailbox?" asked the prosecutor. "Did it already have stamps, was it already addressed?"

"It was ready to be mailed," said Shelly, "and I forgot to mail it at work."

"That entire scenario of your memory wasn't related at all to Sergeant Merrill or Detective Mezzanotte, correct?"

"Yes, it was exactly that."

"Exactly that was relayed?"

"That's what the truth was."

"Did you ever tell either of them that you put anything in the mailbox?"

"I don't recall that."

Then the prosecutor asked her to review the transcripts of her interviews with law enforcement, to see if she had mentioned mailing anything.

"I don't think I told them that," she finally conceded. "I don't see it in the transcript."

Just after 4:00 p.m.—after almost five hours on the stand—Shelly Michael finished testifying, and the defense rested its case.

Then Judge Stone dismissed the jury for the day, telling them that after closing arguments tomorrow, he would charge them with the law and they would start their deliberations.

"Ladies and gentlemen," said the judge, "we have completed the testimony in the case. So, we will recess for the day. We are almost done."

Coming down from the witness box, Shelly Michael believed she had done everything needed for an acquittal. She was certain that she had won the jury over with her testimony, and was full of optimism when Tom Dyer visited her cell later.

"She was absolutely, completely convinced that she had won," recalled the defense attorney, who did not share her view. "At that point, I was a little dejected by my assessment of how Shelly did on the witness stand. So I had lost a certain amount of optimism at that point."

Later, Shelly Michael would be heavily criticized in the media for not displaying any emotion on the stand—something Tom Dyer admits he instructed her not to do.

"I thought it would have come across as rather phony," he explained, "if she had been high-strung and emotional. You didn't see her cry. She was just a relatively hardened individual. The last thing we need to do is to have somebody plant the seed to the jury that [she's] just up to boo-hoo and crocodile tears."

But although he viewed Shelly's performance as a setback, he felt confident he could redress the balance in tomorrow's closing.

"Frankly, I'm notorious for my closing arguments," he later explained. "That's what I'm most known for. I'm very down to earth. Very folksy. Very dramatic. But I don't use a podium. Don't use notes. None at all. My favorite ministers in my Methodist Church are the ones that did neither, and I think that's what brought me to that in my professional career."

CHAPTER 45

"The Cruel and Unusual Manner of This Murder"

Just after 9:00 a.m. on Wednesday, July 18, Monongalia Prosecutor Marcia Ashdown stood up to deliver the State's closing argument. During the next several hours, Shelly Michael hardly looked up, taking copious notes at the defense table.

"Your Honor, counsel, ladies and gentlemen of the jury," began Ashdown. "Yesterday the defendant, Michelle Michael, told you that she doesn't know what happened to her husband, Jim Michael, and she can't agree that he was murdered."

The prosecutor told the jury that now, having heard the toxicology evidence, they knew Jimmy Michael had been murdered by an injection of rocuronium. And although the defendant's testimony had "wanted you to entertain the possibility of suicide," there was absolutely no evidence to support that.

"This defendant hopes that you will believe the façade that she presented to you," said Ashdown, "and find reasonable doubt where there is none."

Ashdown reminded the jury that people who are guilty of first-degree murder don't come to court to confess guilt.

"Instead," she continued, "people who are guilty of, and on trial for, first-degree murder, weave stories. They twist evidence. They try and create confusion. They lie. And one thing you've learned about Michelle Michael is that she has lied, and consistently lied, and continued to lie, and persistently lied throughout the investigation, and now to you."

The prosecutor said it was possible to extrapolate some shreds of truth about what had really happened to Jimmy Michael, from the many lies told by the defendant.

"These lies contain elements of the truth," she told the jury. "She talked a lot about the iron that was in the bedroom. She was worried she had left it plugged in."

The prosecutor reminded the jury that Michael had told both Reggie Ours and State Farm claims adjuster John White that she had left the iron by an open window on HIGH, and perhaps a breeze had blown it onto the bed.

"What the evidence shows," said Ashdown, "is that after she injected her husband with that fatal paralyzing drug, she left that iron in the bedroom on HIGH, plugged in. [She] set it on the floor or the bed, somewhere in the area of the bed or on the bed, assuming that it would set fire to that bed over time. And she would be out of there at work with her alibi."

Ashdown told the jury that at the hospital, Shelly had created her alibi, making certain that people would remember her being there. She had goosed Reggie Ours, left a message on her dead husband's cell phone and talked to Bobby and Kelli Teets.

"And about eight a.m. that morning, while she was at her place of work at the hospital—" Ashdown said, "Tick, tock. No call, 'Your house is on fire.' "

So once again Michael deliberately drew attention to herself, announcing to Dr. Michael Romano and clerk Nancy Buffalo that she was going to morning report. She then told Buffalo she was leaving to get her pager from the car.

"Well, you know she went home," said Ashdown. "Because her neighbor up the street, Shawn Alt, saw her there leaving her residence, somewhere around eight-twenty a.m. He was out and about because he was home from work, and also because he had smelled smoke in the neighborhood.

"Now we have proved to you that that fire started two

hours before being reported at ten-twenty-seven a.m. on November twenty-ninth. And we have proved to you that the defendant was home at the time the fire started. What does that equal? No alibi. You can discount that as a factor in your deliberations."

The prosecutor reminded the jury how many witnesses had testified that Shelly was unhappy in her marriage, no longer wanting a sexual relationship with her husband.

"Shelly Michael was done with Jim Michael," Ashdown said. "And as it happens, divorce would leave her in a position financially that would be certainly less beneficial to her than being married."

The prosecutor also noted that Jimmy Michael had a "brand-new" $500,000 life insurance policy, with his wife as the sole beneficiary.

"If there had been no question about how Jimmy Michael died," said Ashdown, "Michelle Michael would have been written a check for five hundred thousand dollars. Now [she] will say, 'Well, that's just peanuts,' but we know that it's not. That is a nice chunk of change for a thirty-three-, thirty-five-year-old woman to put in her pocket at that point in her life."

And on top of that, said the prosecutor, the defendant and her mortgage company had already been paid $259,000 in fire insurance, as well as applying for a further $195,000 of compensation for the loss of personal items.

"She put a forty dollars price on her wedding vows," said Ashdown. "She wanted money for her dead husband's socks."

The prosecutor described Bobby Teets as an "unwilling catalyst to the defendant's catastrophic steps," saying that if he had done this, he never would have driven by the house after setting the fire.

And she told the jury that if only Shelly Michael had not closed the bedroom door on her way out, after setting the fire, she would have gotten away with murder.

"That whole house and everything in it would have gone down," she said. "Nothing would have remained to examine, nothing to test."

Marcia Ashdown asserted that, although the evidence might be circumstantial, it was also overwhelming.

Then, in a dramatic climax to her closing, the prosecutor brought out a syringe and displayed it to the jury.

"She had injected her husband with rocuronium, and all she had to do takes about a second," said Ashdown, as she plunged the needle into a grapefruit, as Dr. Johnstone had done earlier.

"And to get the fire started, this is all she had to do," she told jurors, as she flicked a Bic lighter.

Finally, Ashdown asked the jury to consider Jimmy Michael's last thirteen minutes on Earth, fully conscious and struggling for breath, after his wife had injected him with rocuronium.

"Dr. Johnstone told you that Jim Michael could have been conscious up to thirteen minutes," she reminded the jury, "knowing that he was dying, and that he had no hope of resuscitation, no hope of rescue, no hope of life, of surviving. And that while he was suffering these thoughts, and suffering this knowledge, he would be able to hear and he would be able to think, and he would be able to know what happened to him.

"That's what happened to kill Jim Michael by the hand of Michelle Michael. We ask you on this evidence to find Michelle Michael guilty of the intentional, willful, premeditated and deliberate murder of her husband, Jim Michael. And to find her guilty of the arson with which she tried to conceal the evidence of this murder.

"And we ask you, keeping in mind that thirteen minutes of suffering and consciousness, to recommend no mercy for Michelle Michael in your verdict of guilt."

After a fifteen-minute break, the jury returned for Tom Dyer's closing remarks. The defense attorney began by telling the jury there was no disputing that Shelly Michael had had access to rocuronium, that the fire had been arson, that the victim had died before the fire, and that his client had had an affair.

"What does this evidence mean?" he asked. "Number one, it means she is an adulterer. She is a cheater. She cheated on her husband. There is no question."

But Dyer reminded the jury that adultery was not a motive for murder.

"I don't mean to impugn Mr. Teets," he said, "but from what we have heard, I am not sure he was the type of person you would kill for."

He said that Shelly had only lied to police about the affair, as she did not want to look bad.

Then Dyer questioned whether the State had gotten everything wrong, and Jimmy Michael had, in fact, committed suicide.

"How does a hundred-pound, one hundred and two-pound woman inject this two hundred and fifteen-pound man with the surgical paralytic? Good question, right? It was one of the first ones I had when I got involved in this case. Very good question. Got a very nice demonstration from the doctor."

Dyer noted that Dr. Johnstone had testified that it would take a minute after the injection to feel anything, and four minutes before walking would be impossible.

"And most importantly," he said, "when you get stuck, it's going to sting. You are darn right it will. You are going to feel it. So why is this guy found in bed? Could it be suicide? I want you to follow me on this carefully. People as nice as Jim Michael, as good a people as he is, aren't usually murdered."

The defender observed he had a "lot of stress in his life," especially his "guilt" after beating his son Drew. He also had the pressures of a new business.

"Lord knows," Dyer said, "if he knows or suspects that his wife is cheating with a good friend."

Then, with Denny and Ruth Michael glaring at him from the public galley, the attorney suggested that their son could have deliberately staged his death so it did not look like suicide. The reason being that the contestable period on his life insurance policy for suicide was a year, and he had only been nine months into it when he had died.

"He knows what rocuronium does," said Dyer. "He is a respiratory therapist. He knows that it's going to give him a little bit of time to start a fire. It won't look like suicide.

"I hate to suggest this. I really do, in front of his family. They are good people. But when you consider . . . all the rest of the evidence, I don't see how you can rule this out as a distinct possibility."

Tom Dyer then described it as "absolutely completely illogical," that Shelly Michael could have plotted and then committed "one of the most diabolical crimes" he had ever heard of.

"Is this young lady, seated over here next to me for the past week-and-a-half, guilty?" he asked the jury. "That's the only question. Is she guilty? And the answer is yes. She certainly is. She is guilty of lying. Cheating. There is no question about that. Is she guilty of murder and arson? No.

"I believe you will agree with me in the end, the appropriate verdict that we can return for this young lady in this case is not guilty."

In the State's rebuttal, Marcia Ashdown attacked any suggestion that Jimmy Michael had committed suicide, noting the defendant's testimony only the day before, that she did not believe in her heart that he'd killed himself.

"If Jim Michael injected himself with rocuronium to commit suicide, and became paralyzed," she asked the jury, "how did he set the fire that burned up his bedroom and practically burned up his body? That would be impossible."

And if he had started the fire before injecting himself with the drug, why hadn't the autopsy shown evidence of either carbon monoxide in his system, or soot or smoke in his airways?

"Suicide by rocuronium under the circumstances you have here is an impossibility," she said. "You can disregard that."

But there were a number of questions, said Ashdown, that the jury should consider in deliberations: Who had access to the murder weapon? Who had access to the victim's home? Who had access to the victim's body? and, Who had motive or something to gain from Jimmy Michael's death?

"Why is the answer to every one of those questions, 'Michelle Michael'?" she asked. "The answer to that why, is, 'Because she's guilty of these crimes.'

"Ordinary-seeming people do unexpected, bizarre and even horrible things all the time. We know that. We see that on TV. They even commit murder, and they commit murder for money. Sometimes not as much money as is involved in this case. That is exactly what Michelle Michael did.

"When we began, we said the case is about death, destruction and deceit. I think I can add a couple of more 'D's' now. One is 'desperation' at the idea that Jimmy Michael would murder himself with rocuronium, and the other people who have been suggested as possible perpetrators.

"And finally, I agree with Mr. Dyer when he says a person who would commit these acts is diabolical. So 'diabolical' is the final and fifth 'D' to be added to the alphabet of 'D's' here.

"In order for justice to prevail for Jimmy Michael and for the State of West Virginia, you must not be deceived by Michelle Michael. You must not. You must find on this evidence that she is guilty of both of these crimes that are charged. And when you come to consider the cruel and unusual manner of this murder, you must return no recommendation for mercy."

Then Judge Robert Stone charged the jury with their instructions. He told them that in respect to the charge of murder in the first degree, they had three possible verdicts: not guilty, guilty or guilty with the recommendation of mercy. A guilty verdict would automatically sentence Michelle Michael to life in prison, but guilty with mercy meant she would be eligible for parole, after serving 15 years.

But on the first-degree arson charge, there were only be two possible verdicts: guilty and not guilty.

"When you have reached a unanimous agreement on both counts," Judge Stone told them, "fill out the form. The foreperson signs it, dates it, knocks on the door and advises our bailiff that you have reached a verdict. And we will bring you back and receive your verdict."

Then the judge discharged the two alternates from jury service, thanking them for their diligence.

At 1:45 p.m., after taking a lunch break, the twelve members of the jury began their deliberations, deciding whether Shelly Michael would spend the rest of her life behind bars or go free.

Inside the long, narrow jury room, the six men and six women could at last discuss the case openly, as they had been forbidden from even talking about it to their families.

"We were not to watch the news, read the papers, surf the Internet, or listen to the radio," noted one of the jurors, who later anonymously published a trial journal online. "We could not express our worries, frustrations, or confusion to anyone."

And that afternoon, the jurors finally got the chance to vent their opinions about Shelly Michael.

"Everyone had a lot to get off their chest," said the juror, who "sensed" that afternoon that the jury was split, with six thinking the defendant was guilty, and the rest leaning towards not guilty.

At 5:15 p.m., after three-and-a-half hours of deliberations, Judge Stone summoned the jury back into court, asking if they wanted to continue into the night, or go home and resume in the morning.

Jury foreman Patrick Farry told the judge that they wished to go home.

"That's fine," said the judge. "Get a good night's sleep, come back and pick up. That's what we will do. I will excuse you until tomorrow morning at nine."

First thing the next morning, the jurors took a poll. Now nine thought Shelly Michael guilty of murder and arson, while the remaining three voted not guilty.

Then they began sifting through all the evidence. Several hours later, they requested a DVD player to replay Detective

Mezzanotte's compelling December 8 interview. They also discussed the fire, and timelines for the morning of November 29, 2005, paying special attention to the defendant's trip to and from Ruby Memorial Hospital.

"We rehashed witness testimony," said the juror, "particularly the neighbor who swore that he saw Michelle Michael pulling out of the driveway on the morning of the murder."

They also focused on the availability of rocuronium at the hospital, and whether anyone else could have committed the murder/arson.

Back at the hotel, the attorneys from both sides were anxiously awaiting a verdict.

"We'd kind of pace around and be sick to our stomachs," recalled Perri DeChristopher. "And then we'd start thinking, 'What's taking them so long?' We knew it was going to take hours, if not days. And every time someone says, 'What do you think?' we knock on wood. I bet we knocked on wood three hundred times while we were waiting for that verdict."

Below the courthouse in the cells, Shelly Michael was waiting with her lawyer Tom Dyer and P.I. Gina Lopez, who had become like a sister to her during the trial.

And although the defense attorney had had his reservations after Shelly's testimony, he was now confident of an acquittal.

"As I sat down at the close of my argument, I thought to myself, 'Congratulations,'" he recalled. "'The closing went as well as it could.' I thought that I brought the verdict back into question with the closing."

But by Thursday afternoon, with no sign of a verdict, Dyer began to feel concerned.

"Well, I was surprised that it was taking so long," he recalled. "I knew that there were going to be some issues that the jury would grapple with. We were tired, frankly, by that time."

After lunch, the jury had taken another vote, with ten now in favor of finding Michael guilty and two hold-outs. By late afternoon they found themselves at an impasse, and at 3:27 p.m., Foreman Patrick Farry summoned the bailiff to take a note to Judge Stone.

"Your Honor," it read. "We cannot reach a unanimous decision. Are there any directions or suggestions you can give us?"

Back in court Judge Stone read the jury the dynamite instruction, reminding the jury of the oath they had taken, and urging them to take a little more time to reach a decision.

"So, at this time, I am going to ask you again to retire," said Judge Stone, "taking as much time as necessary for further deliberations on the issues that have been submitted to you for your determination."

Back in the jury room, they continued deliberating, desperately trying to break the deadlock. Each juror now shared his or her personal theory about what had happened to Jimmy Michael, and why each believed the defendant innocent or guilty.

"The process left us exhausted and emotionally drained," wrote the anonymous juror later. "However, we moved to take another vote."

This time, they unanimously agreed that the defendant was guilty of both first-degree arson and first-degree murder. But they decided to go home and sleep on it, before rendering a verdict.

Just after 5:00 p.m., Jury Foreman Farry sent another note to Judge Stone.

Your Honor, We are making progress, however the jury request permission to retire for the day and return in the morning at 9:00 a.m. We feel an evening to collect our thoughts alone will assist in finalizing our verdict.

CHAPTER 46

The Verdict is Unanimous

At 9:00 a.m. on Friday, July 20, the twelve men and women of the Kanawha County jury reconvened in the jury room. They took one final vote, standing by their unanimous decision to find Shelly Michael guilty of both charges.

But they now had to discuss whether or not to recommend mercy in their guilty verdicts, giving the 35-year-old defendant the chance of parole after serving 15 years.

"Everyone discussed the fact that James Michael died without mercy," the juror later wrote, "but I felt that sending Michelle Michael away for life—locking her up and throwing away the key—was too simple."

The juror decided to vote for mercy, thinking it would mean a "much harder" sentence, as she spent each day wondering if she would ever be released.

"I knew that she would have to do more in prison to be set free," the juror theorized, "meaning she would have to adhere to rules that she seemed to ignore in the days leading up to this case."

Other jury discussions focused on Michael's two children, and their suffering, as well as whether a long term of imprisonment could rehabilitate her.

Finally, after a further hour of deliberation, they agreed to recommend mercy.

"Your Honor," read the final note. "We are requesting a short break and also want to let you know we have a verdict."

It was just after 11:00 a.m. when the word came down that the jury had reached a verdict, after more than eleven hours of deliberations. Over the next few minutes, the ceremonial courtroom slowly filled up. The *48 Hours* camera crew, who had been filming the entire trial, set up their equipment, and news reporters and photographers took their places.

Marcia Ashdown and Perri DeChristopher had been waiting in their little office, just off the ceremonial courtroom, when they heard the news. They then took their places at the prosecution table, where they were joined by Detective Paul Mezzanotte. Behind them sat Jimmy Michael's parents, brother Steve and son Drew.

To their left, at the defense table, sat Shelly Michael, wearing a fashionably sedate plaid trouser suit, with a white shell top underneath. A delicate gold pendant lay in her open neckline, her long hair held in place by a hair band. To her right sat Tom Dyer, looking far more nervous than his client, who had a blank stare.

Behind them were Shelly's parents, Michael and Kathi Goots, her sister Jennifer and Gina Lopez.

At about 11:30 a.m., the court rose as Judge Robert Stone entered the courtroom.

"A verdict is going to be read," said the judge, after summoning the jury. "It's going to be emotional. It's going to affect a lot of people, and I want to remind everyone to maintain proper decorum in this courtroom. We don't want any outbursts or anything of that nature."

Then the jury filed into the courtroom, taking their places in the jury box.

"Has the jury reached a verdict in this case?" asked the judge.

"We have," said Jury Foreman Patrick Farry.

"Is the verdict unanimous in each case?"

"Yes, sir, it is."

Then the foreman handed the signed jury verdict form to the bailiff, who brought it over to Judge Stone.

"All right," said the judge. "Will the defendant please stand?"

It was as if the air had been sucked out of the room, as Shelly Michael stood up, her face a complete blank.

"The jury has returned the following verdict," said the judge. " 'With respect to the charge of murder in the first degree, we, the jury, find the defendant, Michelle Michael, guilty with a recommendation of mercy.

" 'In count two, with respect to the charge of arson in the first degree, we, the jury, find the defendant, Michelle Michael, guilty.' "

Suddenly the court was awash with emotion. Ruth Michael tearfully flung her arms around Denny, as little Drew welled up in tears alongside them. Gina Lopez comforted Kathi Goots, who wept uncontrollably, as Michael Goots and Jennifer Barker just sat there stunned.

But at the defense table, Shelly Michael displayed no reaction whatsoever to the guilty verdict.

"It was a perplexing reaction, to say the least," Tom Dyer would later say. "Just numb. Just numb."

After polling each of the jurors, Judge Stone thanked them for their due diligence, before excusing them for the final time.

Then Michael was handcuffed by sheriffs, as the judge signed a mandatory order for her blood to be drawn for the West Virginia DNA database.

Marcia Ashdown then requested that bail should be formally withdrawn, which Tom Dyer did not oppose.

"The previous bail was revoked, so there is no bond," the judge told Michael. "I would remand the defendant back to the custody of the regional jail until our sentencing hearing."

Outside the court, an emotional Ruth Michael told reporters she was relieved at the guilty verdict.

"I was just praying to God," she said, "that it would be guilty, guilty."

Asked about the defense's suggestion that her son might have committed suicide, Ruth bristled with anger.

"I know my son," she said. "She killed him."

Tom Dyer told reporters that he was disappointed with the verdict.

"Academically speaking," he said, "I felt as if the State did not put on enough evidence to convict. However, I respect the jury's verdict. I disagree with it, but I respect it."

Later, Detective Paul Mezzanotte would recall his mixed emotions on hearing the verdict.

"I felt a sense of closure to the family," he said. "I was obviously happy with the verdict, but then again, we have two kids that have lost a father, and two kids that lost a mother. So you couldn't help but feel for them."

Kathi Goots remembered being shocked at the verdict, possibly sending her daughter to prison for the rest of her life.

"I could not believe they found her guilty," she said. "I don't remember a whole lot from that point. I just knew that I left the courtroom and somebody was helping me walk."

Later, Shelly's sister Jennifer said she had blocked the verdict out of her mind.

"I don't want to remember," she said. "I don't want to remember."

Back at the Embassy Suites Hotel, Prosecutors Marcia Ashdown and Perri DeChristopher posed for photographs, mimicking Shelly Michael's thumbs-up sign the first day of the trial.

"That was kind of a sore spot for us," said DeChristopher. "As you can imagine, after that verdict we were very happy, and we gave ourselves the thumbs-up . . . and maybe had some pictures taken."

In the days to come, various members of the jury would explain how they had arrived at their guilty decision. The anonymous juror wrote of "silently begging" the defendant to take the stand, to persuade her she was incapable of such a horrific crime. But then Michael's arrogant testimony probably damaged her case more than anything else.

"She continued to lie," wrote the juror, "and continued to suggest scenarios that simply weren't logical. When Michelle Michael stepped down from the witness stand, I sat numbed by the experience. I had no choice but to find her guilty as charged."

Juror Gloria Newman described the defense's theory of Jimmy Michael committing suicide as "crazy." The 44-year-old told a reporter that the defendant had "lied" and was "not remorseful.

"The only thing people could say good about her was that she was a good mother," said Newman.

CHAPTER 47

"There Is a Very Dark Side to Your Character"

One week after the verdict, on July 25, 2007, the West Virginia Board of Examiners for Registered Professional Nurses officially notified Tom Dyer that Shelly Michael's nursing license had been suspended.

"The health and welfare of the public is at risk as long as Michael continues to possess a license, allowing her to practice as a registered nurse," wrote Executive Director Laura S. Rhodes in an accompanying letter. "Please have Ms. Michael return her registered professional nursing license to the Board office immediately."

In the weeks following the verdict, Shelly Michael fell into a deep depression, as she tried to come to terms with the prospect of spending the rest of her life behind bars.

"She seemed so upset and depressed," said her oldest friend Renee Del Viscio. "I try to give her hope."

But she was also determined to lodge an appeal as soon as possible. She began studying legal websites, to help Tom Dyer build an appeal case for a new trial.

"She's one of the strongest people I think I've ever known," said her mother. "I couldn't do it. There's no way I could do this."

The first week of August, Judge Robert Stone signed an order moving the Michael case back to Morgantown.

Sentencing was now scheduled for September 12, at Monongalia Circuit Court.

On August 17, Shelly Michael, who was back at the North
Central Regional Jail, had the first of three interviews with
probation officers for her pre-sentencing report. And, still
proclaiming her innocence, she complained to Probation
Officer Frank Wolfe that police had misled her.

"My husband was found dead in the family home after a
fire," she maintained. "In December 2005, the police began
questioning me."

Michael said that she'd left the police station on December 8 "confused," after detectives had told her that her husband's death was not an accident, without giving her the
information she felt she needed.

"The police asked me about my whereabouts the morning of the fire," she said. "I did admit I lied to the police
about leaving work, but I did tell them at the end of the interview that I did indeed leave work that morning."

She had then found an attorney, who advised her to have
no further contact with law enforcement.

"After not cooperating, lying about leaving work and
my affair," she said, "the police made me the number-one
suspect."

Questioned about her future goals, Michael said that her
most important one now was to discover the truth about
what had happened to her husband, and to be back with her
children. She said that before Jimmy's death, she had wanted
to get a Ph.D. in Nursing Research, using it to improve parent education and injury prevention, and start a child development education program in a state clinic.

"Jimmy and I wanted to take the kids on a mission trip to
Africa," she told the probation officer.

Several weeks later, Michael wrote to Chief Probation
Officer Phyllis Stewart, saying she was "uncomfortable"
with the version of the offence she had previously given and
wanted to edit it. She thanked her for all her help in the sentencing process, saying that Stewart would soon be receiving a copy of Shelly's Curriculum Vitae.

"I hope that you can forward me a copy of the completed evaluation at some point," she requested.

In her handwritten two-page amended version of events, she wrote:

> I must begin by stating I do not know why I am here, because I am not guilty of these heinous crimes. I did not kill my husband and I did not set fire to our home!
>
> I do not understand how in the year 2007, with our scientific and technologically advanced country, how we do not have the necessary means in place to protect and prevent innocent people from going to prison for something they did not do.

On Wednesday afternoon, September 12, 2007, almost two years after the fire, more than one hundred friends and supporters of Jimmy Michael filed into a Morgantown courtroom. Wearing "Justice for Jimmy" badges, with his photograph on them, and "Forever in Our Hearts" engraved bracelets, they had come to see Shelly Michael be sentenced for his murder.

There was a feeling of closure, that the nightmare was almost over and justice had prevailed.

The convicted murderess was slowly led into the court by sheriff's officers, in handcuffs and ankle shackles, and was almost unrecognizable. The designer outfits she had worn at trial had been replaced by a prison-issue orange jumpsuit, and without the heavy make-up, her once beautiful face looked haunted and anemic.

But before sentencing, Judge Robert Stone first considered a motion by Tom Dyer for a new trial.

During the trial, as an experiment, Dyer had had his teenage stepson Alex Guy order $259 worth of rocuronium over the Internet. But it had arrived too late for it to be considered as evidence.

"It's from a location in the country of Turkey," Dyer told the court. "It is a set of twelve vials of a drug known generically in that part of the world as Esmeron, but the active ingredient is rocuronium bromide."

Dyer said he wanted it entered on the record that the drug had arrived, and was easily available over the Internet. Marcia Ashdown responded that even if it had arrived in time, it would first have to have been examined by experts to confirm that it was rocuronium.

Judge Stone agreed to put it on the record, noting that it only showed that it had arrived in the mail.

Tom Dyer then argued for a new trial, on the grounds that the defense had never been informed of the true identity of the anonymous caller who had suggested police check Jimmy Michael's remains for rocuronium. He said the defense only learned it had been Rob Angus during his testimony at trial.

Lieutenant Kevin Clark, who had first received the tip-off, was then called to the stand. The officer said his friend Rob Angus had called him, saying he had some pertinent information after Jimmy Michael's death. Clark then told him to speak to Detective Paul Mezzanotte.

More than eighteen months later, in June 2007, he had received a subpoena from the defense, followed by a call from Tom Dyer.

"I had no idea why I was being called to testify," Clark told the court.

When Dyer explained that he wanted to address the issue of the anonymous call logged in the police report, Lieutenant Clark said he had forgotten, and knew nothing about it.

The defense attorney then argued to the judge that if he had known earlier that his client's ex-husband had made the anonymous call, he would have raised it in his cross-examination.

"And that's at the crux of this motion for a new trial," he explained. "[We] were not permitted the opportunity to develop evidence pertinent to what may be considered the most critical witness . . . in this case. That may well have had significant bearing on the outcome of this case."

Arguing against the motion, Prosecutor Ashdown

agreed that Detective Mezzanotte's report terminology had been "unfortunate or inaccurate." But she said it was a running account of a fast-moving case that was changing by the hour.

She also noted the defense could have cross-examined Angus after her direct, but chose not to.

"So all of these opportunities," she said, "were missed, I believe—were passed by by the defense."

Judge Stone then produced the report, chiding Dyer for not joining the dots in Mezzanotte's report, where Angus is named two pages later, although not specifically as the anonymous caller.

"As a matter of fact, the defense was advised who the anonymous caller was," he told Dyer. "You just didn't know it. Because you were advised two pages later. That's what the evidence shows, overwhelming evidence shows that Rob Angus made the call."

The judge denied the motion for a new trial, proceeding straight to the sentencing.

It was 5:00 p.m. when Judge Stone turned his attention to sentencing Shelly Michael for first-degree arson and the murder of her husband. He first noted that he had received the amended pre-sentencing report, as well as witness impact statements from members of Jimmy Michael's family and Shelly's parents and sister.

The judge then told the defendant that she had a right to address the court, if she wished to.

"Your Honor," said her attorney, "after consultation with my client, I have decided to decline to offer any remarks as counsel on her behalf, but I know Ms. Michael wishes to address the court."

Then, in shackles, Shelly Michael stood up to deliver an impassioned speech, proclaiming her innocence. It was the first time she had shown any emotion inside a courtroom.

"I would like to begin by saying that I debated a long time whether to speak or not, because I don't want to create any more pain or discomfort for the Michael family.

"However, I have been instructed on how to talk, think, act, feel for a long time, and I feel that my frustration with the system and how it's failed me, and my anger and my sadness and everything has overcome me to the point where I need to speak. And I hope that I don't offend anyone in the courtroom. I don't intend to.

"I would just like to begin by saying that I in no way, absolutely did not kill my husband. I did not inject him with any drug. I did not set fire to my own home. I did not destroy my whole family and our lives.

"I loved my family tremendously. I loved my husband tremendously. And I know a lot of people are going to roll their eyes about that, because I made mistakes and I did some wrong things, but marriage trouble doesn't mean no love, and I truly loved him and I would never hurt him.

"And it's sad, because Jimmy is the ultimate victim, and I can't for the life of me understand why he would be taken from us—why anybody would want to take him. Everybody was reminding me that God has a plan, that he has a purpose, and for the life of me, for Jacie and Drew and Ruth and Denny and for me and Alec and Kylie, I can't imagine what the plan would be.

"But I'm holding on to that faith, and I'm holding on to the fact that the truth will prevail some day. Someday I will have peace in knowing what happened. And for Ruth and Denny, I don't know where you are, but I swear from the bottom of my soul, Steve, you guys, I did not take Jimmy's life. I swear to you. I don't know what happened. I wish I did.

"I don't blame you for hating me for cheating on him. I don't blame you. If you want closure, you need justice served. If you want to believe I did it and it helps you heal and— because I don't want you in pain anymore, because I love you. I've loved you from the minute I met you, but I don't want you in pain anymore.

"I want you to feel better, and if you want to blame me and believe it, then go ahead.

"But I didn't. I did not do it. And I would just like to, as far as for sentencing purposes, whoever is responsible deserves to be thrown in jail, locked away forever and the key thrown away.

"The death penalty wouldn't be easy enough or hard enough or whatever, but just please keep in mind that the sentence that comes upon me today is not only a sentence for an innocent person to be incarcerated, but it's also a sentence for my two children and my family, who are also victims. Because we are victims, too.

"We lost a lot. I lost my husband, our home, our family, everything. And I ultimately lost my own children, too. And they have lost their mother. And, so, that, whatever sentence I get is a sentence for them as well. And we are all innocent. Nobody except God and Jimmy, and perhaps a fly on the wall that day and the murderer themselves, know what happened that day.

"And I pray every night that the truth will come out. I wish we could give truth serum to everyone involved. I just want everybody to tell the truth.

"But just my only last thing I need to say is, everybody's mind is made up that I'm guilty, and I'm not, and innocent people do get charged, and innocent people do get convicted. It's a known fact.

"I was going to bring a picture out of Alex and Kylie, but that wouldn't be fair not to bring a picture of Jacie and Drew, as well, because they are all four the innocent victims in this. And I just please ask that the Court remember that, and the media please remember that as well."

Then Judge Stone invited Ruth Michael, who had been sobbing throughout the speech, to come to the podium and address her son's killer.

"First of all," she began in a shaky voice, "you never, ever defended yourself to me. Your family never contacted Denny or I to see how we were doing, to say, 'Our daughter couldn't do this.' "

She said if the situation were reversed, she would have been calling Mike and Kathi Goots every day, defending her son.

At first she had thought Jimmy had died in the fire, but

when she discovered that he had been murdered by someone she had thought had loved him, her heart had been broken.

"How could you watch him struggle to breathe?" she asked Shelly, now crying in the dock. "You knew what that drug would do. How many minutes did he struggle to breathe before he went unconscious?"

Since the fire, she said, she can't sleep and has "bad dreams" every night, thinking about Jimmy suffering.

"Why?" she asked her daughter-in-law. "What was so horrible about your life, that you had to take his, and inflict this pain on so many people's lives? I try not to think of what Jimmy was thinking as he was struggling to breathe. I can't think of a death more cruel than what he suffered. The fact that she set him on fire to try to hide the murder has robbed me of the finality of his death.

"It's hard for me to have closure, when I have never, ever been able to view his body. It's like he went away, and I'm waiting for him to come back."

She then asked Judge Stone to give Shelly Michael the maximum possible sentences for the arson, to run consecutively with the mandatory life sentence for murder.

Then Denny Michael—the only family member to have seen Jimmy's charred remains—walked over to the podium.

"Michelle," he began, "I loved you like a daughter. I said you were a breath of fresh air. How many days I've laid awake at night, praying you would call me and say, 'Denny, I didn't do it.' I've got to come to you. Your family never called me."

The former pastor said the love of money had led to his son's death.

"Everything was about money," he told her. "My heart is broken. I will never be the same. My family will never be the same."

Then, citing First John 1:9, Denny told her that her only way to redemption was to confess her sins.

"I want you to go home," he said—prompting Kathi Goots to cry out, "She can't go home!"—"and I want everybody in the sound of my voice to read that verse and read it continuously, because I have the forgiveness in me to forgive you, but forgiveness cannot be achieved unless we confess."

He told Shelly that he did not hate her, but only hated what she did to his family.

"Your hope is not that you will get paroled in fifteen years," he told her. "Your hope is not that you will get out in twenty years. Your hope is not that you will get off. Your eternal hope is that God is willing to forgive you. You can't just tear the roof and get right with God. You have got to tear the walls down and get right with the family, and the fellowship of the people that you have harmed.

"Shelly, I love you, and hope you read that verse tonight."

Then Marcia Ashdown stood up and read out a letter from Jimmy Michael's 10-year-old daughter Jacie to Judge Stone.

"Shelly Goots has a cold-blooded heart and an evil mind," it read. "She deserved every minute in her jail cell. My dad wasn't perfect but he didn't deserve to be killed. I hope you give her the maximum by law. Also, I hope she knows she has hurt my family, and especially my brother. Love, Jacie Michael."

The prosecutor then told the judge that, although the defendant still maintains her innocence, a jury had found sufficient evidence at trial to find her guilty.

"Michelle Michael is tearful now," Ashdown told the court, "on this day when she is facing the very imminent imposition of a life sentence."

Ashdown said although Michael may now theorize that it was all part of God's plan for her, the court knows better.

"Certainly here on Earth," said the prosecutor, "this murder and this arson were the plans of Michelle Michael. She planned and premeditated and cold-bloodedly carried out the crime of murder . . ."

"No, I didn't!" Michael shouted from the dock, but Ashdown continued without missing a beat.

"We know from her background that she is a person capable of looking death in the face. She had to do so frequently in her place of work. And so, when the question is asked, 'How could she do what she did to her husband?,' that, perhaps, is one of the answers."

Then turning to the jury's recommendation of mercy, Ashdown said it was hard to know exactly what was in their hearts and minds.

"Your Honor," she said, "we ask you to assign the full penalty for the first-degree arson that the defendant was found guilty of. And we ask you to add a twenty-year sentence to her life sentence, so that that will be an additional factor for some future parole board to consider."

Then Judge Stone addressed Shelly Michael, saying that he had read through all the witness impact statements, mostly from Jimmy Michael's family, seeing her crime described as "evil, mean, demented and diabolical."

"I've kind of settled on one word," he told her, "and that is just 'cold.' I don't know why that hits me, but that's what hits me. It is just cold."

The judge said that her guilt or innocence were not a factor today, as she had been found guilty by twelve good jurors. And there was nothing he could add to what Jimmy Michael's parents had told the court, about the "devastation" she had caused so many people.

"My perception is that our community is just appalled and outraged at these crimes," he told her. "I've [never] seen anything like it in my twenty-two years of being a judge. I don't think I've seen anything as remotely as bizarre in some aspects of this, hard to understand. You know, people talk about marriage trouble and money as the root of all evil. I mean, nothing could justify what happened here. Absolutely nothing.

"Somehow, there is a very dark side to your character. And the question is asked—a person who is trained to help people and save lives doing something like this. It's senseless. Totally senseless.

"You do not deserve leniency. The sentence of this court for murder in the first degree is the sentence that is required by law when a jury finds that they recommend mercy, and that is a sentence of life in the penitentiary with a notation that the jury has recommended mercy, so it is with mercy.

"For the conviction of arson in the first degree, the court sentences you to the penitentiary term of twenty years, and I would order that it run consecutively to the life in prison."

Then, after being sentenced to the maximum possible imprisonment, meaning she won't be eligible for parole for twenty years, the defendant defiantly stood up to have the last word.

"Your Honor," she said in a clear resonating voice, "I would like to say one more thing. I don't intend any disrespect to you whatsoever, but I am not cold. I am not calculated. And I did not kill my husband. And you saying that is . . . It's wrong."

Judge Stone told her that she had made her statement to the court, and so had he.

"And, as I indicated," he said, "your guilt or innocence is not an issue. It's been decided. The jury decided it and, quite frankly, I agree with the jury."

Ten days later, Michelle Michael granted Brandy Brubaker of *The Dominion Post* a one-hour jailhouse interview. With her private investigator Gina Lopez present as a witness, the new inmate held the interview behind a Plexiglas partition.

She announced that she had already started working on her appeal with Tom Dyer, saying she was confident of getting a new trial. And she spoke of her love for Jimmy Michael, and her struggle with coping with his loss and the loss of her children. She claimed to have been misunderstood, saying that the public perception of her had been totally distorted by the media.

"I'm not some killing stone heart, cold, immune-to-death person," she told Brubaker.

She maintained that the thumbs-up sign had been directed at her father, a few seconds after hearing that he had arranged for a jailhouse visit that night.

"It was so misconstrued," she said. "Normal, innocent things are taken so out of context."

CHAPTER 48

Justice4Michelle

In early 2008, Shelly Michael was transferred to Lakin Correctional Center, an all-female state prison on the banks of the Ohio River. The tough state penitentiary opened in 2003 and houses 450 female inmates, including thirty serving life sentences.

Now officially designated inmate #45996-1, Shelly was placed in general population, her fame preceding her because of the notoriety of her case. She now lived by herself in a tiny 6-foot–by–9-foot cell with cable television, and given a prestigious job as a teacher's aide, helping inmates study for their GEDs.

During her initial processing, the guards impounded the wedding ring Jimmy had given her, because of the diamonds. She now wore a regulation cream-colored short-sleeved prison uniform, with her name and inmate number embroidered over her breast pocket.

As Lakin Correctional Center was three hours away from Clarksburg, Shelly's parents and sister took it in turns, visiting her every other weekend. Convinced of her innocence, her family members were standing by her, bringing her news of her children and providing moral support.

"We try to spread it out so somebody is there every weekend," said her sister Jennifer. "She puts up a good front."

* * *

In March 2008, Tom Dyer asked the West Virginia Supreme Court of Appeals for a new trial, on the grounds that prosecutors had failed to tell the defense the identity of the anonymous caller. The defense attorney also claimed that Judge Stone had refused to allow the defense to introduce evidence at trial that rocuronium could be purchased over the Internet.

That May, Shelly sent Tom Dyer a detailed handwritten analysis of the appeal brief she wished him to file, listing various points she felt needed to be clarified for the state supreme court.

In a cover letter she wrote,

> Please remember that I've been convicted of a crime I did not commit, and on top of all the other trauma and loss I have endured, now I have to live in 6×9 block cell surrounded by nothing [but] steel, concrete and razor wire, isolated from my children and family, treated worse than an animal, and left to rot away all alone.

On June 11, the West Virginia Supreme Court of Appeals agreed to review her grounds for a new trial.

"Michelle Michael appeals her conviction for First Degree Murder with a recommendation of mercy and First Degree Arson," read the docket, "and the court's denial of her various motions. She asserts the court erred in excluding her evidence that the drug which caused the victim's death could be purchased over the Internet without a prescription; and that the State suppressed material, exculpatory evidence of the identity of the caller who told police to check for the presence of this drug."

Six weeks later, while still awaiting a decision from the state supreme court, the Goots family and a friend formed the Michelle Michael Defense Group, launching a website to campaign for her freedom.

On the home page of Justice4michelle.com, beneath two smiling photographs of her and Jimmy, came this invitation:

Read this compelling story about a family tragedy and a case of true injustice.

Join our group as we stand together in the fight for justice and truth, and become a warrior for Jimmy by helping free his wife and open the door to finding the real monster responsible for this heinous crime.

On another part of the site were Shelly's high school basketball photographs, as well as half-a-dozen others featuring her wedding pictures to Jimmy. There was also a thirteen-page single-spaced case report, and a prayer poem Shelly had composed in Lakin that read, in part:

> *So, what's the point of all this heartache?*
> *We need answers, we need a break.*
>
> *Oh, from this nightmare I wish I could awake.*

Her prayers finished off by asking God to

> *Please take care of my Jim(my)*
> *Tell him how much I love him & miss him!*

On September 23, the West Virginia Supreme Court denied Shelly Michael's appeal for a new trial, by a unanimous 5–0 ruling. Chief Justice Elliott Maynard found that the identity of the anonymous caller, Rob Angus, had been available to the defense in writing weeks before the trial.

"I suspect no one saw any merit in the defense's petition," said the chief justice, "or any good grounds for the case to be reviewed."

The supreme court ruling effectively shut out any further appeals for a new trial, but Tom Dyer said his client was determined to continue the fight.

"I have spoken to Ms. Michael," he told *The Daily Athenaeum*, WVU's student newspaper, "and though she is very disappointed, she is determined to look at all post-conviction remedies necessary."

* * *

Over the next few months, Shelly Michael's relationship with Tom Dyer deteriorated rapidly. There had been much tension and resentment building since the trial, with Shelly's parents, who had put up hundreds of thousands of dollars for their daughter's defense, bitterly disappointed with how it had been handled.

"He was very expensive," Michael Goots complained. "But when you pay good money, you want a good attorney."

After her appeal was denied, Tom Dyer began to distance himself from his "controlling" client.

"Shelly had basically got under my skin," he explained, "where I was not tolerating her very well."

Finally, in late 2008, Tom Dyer drove to Lakin Correctional Center for his final meeting with Shelly Michael. In a visiting room with several other inmates present, he told her that, in a sense, she had won the trial, because the guilty verdict with mercy meant the jury had disagreed.

He then advised her to confess her guilt now, reasoning that if she served 20 years, before being released in her mid-fifties, she would still have a lot of her life ahead.

"I told her, 'You need to begin now to acknowledge guilt,'" he recalled. "'Beg for forgiveness, and over the course of those twenty years, you will get out. But if you wait until six weeks before your first parole hearing . . . it's going to look pretty disingenuous, and you're probably not going to get out for several more years.'"

According to Dyer, Shelly then flew into a fury, having to be restrained by a guard.

"She started to rant and rave," he recalled. "She screamed at me. Well, she flipped out to a point where one of the correctional officers in the facility had to come over and calm her down."

After she quieted down, he advised her that her only course of action was to file a writ of habeas corpus, accusing him of ineffectual representation at trial.

"I'm not the man to continue to pursue these frivolous appeals," he said, "because my heart is no longer in this.

And I told her, 'Your best pitch under any circumstances, now that you've lost the direct appeal, is going to be to point the finger at one or both of your trial lawyers.' I had never lost before, so this was new to me."

Soon after that, Tom Dyer severed his ties with Shelly Michael, and at the time of going to press, she had no criminal lawyer representing her.

In April 2009, Shelly Michael petitioned the federal court, seeking to prevent Jimmy Michael's $500,000 Northwestern Life Insurance money from being distributed to their four children. She also did not want the children's respective parents, Rob Angus and Stephanie Estel, as trustees, asking that Renee Del Viscio be reinstated, as her late husband had originally intended.

Although her murder and arson conviction disqualified her from receiving any money, she noted that she had a petition of habeas corpus pending. She pointed out that if the Supreme Court of Appeals were to grant her petition, she would be eligible to a portion of the insurance money.

EPILOGUE

For her first Christmas in Lakin, Shelly made stockings for every inmate in her block, placing them on their cell doors with candy and small presents inside. She also made graduation certificates for the students she coached through their GEDs.

She attended craft classes, making "prison bags" for her children and various friends out of yarn her mother brought in.

"She does whatever she can do to stay busy," said Kathi Goots. "I mean, she's always done crafts and stuff like that, but does a lot more of that now."

She's also one of the stars of the prison volleyball team, delighting in showing off her cheerleading moves to the other inmates.

"She still does back-handsprings at the prison," said her mother proudly.

Although she has no legal representation, Inmate Michael still works hard on her appeal every day, using a computer in the prison library for legal research. She reportedly also pursues several pen pal relationships with men she meets online, sending them pictures of herself taken by another inmate.

Michael has a good relationship with her fellow inmates,

some of whom are also serving long sentences for murder. She treats inmates medically in what she calls "under-the-table nursing," which she has to keep quiet, as it is against the rules.

"It's not like television," she said in a prison interview in January 2009, one week before her thirty-seventh birthday. "The ladies here are really mean, but I don't get picked on. I respect them and keep to myself."

She said the worst thing about incarceration was the guards treating her like "an idiot," and not taking her seriously.

"Because you're an inmate, your word is crap," she said. "I find this really hard to handle."

Still confident of getting a new trial and having the verdict overturned, Michael claims her private investigator has recently uncovered new evidence, which she refuses to divulge at this point.

She still vehemently denies murdering Jimmy Michael, fondly describing him as the first man she ever truly loved.

"He was my Mr. Right. My dream man," she said, wiping an imaginary tear from her eye. "He was my Tom Cruise. I've only had four or five boyfriends in my life, and I never cheated on any one of them. Jimmy was the first man I ever really loved. And he was the first one I ever cheated on."

She vowed to fight to find his real killer, saying he would have done the same, if their roles had been reversed.

"What keeps me going," she said, "is that I know if I had been the one that had been killed, Jimmy would be there fighting for me tooth and nail. The thing I struggle with is how people that were friends could just turn against you, and believe you're capable of something like this. They were brainwashed. If Jimmy could have heard the testimony in court, he would be turning in his grave. I've been very betrayed."

Asked about all her lies to police over the course of the investigation, Shelly says she wants people to know she is not a liar.

"I value honesty so much," she said. "So even with the tiniest white lie, I get the biggest pangs of conscience. It's my whole personality."

To keep herself occupied in prison, she takes culinary and crafts classes. She reads an average of twenty books a month, and her favorite author is John Grisham.

"I survive by keeping busy and praying a lot," she said. "I speak a lot to the chaplain, who counsels me. This has strengthened my faith. I believe in Jesus Christ and read the Bible every night."

She said she finds it hard to sleep at night, often having a recurring dream of her dead husband.

"It's a nightmare," she said. "I keep thinking that Jimmy's going to come back. Two nights ago I had a dream that I came home and he was lying on my couch in our home. And I came in and he said, 'Shelly.'

"And I'm shaking him. 'Where were you! Where were you!' I kept asking him. He said, 'I was held hostage in a concentration camp in Kentucky.'

"I dream about him a lot, and I hate to wake up. I get so angry. I've had this dream a couple of times since the fire."

Renee Del Viscio talks regularly to her oldest friend, trying to lift her spirits, as Shelly comes to terms with the likelihood of spending the rest of her life behind bars.

"Some days I think that it might be the last time that I'll talk to her," Renee said, "because she seemed so upset and depressed. And then some days it's just as though she had a normal day, coming home from work and she's as happy as can be. She definitely spends a lot of time going over her thoughts, and a lot of time writing and researching."

Now, after everything that she's found out about Shelly, Renee no longer knows what to think.

"I mean, people want to call her the Black Widow," said Renee. "At the end of the day, I do not know what happened. And I truly don't know what I believe. Ten years ago, the Shelly that I knew . . . I would never have thought she'd be in this situation. And since then, I've heard so many things about kind of another life that she was leading. But again, that other life does not mean that she would kill somebody."

Her husband Eric has his own theory of what could have happened, if she is guilty.

"This is a perfect mystery," he said. "I don't think they ever chased down anybody else, and maybe that's Shelly's own fault. She was her own worst enemy through this whole process, I think.

"And I've said to Renee—if she did it, the thing that angered her was: Jimmy finds out about the affair that Monday, tells her he's leaving. And the lack of control would piss her off. Not the money, I don't think the money has anything to do with it. Because she had talked to me and said, 'It's really going well, everything's going fine.' I said, 'This business is going beautifully, you've nothing to worry about.'"

Eric Del Viscio believes that the only reason Shelly might have killed Jimmy is if he'd discovered her affair with Bobby Teets, and wanted a divorce.

"That's the only thing I could see that would put her over the edge," he said. "Because I don't think it was money. So who knows? It is a real whodunit."